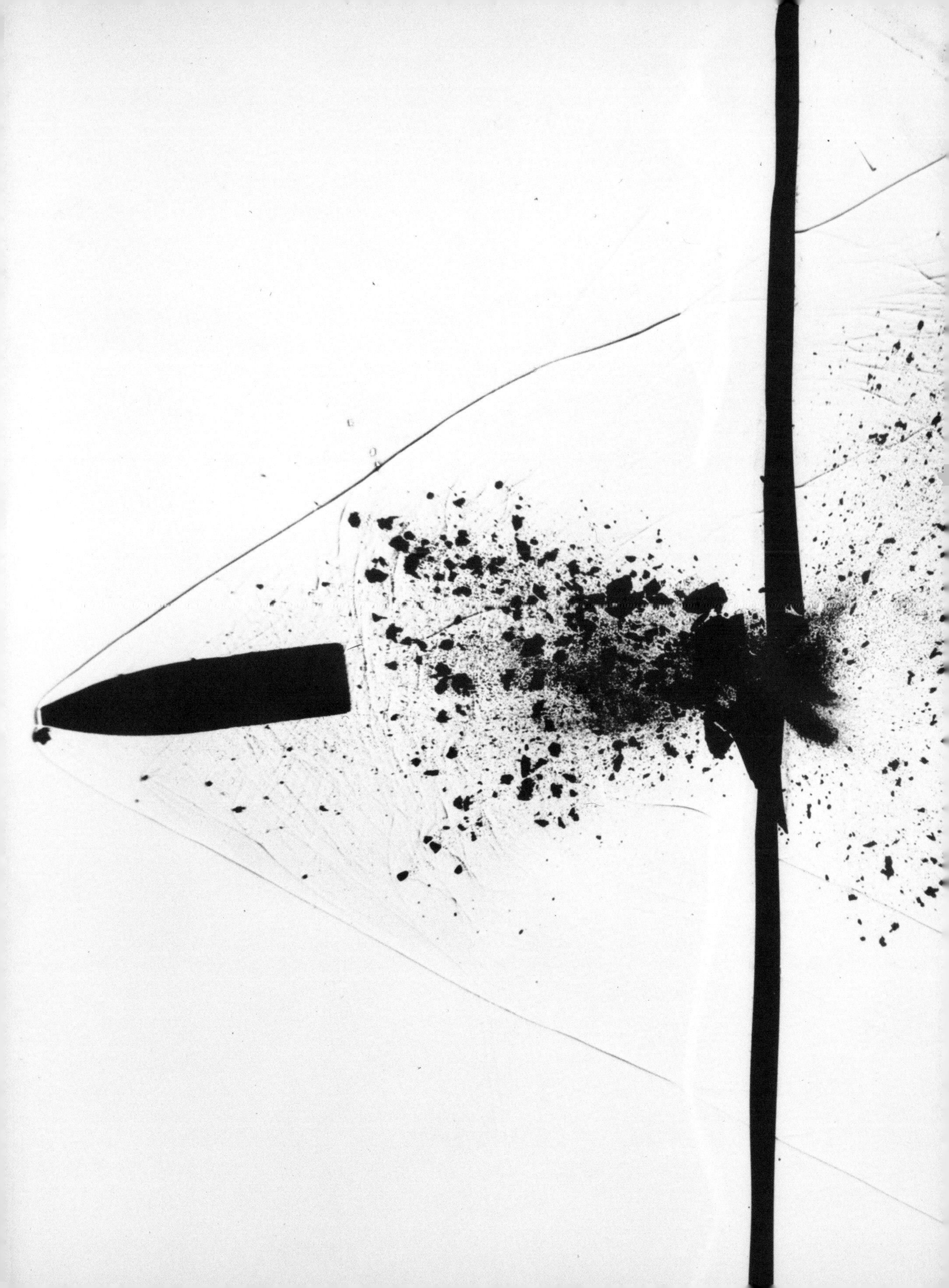

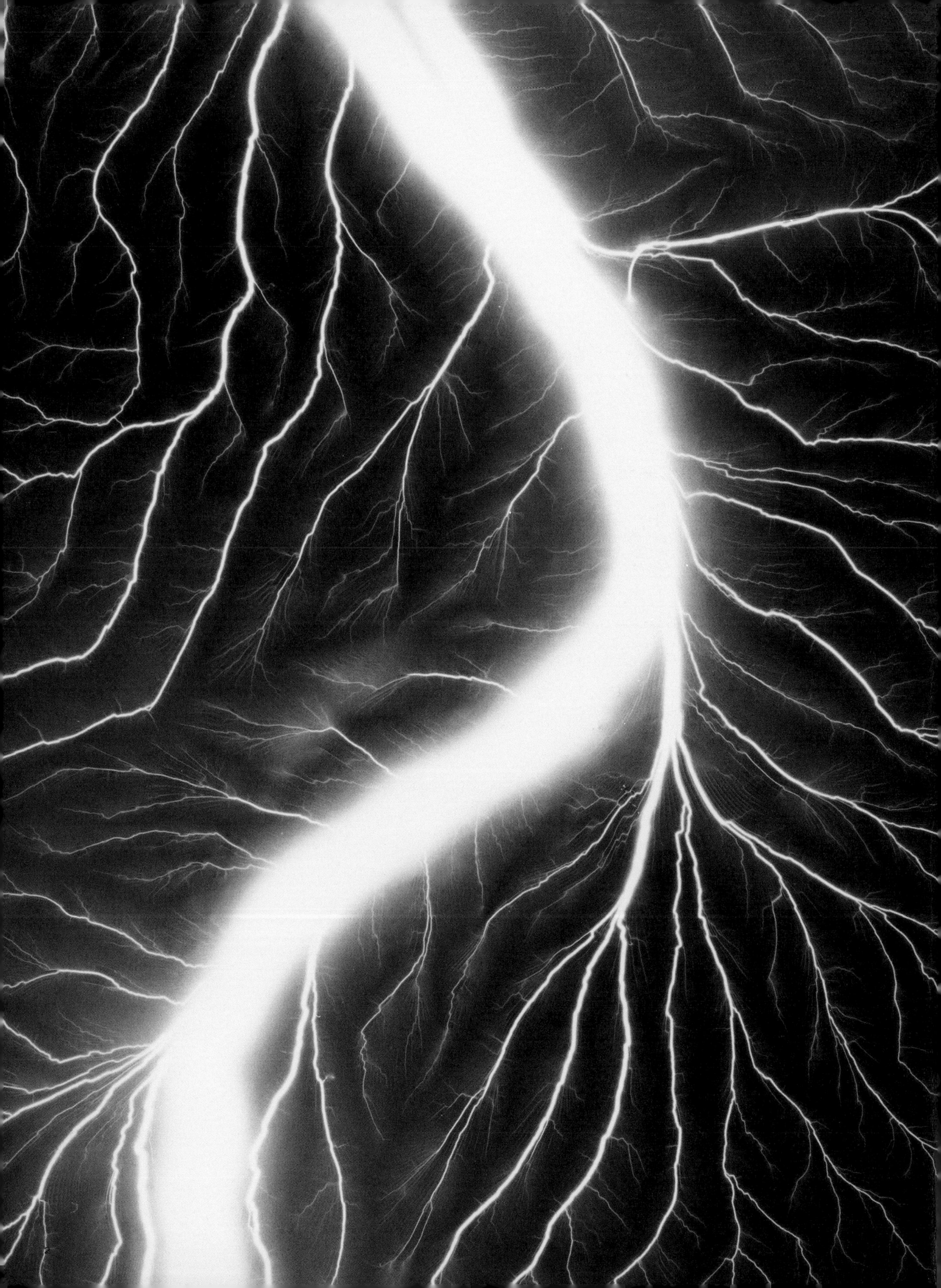

V&A Photography Library

Cameraless Photography

Martin Barnes

Thames & Hudson

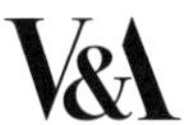

With 141 illustrations

Published to accompany the opening of the V&A Photography Centre at the Victoria and Albert Museum, 12 October 2018

Designed by Loose Joints

First published in the United States of America in 2018 by Thames & Hudson Inc, 500 Fifth Avenue, New York, New York 10110.

www.thamesandhudsonusa.com.

Library of Congress Control Number 2018945322.

ISBN 978-0-500-48036-6

Printed and bound in Slovenia by DZS-Grafik d.o.o.

V&A Publishing

Supporting the world's leading
museum of art and design,
the Victoria and Albert
Museum, London

Titles in *italics* have been assigned by the photographer or artist. Those in roman are descriptive titles.

On the cover: Detail of Curtis Moffat, *Abstract Compositions*, *c.*1925 (see p.60).

p.1 Detail of Harold Edgerton, *Bullet Through Plexiglas*, 1963 (see p.84).

p.2 Detail of Hiroshi Sugimoto, *Lightning Fields, 225*, 2009 (see p.181).

p.6 Detail of William Henry Fox Talbot, Ferns and leaves, *c.*1852 (see p.32).

p.12 Detail of Helen Chadwick, Study for *Of Mutability*, 1986 (see p.109).

Contents

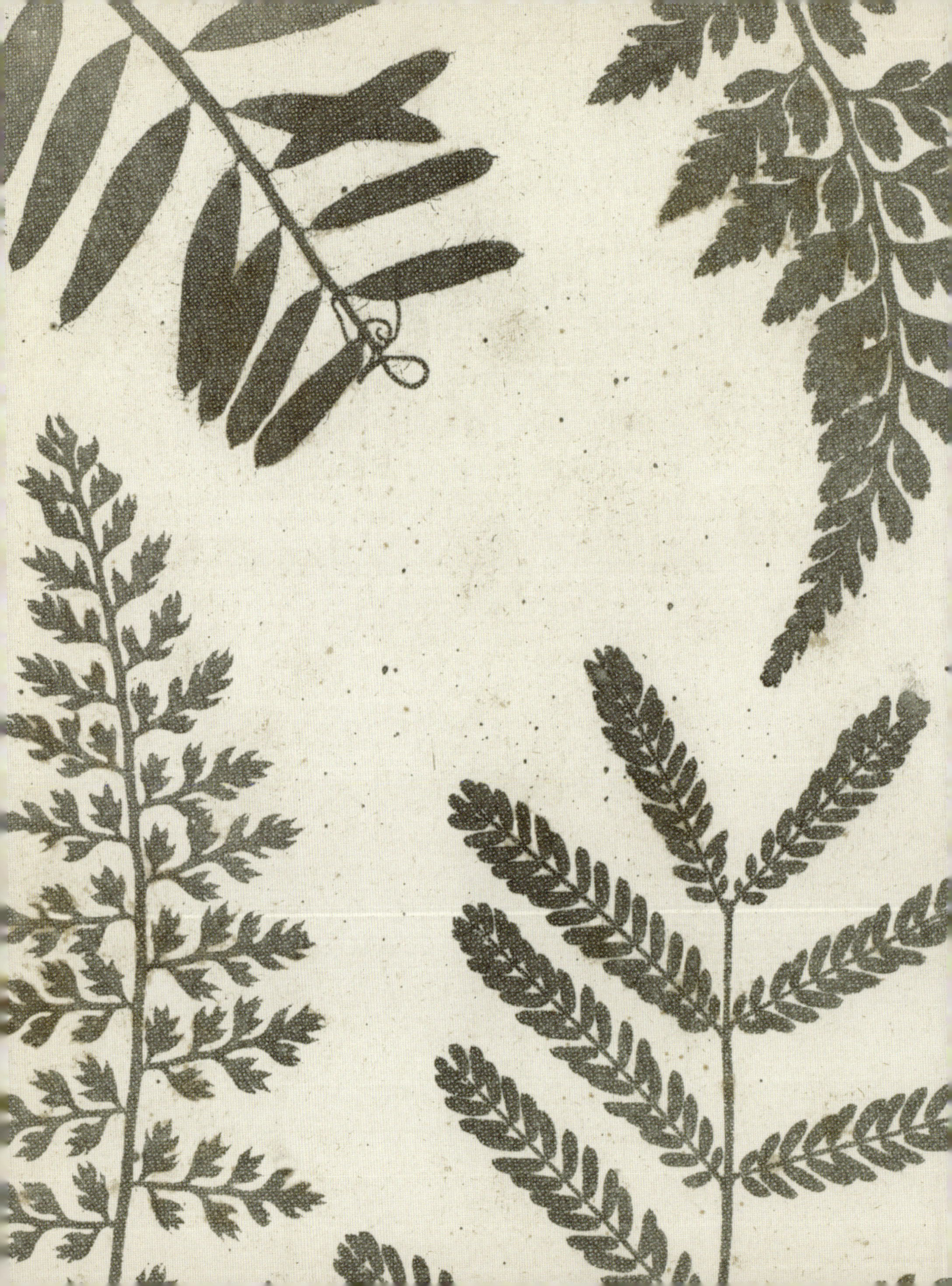

Martin Barnes

Cameraless Photography

The camera has become so closely associated with photography that it is easy to assume one is always necessary to make a photograph. But just as a painting can be made without a brush, so a photograph can be made without a camera. At its most basic, a photograph is simply an image produced by the action of light on a light-sensitive surface. The word 'photography' comes from the Greek words for 'light' and 'writing'. In this sense, its definition can encompass many variations on the theme. The earliest surviving photographic images by Joseph Nicéphore Niépce (pp.14–16) and William Henry Fox Talbot (pp.18–25, 27–33) were made without a camera by placing objects such as engravings, leaves or lace directly onto sensitized metal or paper, which was then exposed to light. Far from remaining an evolutionary stage in photography, cameraless techniques have been explored and reinterpreted by successive generations of image makers and continue to be used by contemporary artists today. While related to the conventional practices of photography, cameraless images offer an alternative, experimental, radical and often revelatory form of vision.

This book gathers a roughly chronological sample of cameraless images. What constitutes a cameraless photograph has been broadly defined. In general, any images that employ the use of conventional cameras and lenses have been excluded. The choice and range is not intended as comprehensive. Some artists are represented with more examples than others, primarily because their practice is dedicated to cameraless work. Many other image makers and types of cameraless process could be included under this book's title, but the selection is determined by the permanent collection of the Victoria and Albert Museum from which it is drawn. It is intended as an introduction to the richness of the subject, the creativity it inspires, and the depth and variety of the Museum's collection.

Most photographs are created today using phones or other multifunction digital devices. The types of camera that once dominated the analogue era will likely retain a niche use, but for most of us they are already obsolete. The transition from analogue to digital made over the last few decades, across all forms of communication, is particularly dramatic. It prompts excitement about future possibilities but is mixed with nostalgia for vanishing crafts, mechanical devices and the tactile world. Artists, curators and writers who have propelled the current renaissance in cameraless photography respond in some degree to this nostalgia – an urgent realization that analogue materials in photography are becoming rare or extinct. There is also a desire to reconnect to the rudiments of photographic technology, to rediscover and resurrect some of its alchemy. Overloaded with the possibilities and multiplicity of a digital and global economy, a growing number of creative image makers using photography are seeking inspiration from the medium's origins, its defining principles and physical materials. Within the history of photography, this might be placed as the latest chapter in a continuing story: a cycle of innovation followed by technical or commercial obsolescence.

Since the official announcement of photography's invention in 1839, manufacturers of photographic equipment, and most of its consumers and producers, have striven for greater clarity, detail, permanence, speed of production, portability and reproducibility. The camera – and its associated plates, negatives or transparencies and prints to capture the images – helped realize these ambitions. Refinements were made over the years: first with the use of daguerreotype plates, giving a direct positive image on metal; then with negatives made of paper, then glass, then plastic; and today with images formed on digital sensors. By the 1850s, monochrome photographs made using glass negatives had already reached a level of perfection that has rarely been surpassed. Yet the materials and equipment used to produce them were fragile, heavy, flammable and even poisonous, and did not yield results in colour. The quest for a practicable form of colour photography saw rapid advances in the early twentieth century but were arguably not fully achieved until later in the century. Throughout these and many other developments, photography's technical, practical and aesthetic advancement was predominantly wedded to the camera. The camera – and latterly the mobile phone, or other device incorporating a camera – can be a tool, a toy, a design item and a status symbol. Each of these definitions suits market forces and drives the marriage of art and commerce that photography has always been.

However, a history of photography divorced from the camera largely evades these definitions. It offers a parallel narrative, one that has often been subordinated or seen as marginal but that has, at times, emerged into prominence to push or re-establish the boundaries of photography and rethink its possibilities as an expressive medium. Its trajectory is less concerned with technical advances and replicating the world as seen by the human eye or its surrogate, the camera lens. The great American photojournalist and documentary photographer Dorothea Lange declared, 'The camera is an instrument that teaches people how to see without a camera.'[1] Her words imply that conceptual vision is more important than technical method, even if the attainment of that vision is dependent on the tools. Cameraless photographers take up the implied challenge of her statement quite literally, abandoning the camera at the outset in favour of a more direct, haptic and readily metaphorical rendering of photographic phenomena.

1. Quoted in Milton Meltzer, *Dorothea Lange: A Photographer's Life* (Syracuse, NY 1978), p.vii.

Compared to traditional photography, the unorthodox techniques of cameraless photography can seem rudimentary. There are several ways of making cameraless images – such as photograms, radiographs, luminograms, chemigrams and scannergrams – and the terminology often sounds more complex than the processes are when practised (each is described in more detail in the glossary). The most common is the photogram, a term that encompasses all images made simply by the contact of objects on light-sensitive surfaces. The imprint of a wristwatch left on your skin after a day in the sun illustrates the principle. Photograms are generally one-of-a-kind and reproduce an actual-size image of the object that blocks light from the light-sensitive surface. The resulting silhouette is a trace, a direct translation of the object's touch and presence.

William Henry Fox Talbot was the first to experiment and systematically explore the potential of this technique on paper, the results of which he termed 'sciagraphs' (shadow pictures), then 'photogenic drawing'. Talbot favoured using botanical subjects and samples of fabrics, suitably flat objects that created pleasing patterns when placed under glass on sensitized paper in the sun. He quickly grasped the concept that the inverted tones of these resulting 'negative' images could be copied by placing them into contact with additional sheets of sensitized paper and repeating the process to produce positive prints. This sparked the revolution of mass production in photography. In this respect, we have the cameraless photograph to thank for that innovation. However, it now seems surprising that Talbot simultaneously persisted with camera-made and cameraless images, even after the negative and camera came to dominate the medium he invented. It is likely that, compared with the softness of early paper negatives, the superior crispness of outline and detail produced by cameraless specimens remained both practical and appealing.

Talbot's contemporary, illustrator and botanist Anna Atkins, capitalized on both the practicality and beauty of photograms to specialize almost exclusively in images of botanical specimens (pp.38–42). Atkins employed the same basic techniques as Talbot, but used cyanotype paper, which yielded Prussian blue images that could be developed simply in water. The subjects of plants and fabrics that appear in these early images by Talbot and Atkins have often been repeated in cameraless photography, and appear as a common trope of experimental discovery and primal photographic origins. Contemporary examples can be seen here in the botanical photograms by Angela Easterling (pp.131–3), the digital scanner images produced by Barbara and Zafer Baran (pp.138–9), various photogram interpretations of fabrics by Elaine Duigenan (p.149) or Rebecca Earley (pp.126–7), and the cameraless holograms of Susan Gamble (pp.106–7).

Another common trope of cameraless imagery is scientific or medical investigation. This is primarily because of its association with the discovery of X-rays in 1895. By that date, cameraless imagery pioneered at the start of the century must have seemed almost irrelevant; but the revelations suddenly made possible by the discovery that X-rays acted like an invisible light source and left their trace on photographic plates revitalized and expanded cameraless possibilities. Here was a kind of photogram that not only revealed the silhouette of the object placed in front of the photographic surface, but also penetrated opaque matter and revealed its hidden inner structure. The shadow images produced by X-rays were described initially, in Talbot's term, as sciagraphs, but later became known as radiographs, after the radiation from which they are formed. Radiography instantly created a sensation, and was the subject of intense discussion in both photographic and medical circles during the late 1890s and early 1900s. The medical applications were obvious, but their startling visual impact was also irresistible, with graphic skeletal images of human and animal subjects proliferating (pp.50–53). Moreover, X-rays gave tangible evidence of a formerly invisible world that existed beyond the capabilities of human vision. In recent years, Nick Veasey has perfected X-ray images, often in the context of spectacular commercial graphics, and has achieved an ambitious scale of subject matter, such as motor vehicles, that were beyond the reach of early practitioners (see pp.166–7).

Photograms and radiographs were rediscovered for their aesthetic value in the early twentieth century by artists of the avant-garde art movements including Dada and Surrealism, and those turning their backs on traditional techniques in favour of abstraction. Chief among them was László Moholy-Nagy, advocate of a 'new vision', who began to experiment with cameraless processes in 1922 and coined the term 'photogram' (pp.54–7). He wrote:

> *The photogram, or camera-less record of forms produced by light, which embodies the unique nature of the photographic process, is the real key to photography. It allows us to capture the patterned interplay of light on a sheet of sensitized paper without recourse to any apparatus. The photogram opens up perspectives of a hitherto wholly unknown morphosis governed by optical laws peculiar to itself.*[2]

2. László Moholy-Nagy, 'A New Instrument of Vision' (1932), quoted in *Moholy-Nagy: An Anthology*, ed. Richard Kostelanetz (Cambridge, MA 1970), p.50.

Like many of his peers who began using the method, he capitalized on the unexpected, spontaneous effects created by unusual juxtapositions of everyday objects. By varying the exposure time, he found he could create layers of objects, and that by moving objects as they were exposed tonal variations were created. Significantly, Moholy-Nagy also introduced the photogram in his teaching of art and design at both the Bauhaus in Germany and the New Bauhaus in Chicago. His theories played an influential role and were passed onto many of his students and followers, such as Henry Holmes Smith (pp.78–81) and Arnold M. Gilbert (pp.104–5), who continued refining cameraless techniques into the late twentieth century. In the 1920s and 1930s, Man Ray stylishly applied photograms (or what he termed 'rayographs', after his own name) to his artwork and commercial commissions with great effect. The bold, graphic forms stood out among other advertising imagery (pp.66–70). Fellow American Curtis Moffat worked in Man Ray's Paris studio before moving to London in the early 1920s. Here, Moffat set up a portrait studio and design emporium, exhibited his photograms and used them as schemes in Modernist interior decoration (pp.58–62). After the Second World War, cameraless photography became increasingly accepted practice in European and North American experimental and conceptual art. While camera-made photographs implied a documentary role, cameraless work offered a contrasting photographic language liberated from the restraints of representational realism. The group Fotoform, founded in 1949 by artist Otto Steinert, embraced cameraless photography. The outlet for the Fotoform group's work was a series of exhibitions titled 'Subjektive Fotografie'. Pierre Cordier exhibited his unique chemigrams in its last exhibition in 1958 and has dynamically pioneered and promoted this distinctive form of cameraless photography ever since (pp.113–20).

Chemigrams rely primarily on the physical reaction of substances, chemistry or mark-making on the surface of photographic materials rather than on the action of light alone. Typically, substances such as varnish, oil, syrup or wax are applied to the paper in full light, sometimes inscribed with handmade marks, and processed with photographic developer and fixer. The tints are generally the result of chemical reactions with standard black and white photographic emulsions rather than with colour photographic paper. Exposure to light before development produces 'photolysis', in which the paper turns blue, mauve, brown, reddish or ochre depending on the emulsion. In traditional photography, these phenomena are usually seen as mistakes but in chemigrams they are generally embraced for creative effect. Cordier has described his works as a 'mutation', as 'hybrid' and 'marginal' – fake photographs of an imaginary, improbable and inaccessible world. His chemigrams are full of visual and linguistic puzzles. The artistic signature style is the result of visual and technical research, and is produced organically by the process and technique. In this respect, Cordier's chemigrams appear closer to natural form, or an alien hand, than anything usually associated with photography. The work of Jean-Pierre Sudre occupies similar territory, with intricate images being generated by crystals formed on glass plates, which are then printed, in a variation of the nineteenth-century *cliché-verre* process (pp.101–3). A continuation and variation on such deeply researched, systematic and process-based work can be seen in Marco Breuer's 'photographic recordings', which also employ some chemigram techniques (pp.171–8). Breuer pushes and tests the limits of what different varieties of photographic paper are designed to do, often subjecting them to physical trial by scraping, burning, folding, puncturing or other interventions to create abstract compositions.

Floris Neusüss has dedicated his whole career to extending the practice, study and teaching of the photogram. From 1960, he became recognized for 'whole body' photograms that brought renewed ambition to the form in terms of scale, visual treatment and conceptual forethought. His photograms extended into installation pieces and site-specific works, referencing photographic history, the psychology of the shadow and its use as a metaphor for absence and transience (pp.85–91). From the 1980s onwards, Garry Fabian Miller has likewise devoted his career to a long-term visual and philosophical enquiry, removing the camera as a way of paring back to the fundamentals of photography: light and time (pp.153–63). He has accrued a dexterity and command of his chosen colour materials as a craftsman through years of sustained production and series of works. Many of his works are luminograms, created by shining light through glass vessels and over cut paper forms before registering on the photographic paper. These explorations of abstract form and colour involve exposures in the darkroom ranging from some minutes up to several hours. The powerful capacity of such cameraless imagery to accommodate or evoke metaphorical, psychological or spiritual readings can also be seen in the work of Miller's peers: Susan Derges's immersive wave and water forms (pp.142–7), Adam Fuss's symbolic emblems of creation (pp.123–5) and Christopher Bucklow's otherworldly silhouette figures, glowing with inner light (pp.110–11).

Some artists have opted for cameraless methods, not as their main medium but more for their appropriateness to realize a concept, or as one of several tools within their armoury. Helen Chadwick made sophisticated and unconventional use of photocopies to create sublime collages (pp.108–9). Her use of utilitarian office technology for high art subjects was deft and innovative. Robert Heinecken, who described himself as a 'paraphotographer', made fitting satirical use of the photogram to manipulate found images and subvert the messages of magazines and advertising (pp.92–7). Cornelia Parker has often used photography to harness a conceptual or linguistic idea into visual form that would be difficult to capture in any other way. In her deceptively simple photogram, *Bated Breath: Fluff and Dust from the Whispering Gallery, St Paul's Cathedral, London* (1997), dust, the enemy of conventional photography, becomes the subject and the means of evoking a delicate sound and a sense of awe (p.129). Hiroshi Sugimoto's captured bolt of pure energy, *Lightning Fields, 225* (2009) reads as a primordial creative spark (p.181). For Parker, Sugimoto and many others, the enduring cameraless methods used by Talbot in the 1830s remain relevant, inspiring and vital.

In selecting works for this compilation, common subjects and overlapping themes have emerged that have seemed particularly suited to cameraless imagery throughout its history: natural forms and forces are re-envisaged and revealed; human and animal bodies leave their emotive and visceral trace; and scientific, cosmic, lunar or solar references can be found in pictures that confound or expand a sense of scale. Recent advances in photographic technology and the demise of traditional cameras seem only to have increased both the inventiveness of artists who use cameraless techniques and the growing public fascination for cameraless photography.
Such images challenge preconceptions of photography as a representational and reproductive medium. If at times ambiguous and resisting firm classification, they equally leave open a welcome space for imagination.

Martin Barnes
Senior Curator, Photographs
Victoria and Albert Museum, London

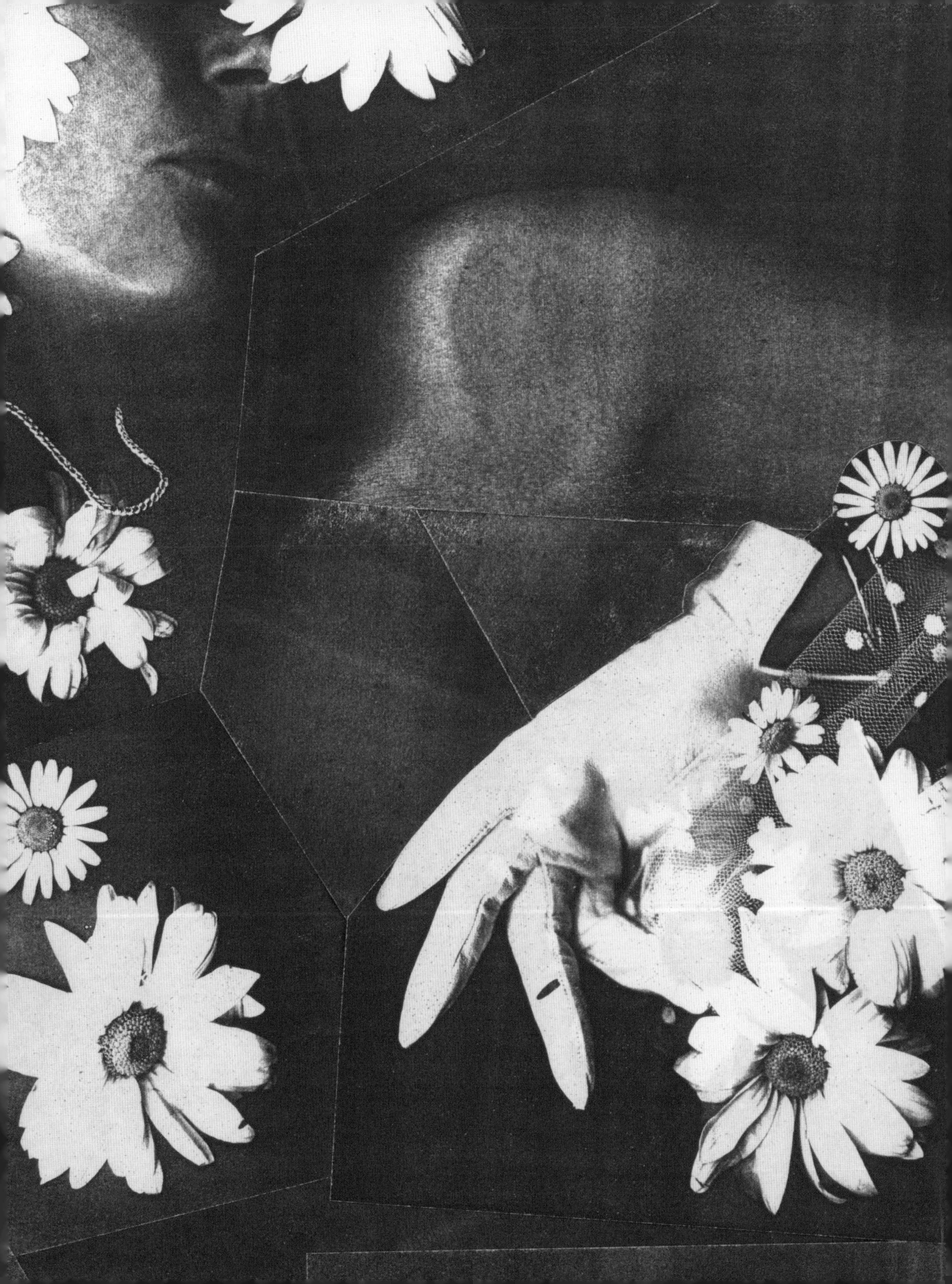

Plates

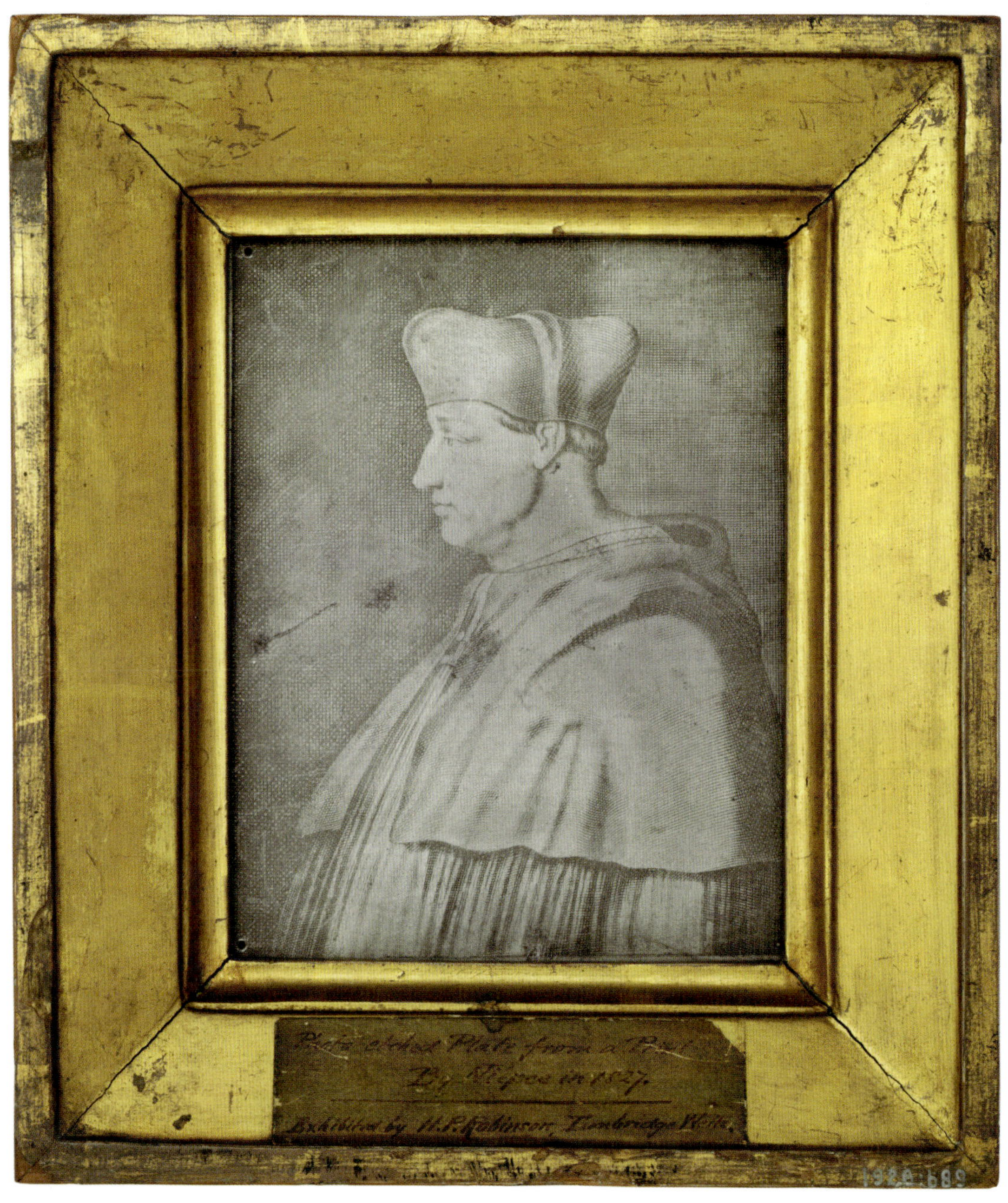

Joseph Nicéphore Niépce (1765–1833)

'Le Cardinal d'Amboise'
1826

Heliograph on pewter plate
27.3 x 24 cm (framed)

The earliest surviving photographic images were made by French inventor Niépce. He called them 'heliographs' or 'sun writing'. Only 16 heliographic plates by Niépce are still thought to exist. Created on metal plates, they were intended to be coated with ink and intaglio printed. Most of his images were derived from pre-existing artworks. This one is taken from an engraving made in 1633 by Isaac Briot (1585–1670).

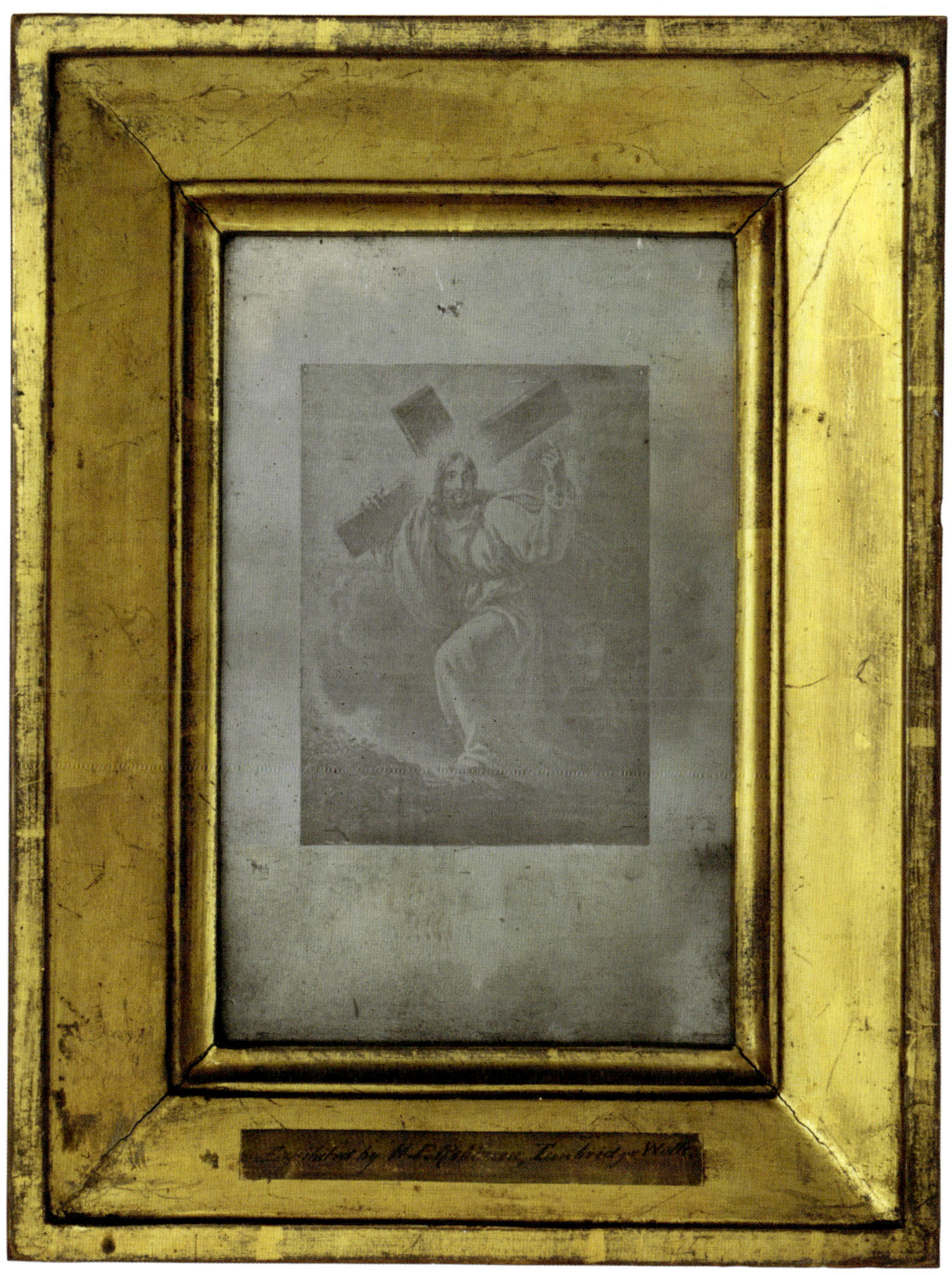

Joseph Nicéphore Niépce (1765–1833)

Christ Carrying his Cross
c.1827

Heliograph on pewter plate
29.9 x 23.2 cm (framed)

Niépce brought his heliographs from France to London in 1827. Their gilded frames appear to have been made at that time. He hoped to display the works and demonstrate his techniques to the Royal Society and King George IV, but the meetings apparently did not take place. Niépce returned home, leaving some plates with a Fellow of the Royal Society. These were presented to the Royal Photographic Society in 1924 by the son of photographer Henry Peach Robinson who had acquired them for his private collection.

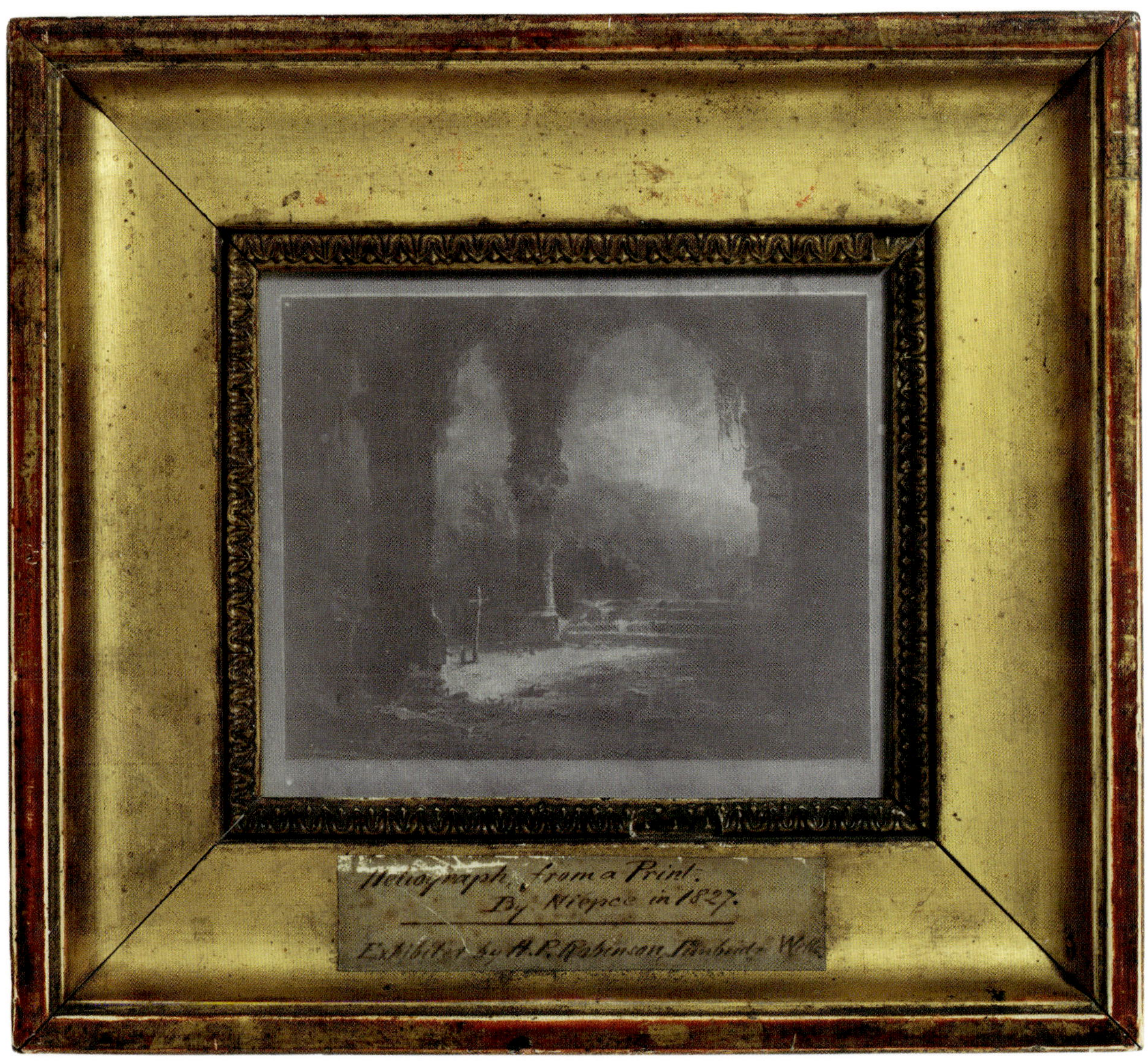

Joseph Nicéphore Niépce (1765–1833)

'Un Clair de Lune' (Moonlight)
1827

Heliograph on pewter plate
22.3 x 25.2 cm (framed)

This image is taken from an engraving of an artwork by painter, inventor and photographer Louis Daguerre (1787–1851). Daguerre had written to Niépce in 1826 after hearing about his heliograph experiments, eager to learn the techniques. The pair entered into business together in 1829. Niépce had experimented using a camera with his heliograph plates, but Daguerre perfected the methodology and the 'daguerreotype' – the first practicable photographic process – was announced to the world on 7 January 1839.

William Henry Fox Talbot (1800–1877)

Astrantia major – the 'Melancholy Gentleman'
13 November 1838

Photogenic drawing negative
17.3 x 9.5 cm

Talbot used the term 'photogenic drawing' to describe his cameraless process as early as 1834. In his private notes of 1835, he described what he set out to invent as 'sciagraphy' – the art of depicting objects through their shadows.

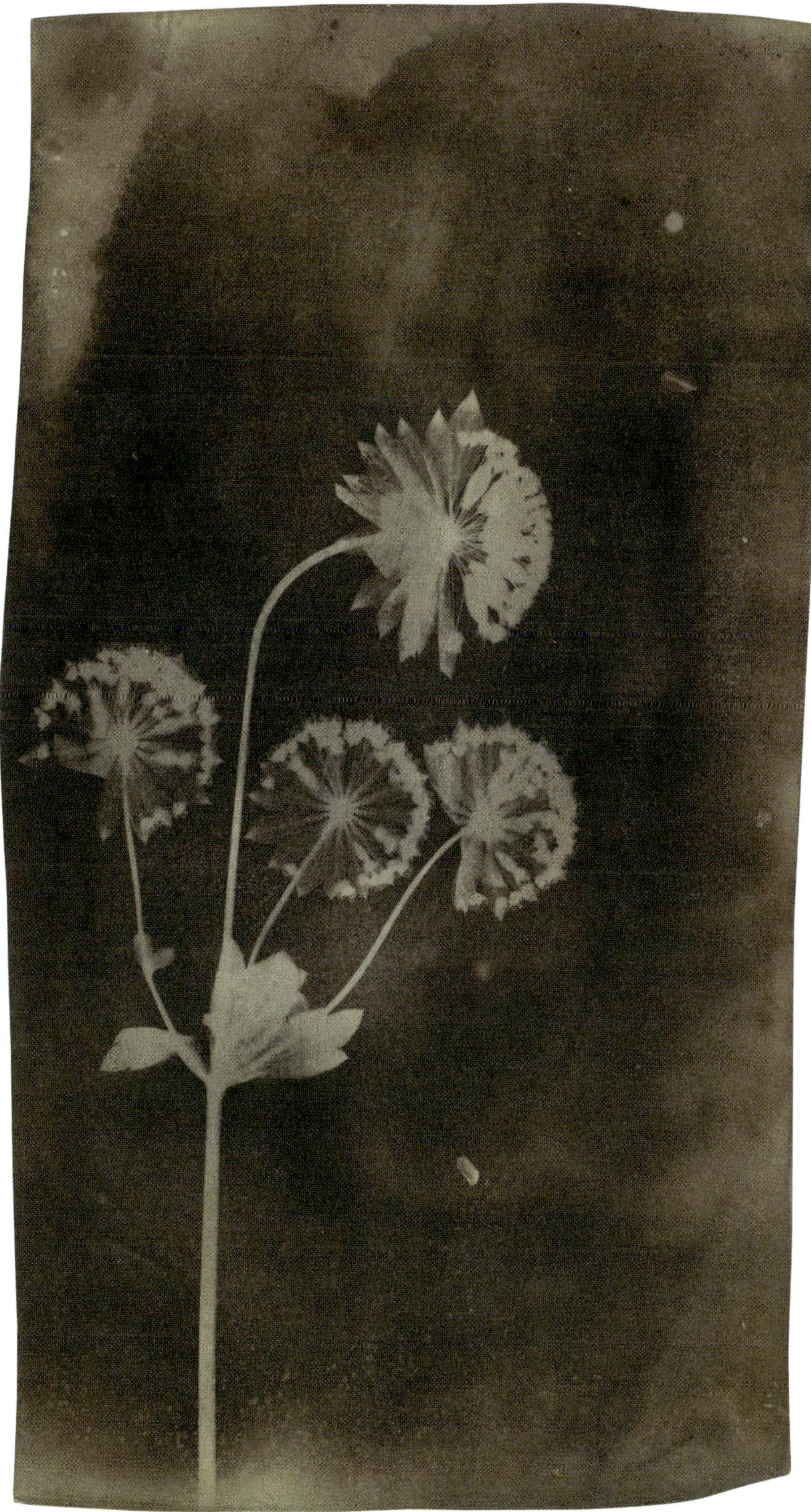

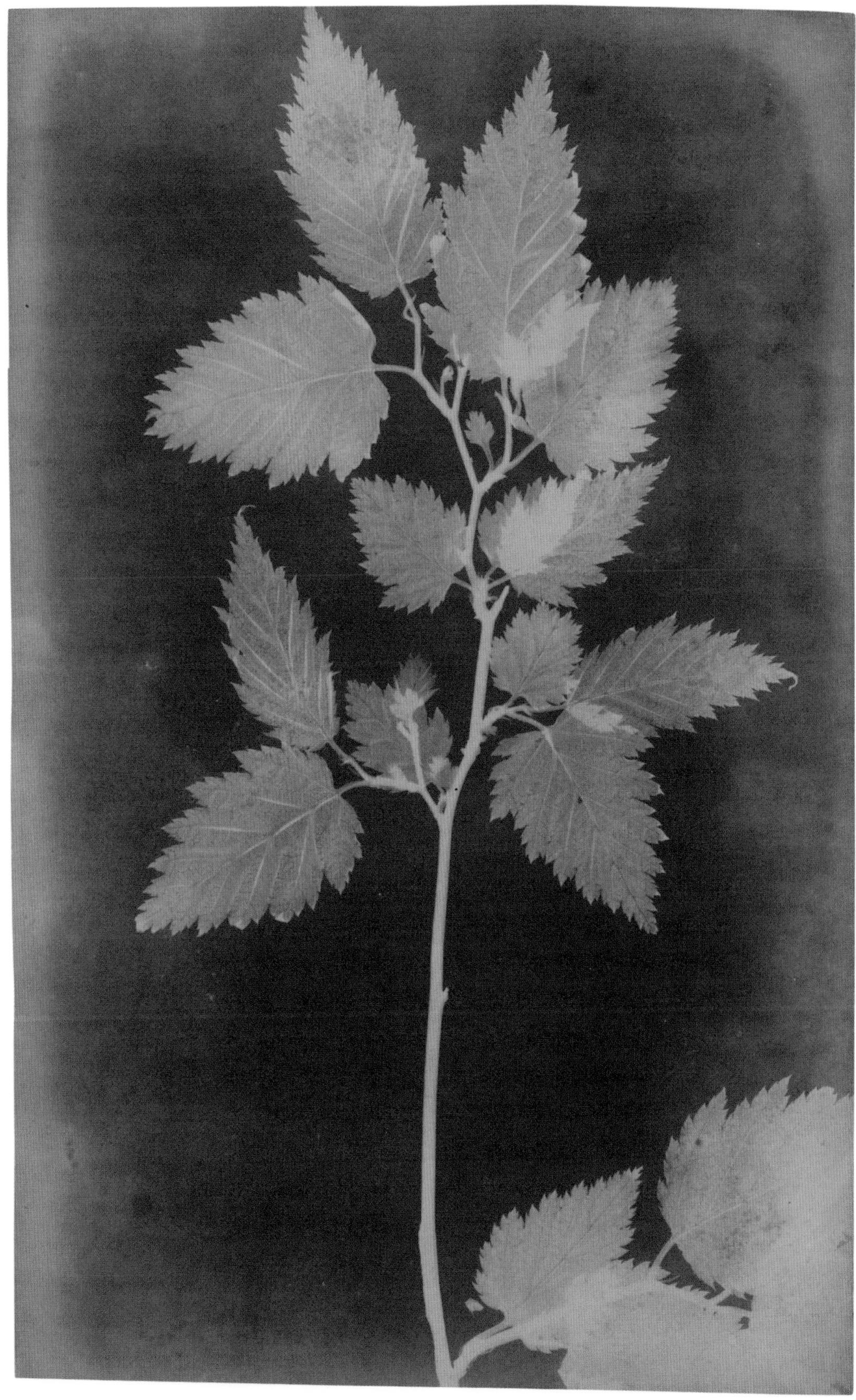

William Henry Fox Talbot (1800–1877)

Leaves on a stem
*c.*1839

Photogenic drawing negative
17.8 x 11.2 cm

Arranging a flattened plant on the surface of light-sensitized paper, Talbot placed his subject under a sheet of glass, usually in a wooden frame, and put it in the daylight for a period of around ten to thirty minutes. The emerging result was visible as a negative, with the plant shielding the paper underneath it while the surrounding areas were darkened by solar energy. However, the image would continue to darken as one viewed it under ordinary light. Almost immediately, Talbot discovered that washing the print in a strong salt solution fixed the image.

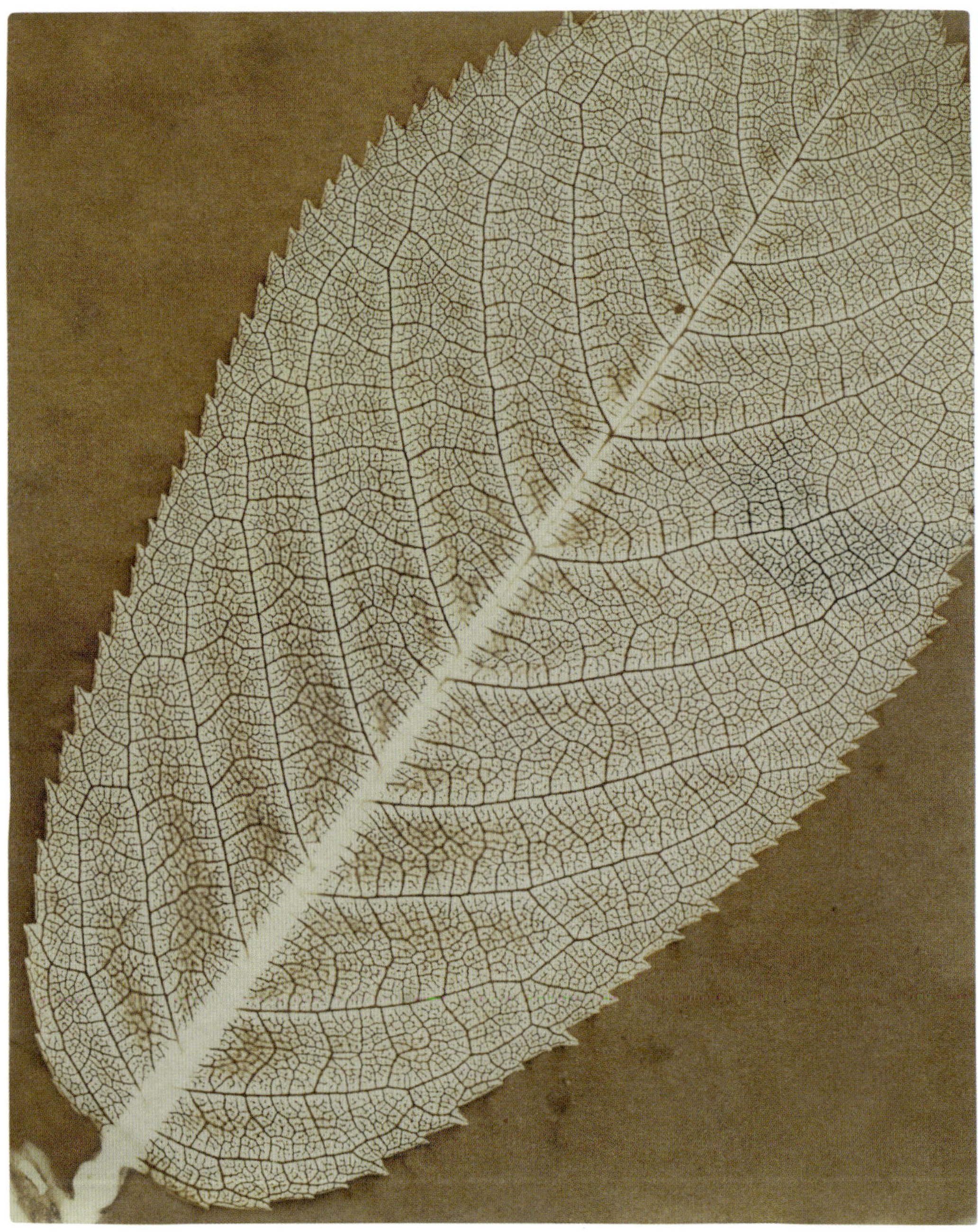

William Henry Fox Talbot (1800–1877)

Leaf
*c.*1839–44

Photogenic drawing negative
9.6 x 7.9 cm

As a talented botanist, Talbot's use of plants for his very first images was a natural choice. Many were gathered from his own gardens at Lacock Abbey in Wiltshire.

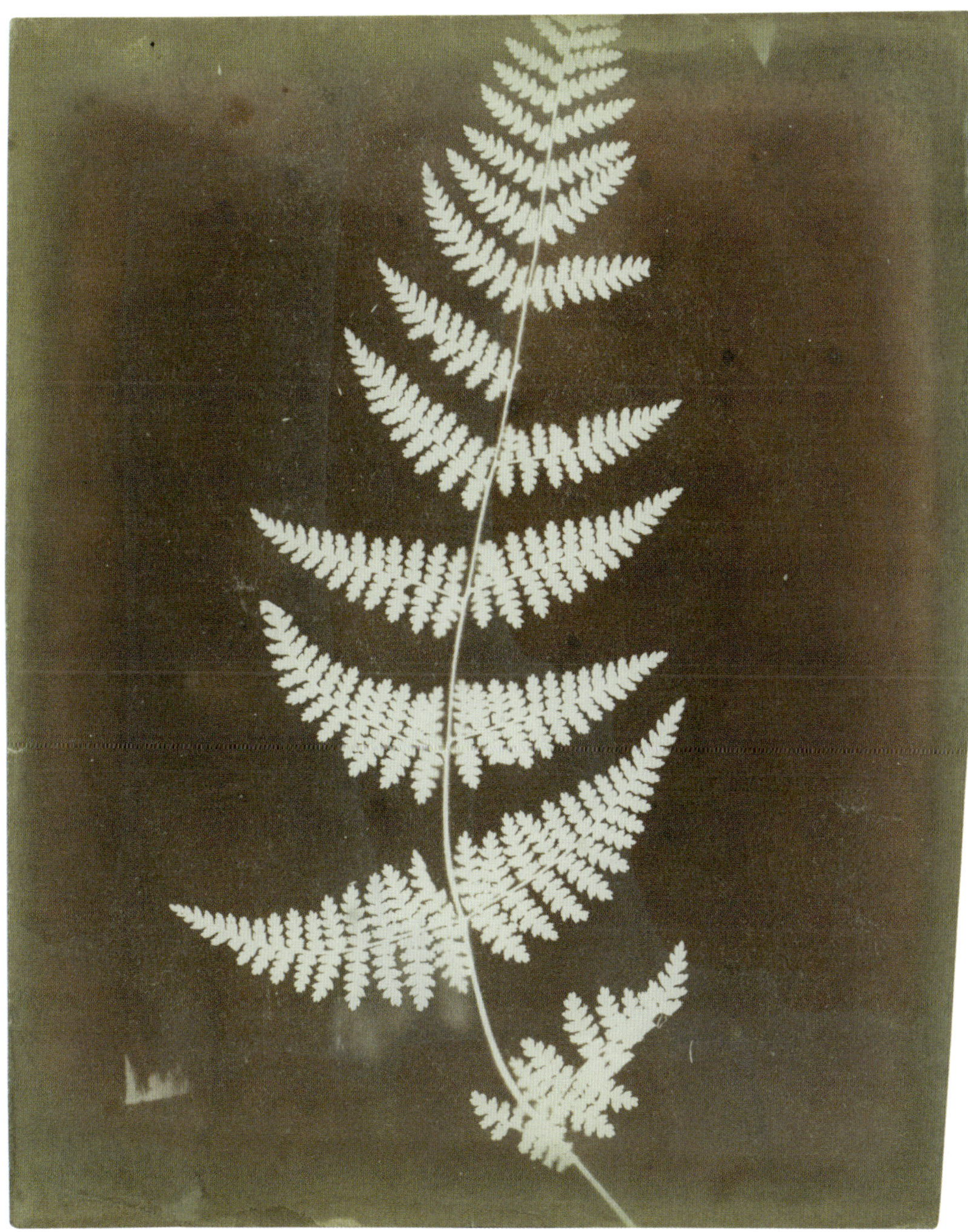

William Henry Fox Talbot (1800–1877)

Buckler fern
March or April 1839

Photogenic drawing negative
22.8 x 18 cm

(detail p.182)

Talbot favoured this particular fern, using it to make at least twenty examples of photogenic drawings in March and April of 1839. It progressively shed leaves and whole branches through handling.

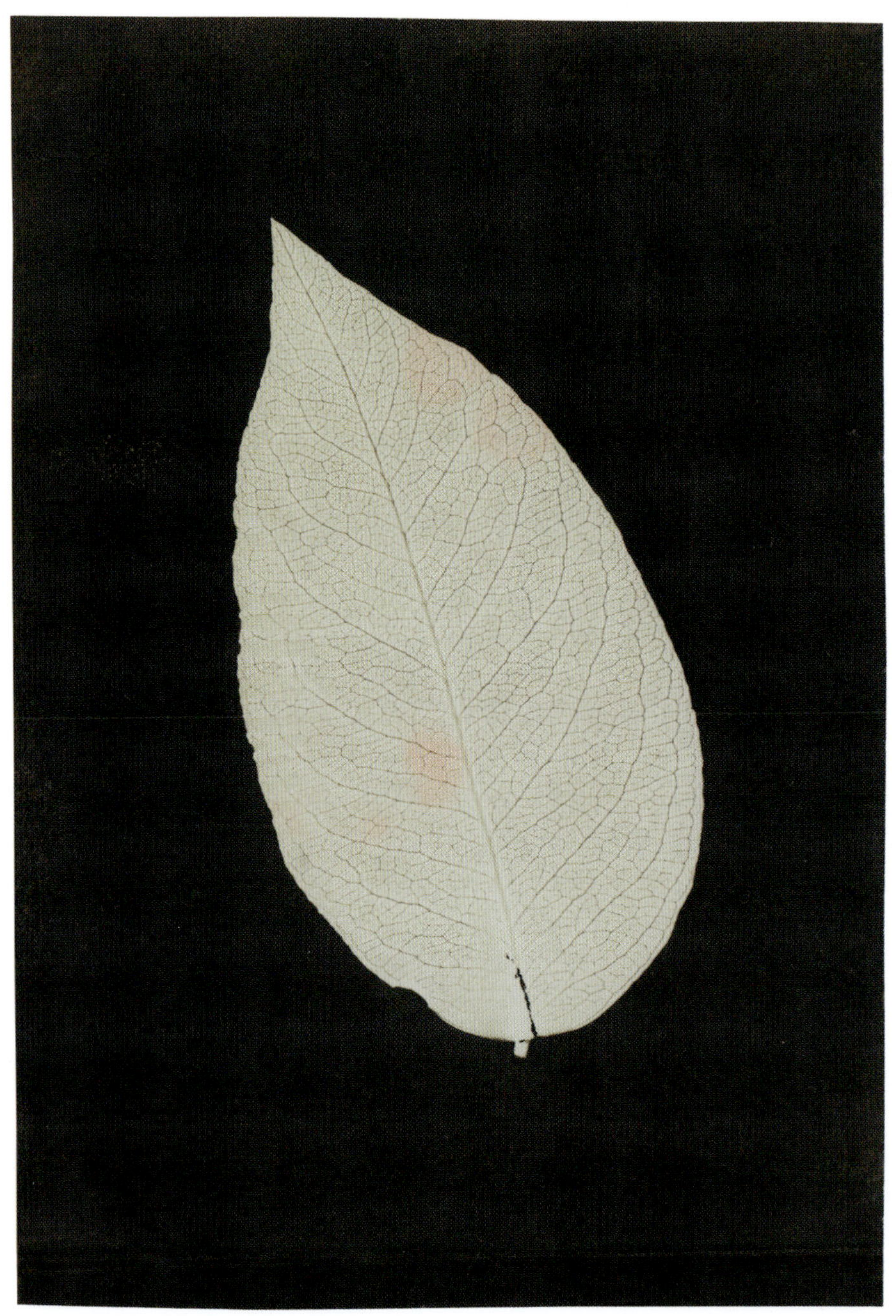

William Henry Fox Talbot (1800–1877)

Leaf
*c.*1839

Photogenic drawing negative
15.1 x 10.5 cm

Unlike a hand-drawn illustration, where an artist could use their imagination to fill in details, photography captured exactly what it 'saw'. In this case, the stem has been torn away, accidentally or intentionally, from the leaf – a loss faithfully recorded by Talbot's sensitive paper. Most of these early negatives were never printed, for Talbot saw them as precious original drawings made by nature. There is one known salt print from this negative.

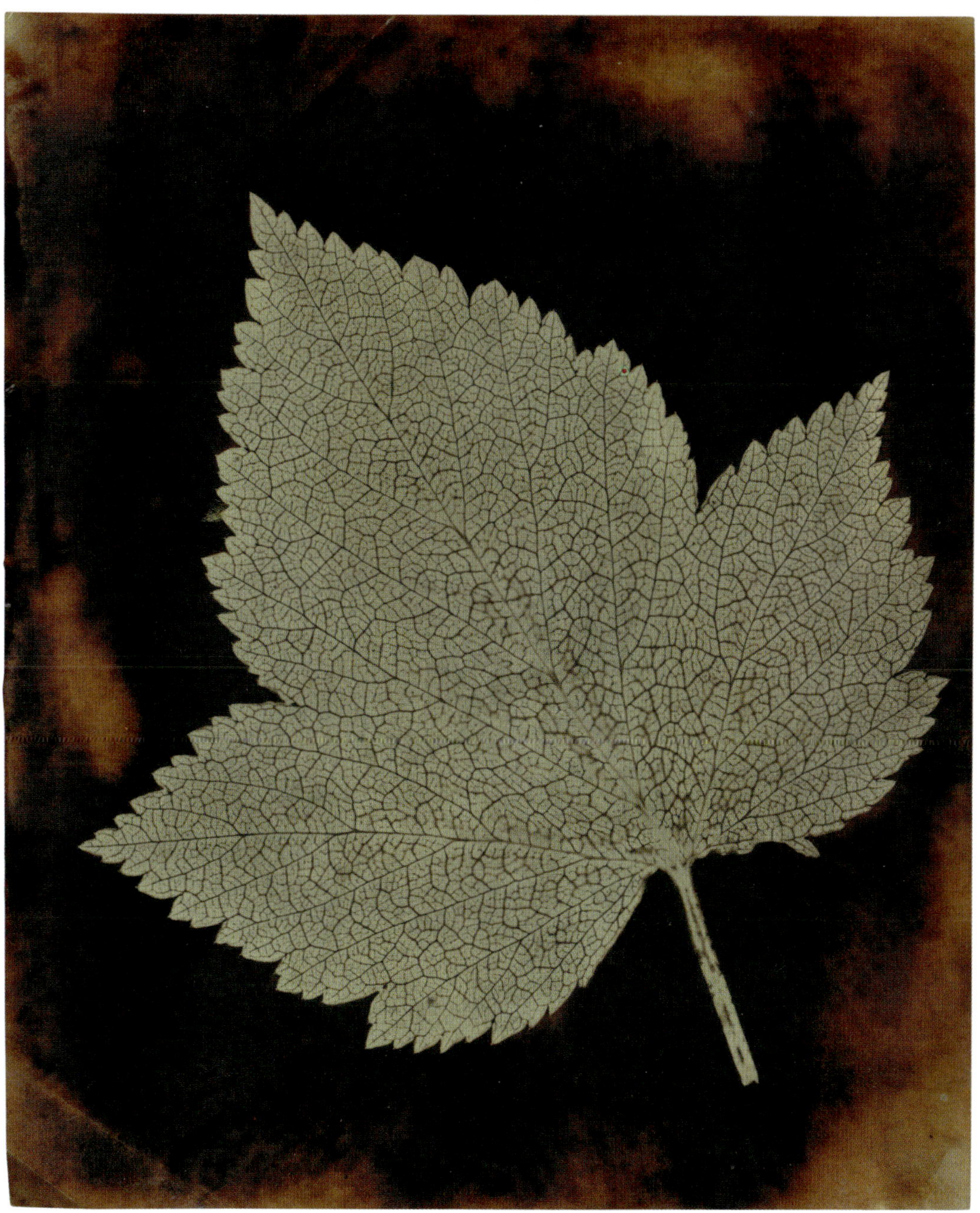

William Henry Fox Talbot (1800–1877)
or Nicolaas Henneman (1813–1898)

Leaf
*c.*1839–44

Photogenic drawing negative, waxed
18.8 x 15.6 cm

Talbot's former valet, Nicolaas Henneman, established a pioneering photographic works in the town of Reading in late 1843. Naturally his choice of subjects was influenced by the practices of the master. Waxing the paper negative made it more transparent, in some cases making it easier to print. This practice was more common at Reading than at Lacock.

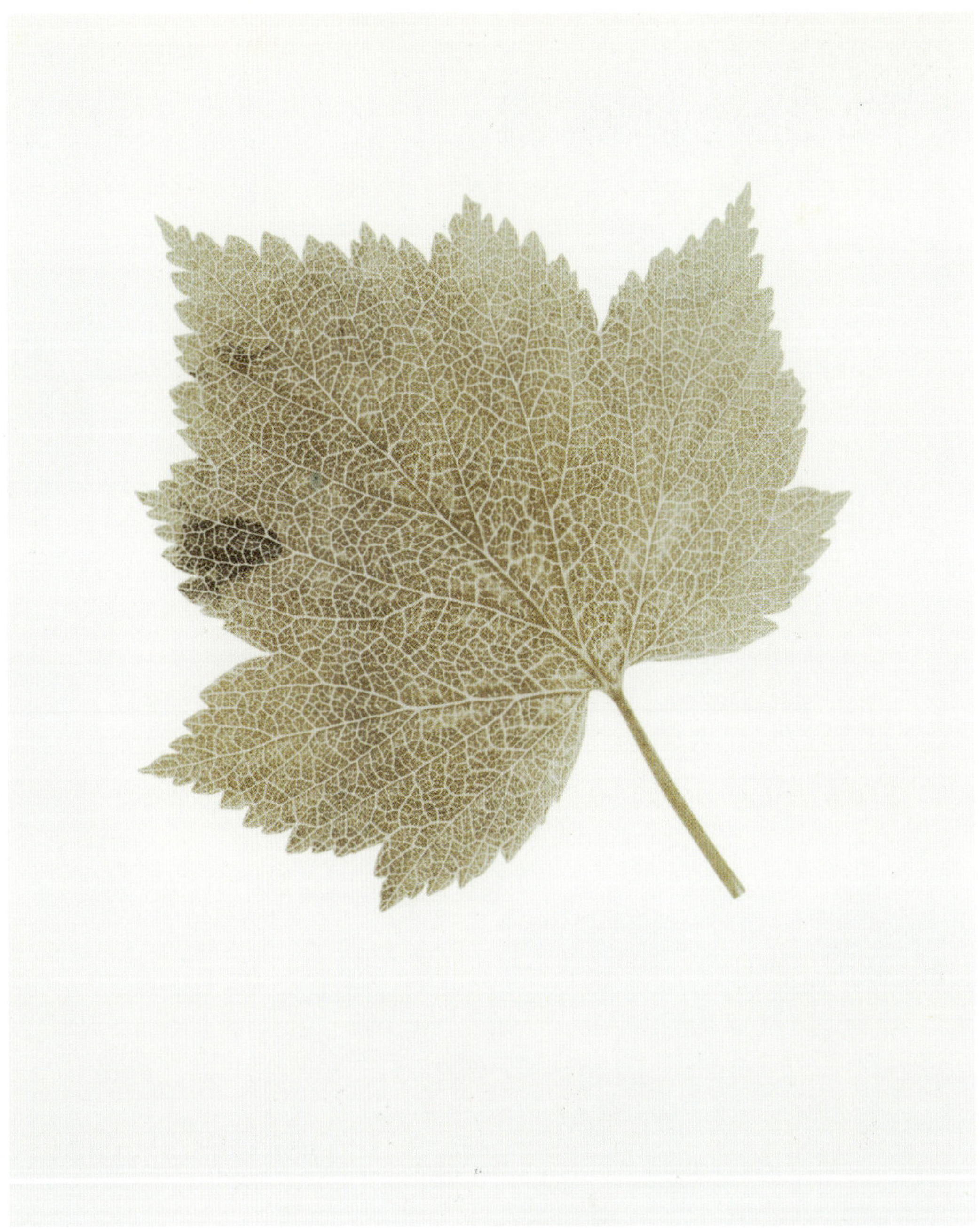

Nicolaas Henneman (1813–1898)

Leaf
*c.*1843–5

Salted paper print from a photogenic drawing negative
18.8 x 15.6 cm

Positive images could be produced by placing a photogenic drawing negative over a second sheet of sensitized paper and exposing the sandwich to daylight. Although this print is very similar to the preceding negative, there are differences in the edges of the leaf, and it would have been laterally reversed in printing. The ink inscription '1/' on the back indicates that Henneman offered it for sale for one shilling. Talbot, being a gentleman, never entered into commerce. There is one other surviving example of this print.

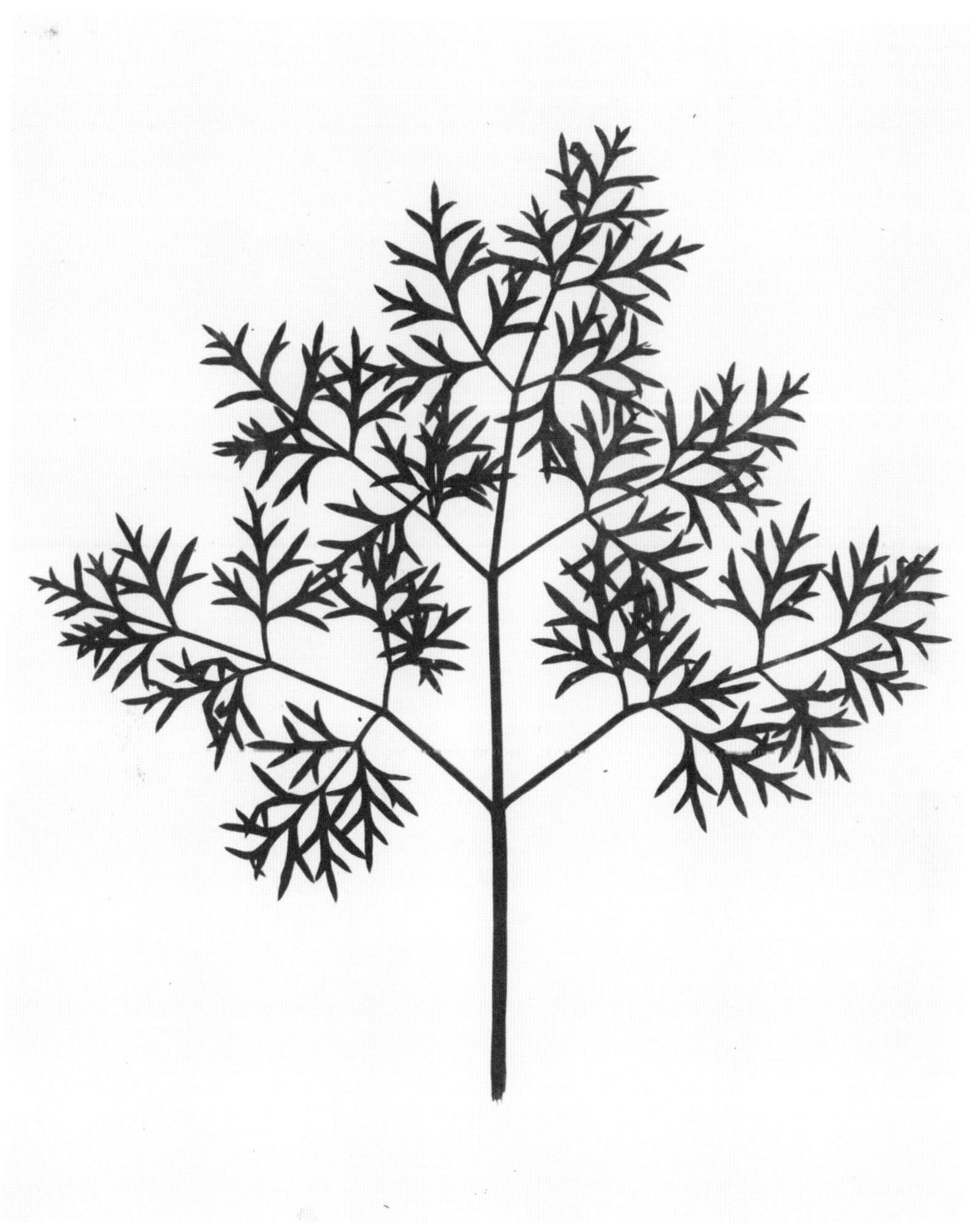

William Henry Fox Talbot (1800–1877)

Fern
printed 1846 or later

Salted paper print
22.9 x 18.9 cm

Although the negative for this is not known to have survived, there are numerous prints from it, some dating to 1839, so it must have been a favoured example. This particular print is on paper watermarked 'J Whatman 1846' – a testimony to the durability of some of Talbot's early negatives.

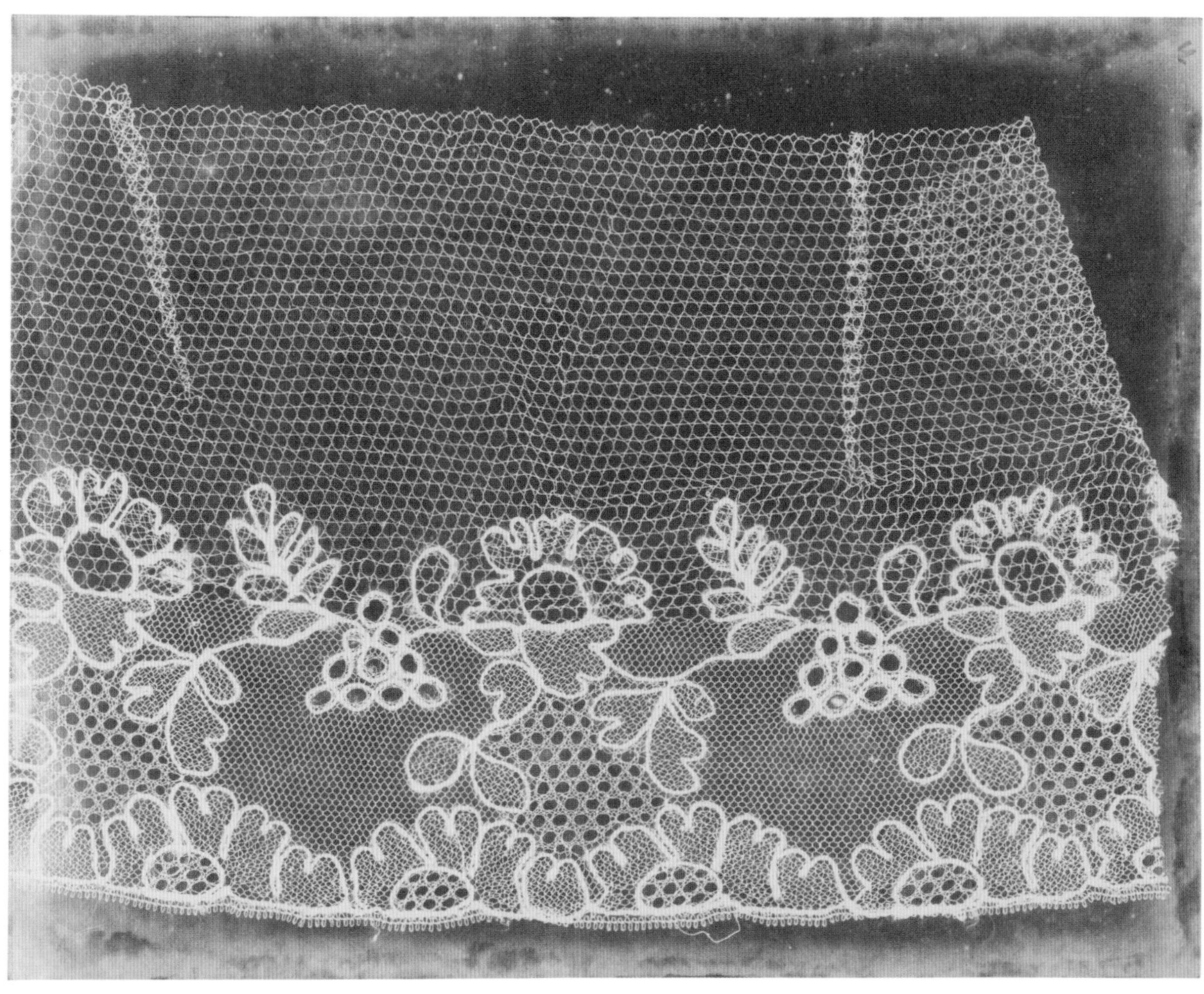

William Henry Fox Talbot (1800–1877)

Lace
1844

Photogenic drawing negative
17.4 x 22 cm

This image was published in Talbot's *The Pencil of Nature*, his pioneering explanation of photography and his manifesto for its possibilities. In the text, he wrote: '... in copying such things as lace or leaves of plants, a negative image is perfectly allowable, black lace being as familiar to the eye as white lace, and the object being only to exhibit the pattern with accuracy.' It is the only plate in *The Pencil of Nature* that was a unique negative in each copy; the other twenty-three plates were prints made from a common negative.

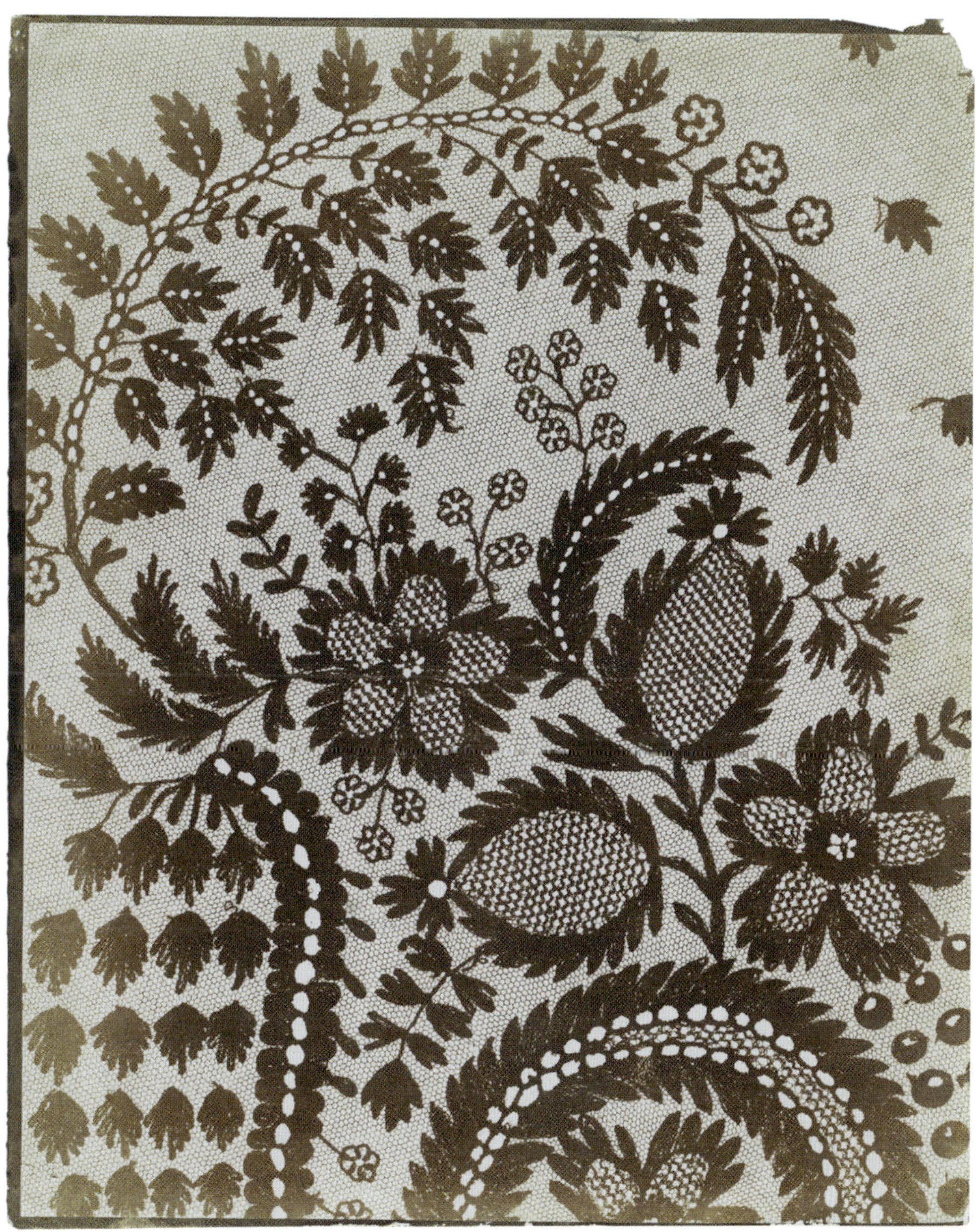

William Henry Fox Talbot (1800–1877)

Black lace
early 1840s

Salted paper print from a photogenic drawing negative
23.2 x 18.9 cm

Although this appears to be black lace, in fact either black or white lace would block the daylight from the sensitive negative paper, yielding very similar results. Talbot exhibited the original negative for this in 1852 at the Royal Society of Arts. It still retains its vigour, even though it was used to make numerous prints.

William Henry Fox Talbot (1800–1877)

Ferns, leaves and fabric
*c.*1852

Photographic engravings
25 x 24 cm

Talbot's silver-based photographs often suffered from fading when they entered the real-world conditions of sunlit drawing rooms and coal-smoke-laden country houses. For the last twenty-five years of his life, he sought to perfect a method of using silver-based photography to capture nature's drawing faithfully, and then photographically producing an intaglio printing plate from this that would allow the final prints to be rendered in permanent printer's ink. As in his earliest photographic experiments, he initially turned to plants and fabric to make contact-printed images on his copper or steel printing plates. He first called these 'photographic engravings' and patented the process in 1852. It was the direct forerunner of the modern photogravure process.

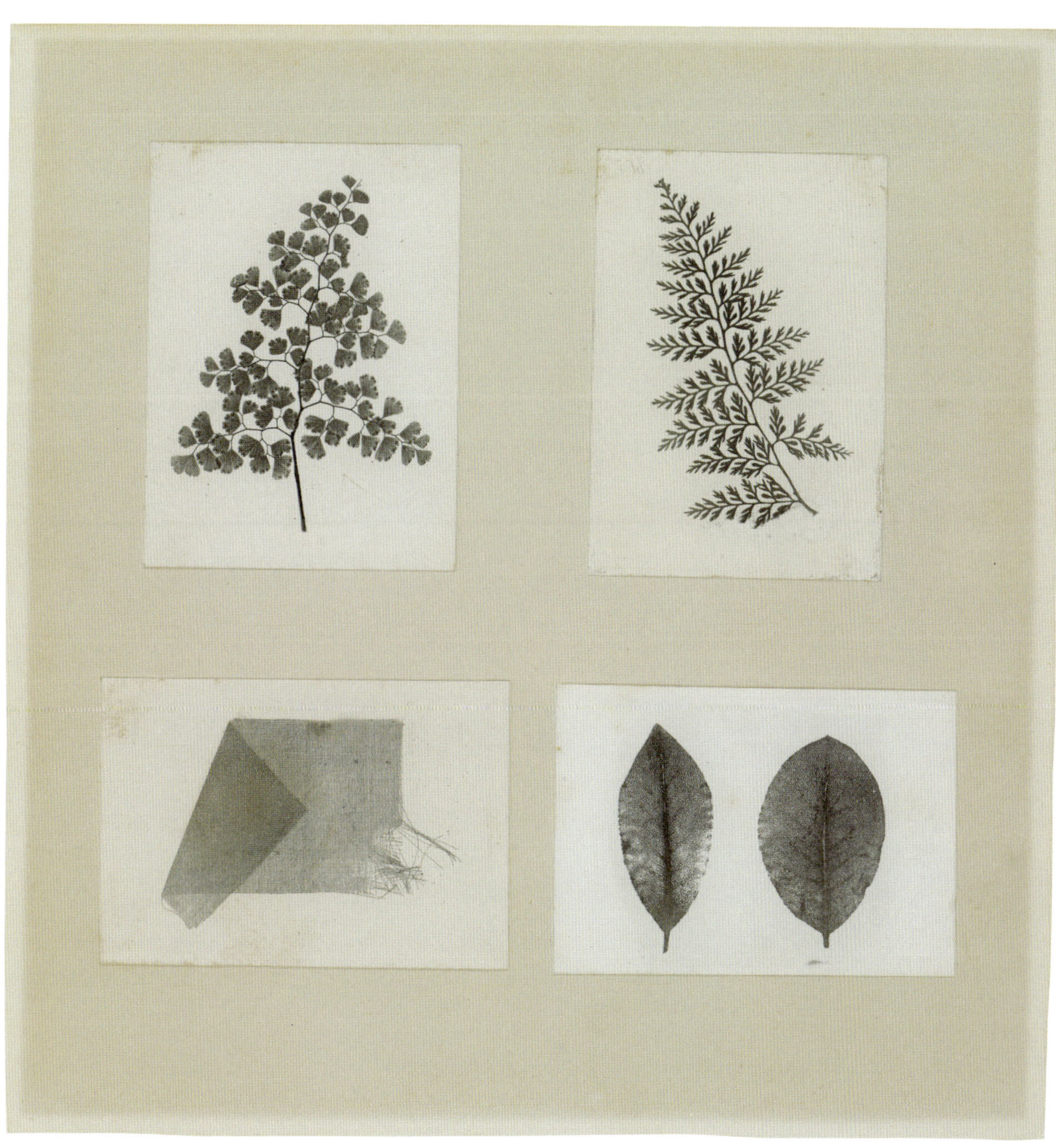

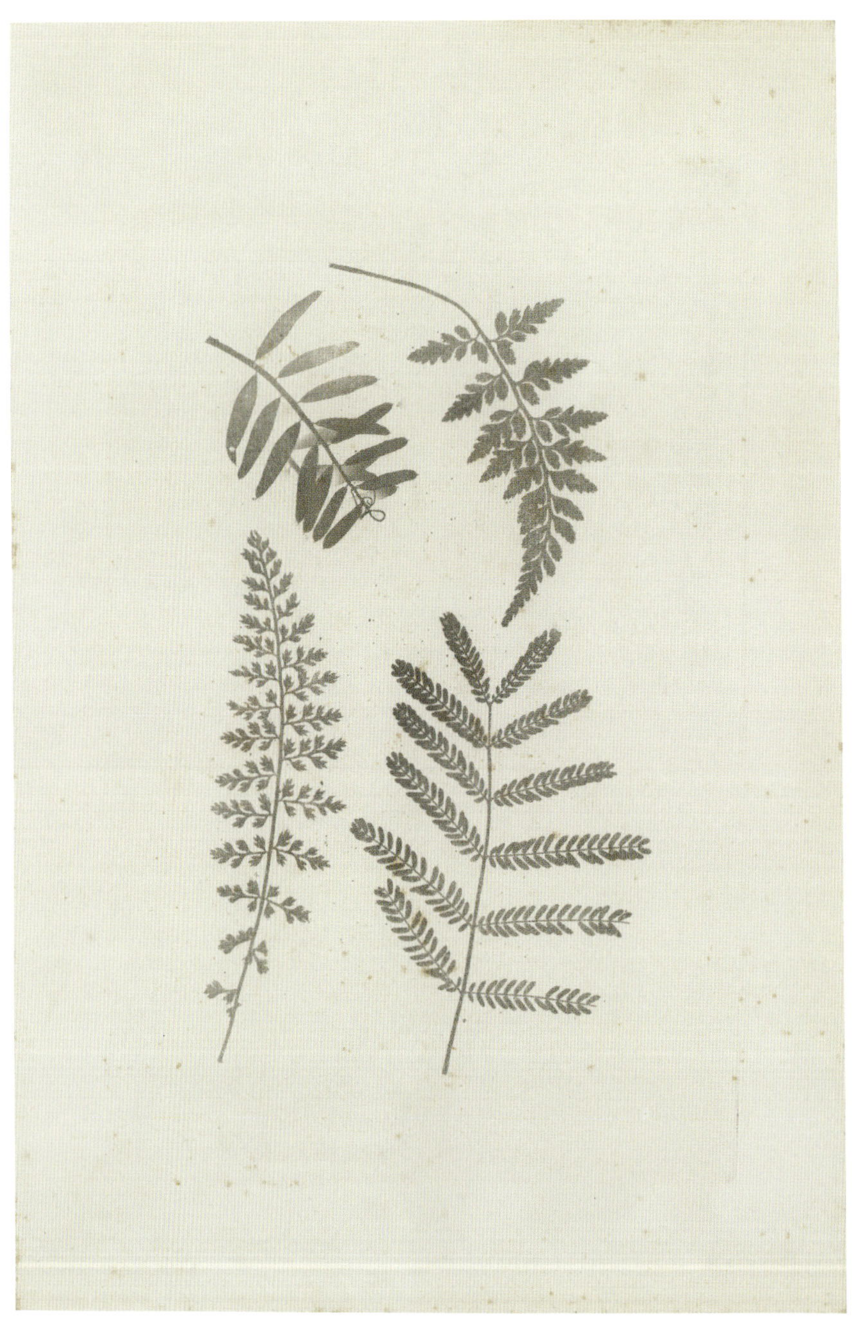

William Henry Fox Talbot (1800–1877)

Ferns and leaves
*c.*1852

Photographic engraving
26 x 21.8 cm

(detail p.6)

Initially, reproducing a range of middle tones was a challenge for Talbot, as any wide channels in his intaglio plates lost some of their ink when wiped over to remove excess ink from the blank areas. His first solution was to create the equivalent of the half-tone dot. Close examination of this print and its plate reveals that he imposed a piece of loosely woven fabric over the image, breaking up the solid areas into small ones that would retain their ink but still give good tonalities to the eye at a normal viewing distance.

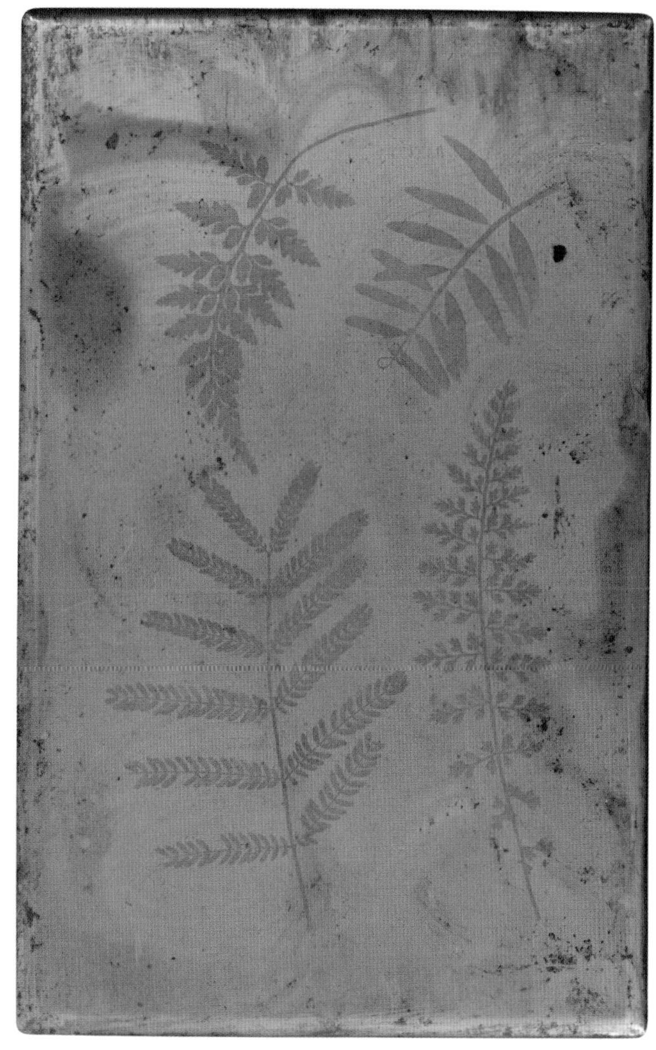

William Henry Fox Talbot (1800–1877)

Printing plate corresponding with Ferns and leaves
*c.*1852

Steel photographic engraving plate
19.6 x 12 cm

The original steel plate reproduced here was used to print the photographic engraving shown opposite. The image of the leaves, seemingly pressed into the plate to leave their mark, can be compared with other direct impressions that rely on touch, like fossils or animal tracks in snow.

Johann Carl Enslen (1759–1848)

Face of Christ superimposed over an oak leaf
1839

Salted paper print from a photogenic drawing negative
16.2 x 13.1 cm

Enslen was a German painter and travelling showman who, aged eighty, experimented with photography after reading about Talbot's work. He sent this example to Talbot and it remained in Talbot's collection. Enslen appears never to have used a camera. Instead, he overlaid engravings, plants and other natural specimens on sensitized paper.

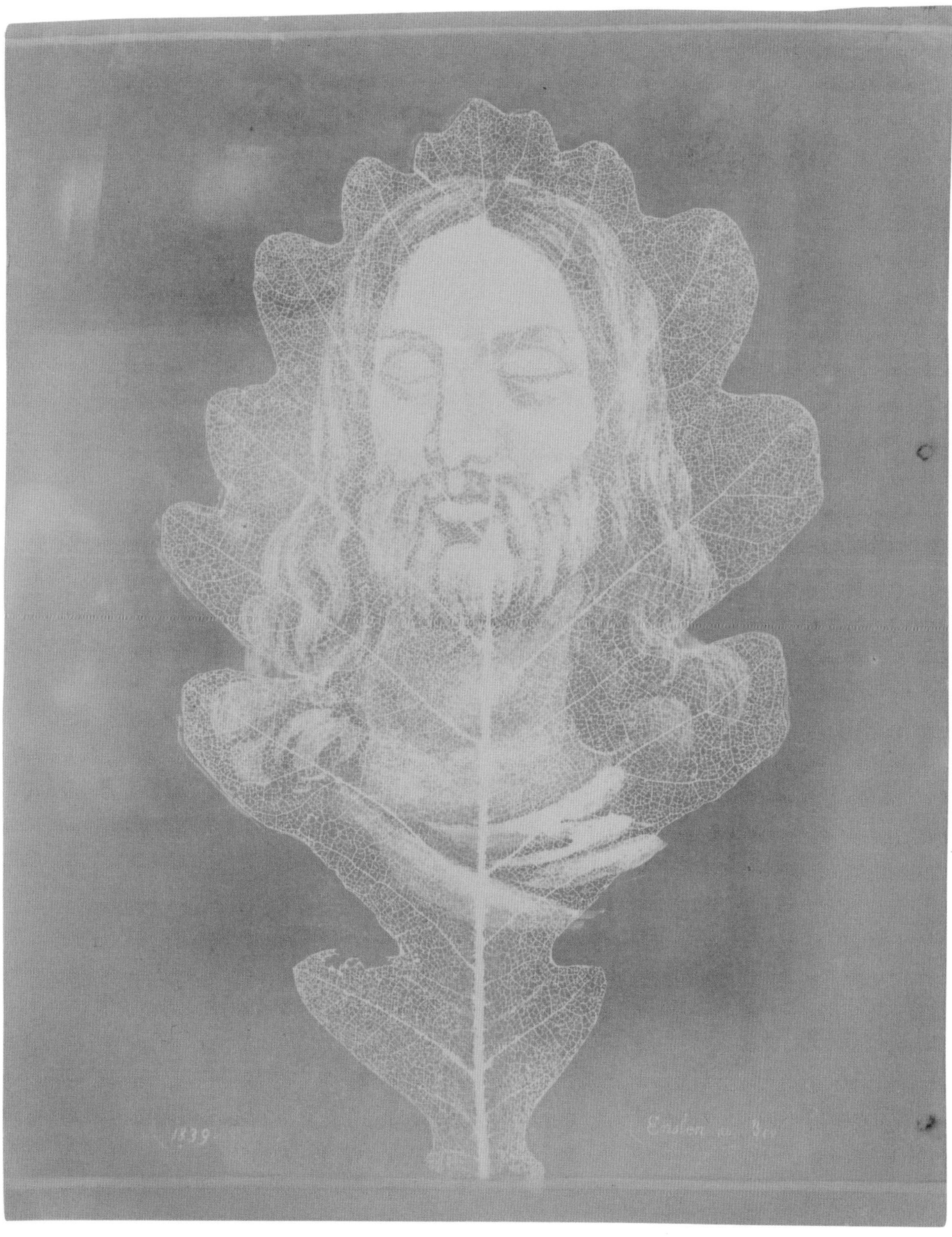
1839.

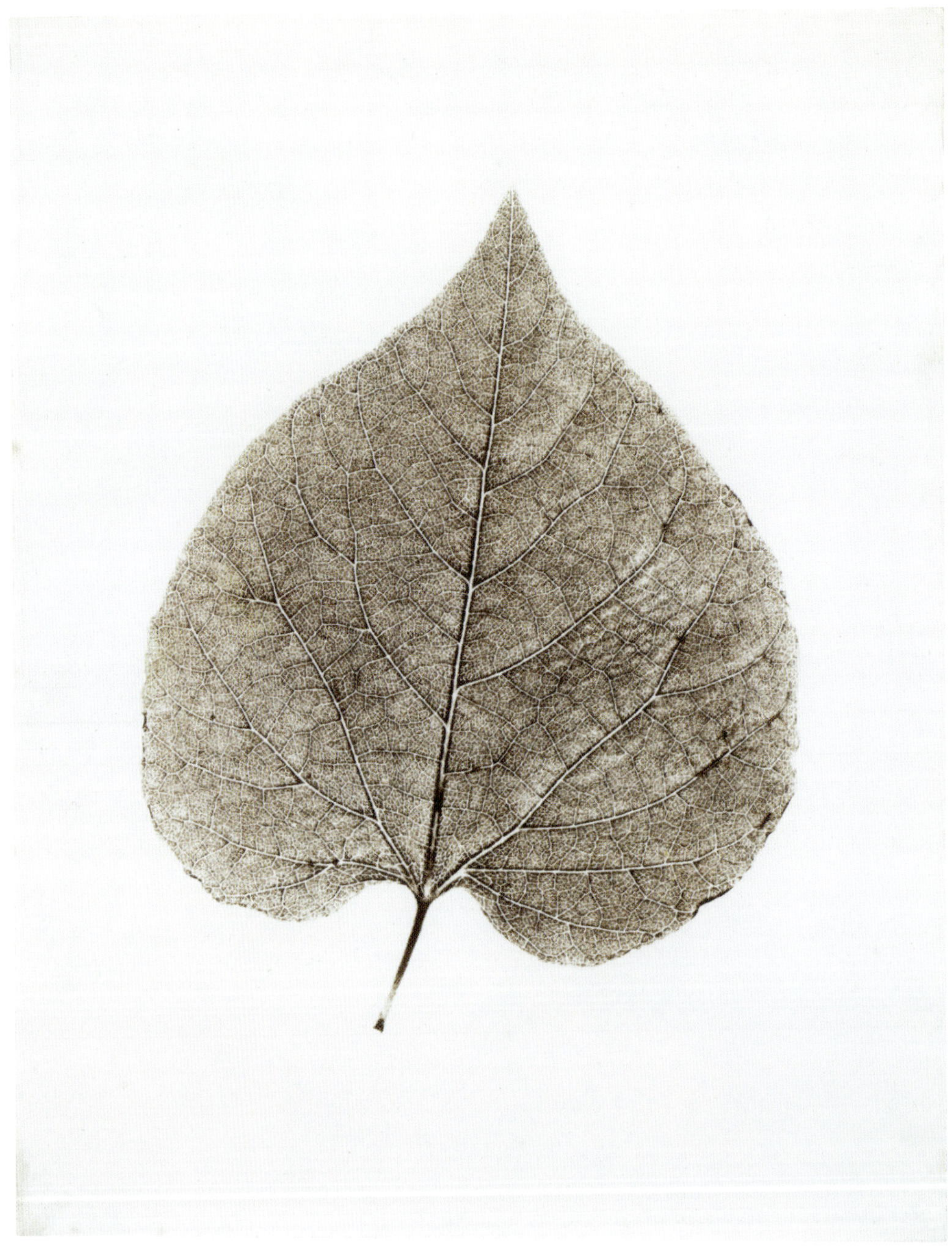

Calvert Richard Jones (1802–1877)

Lime leaf
*c.*1845

Salted paper print from photogenic drawing negative
20.6 x 16.4 cm

Jones was an associate of Talbot, and a skilled painter and photographer who made landscape and architectural studies on extensive European travels. It is unusual to find cameraless images among his work. This one was made in the same way as the examples on pp.26 and 27.

Anna Atkins (1799–1871)

Title page of *British and Foreign Flowering Plants and Ferns*
*c.*1854

Cyanotype
35 x 25 cm

Atkins is credited with being the first woman photographer and the first person to produce a photographically illustrated book, *British Algae: Cyanotype Impressions* (1843). Illustrated here is the title page from a later book, from which the following pages are also illustrations.

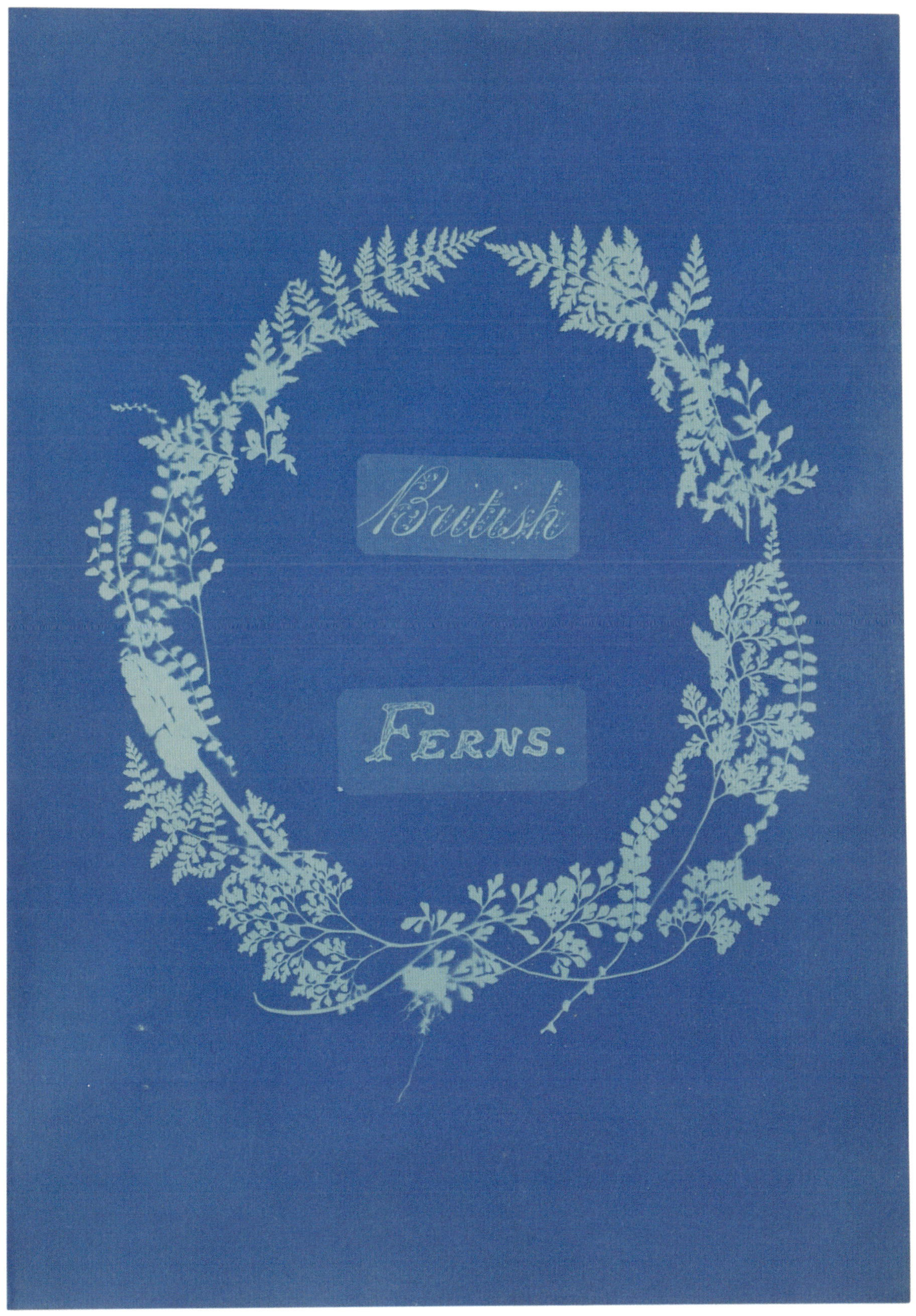
British
Ferns.

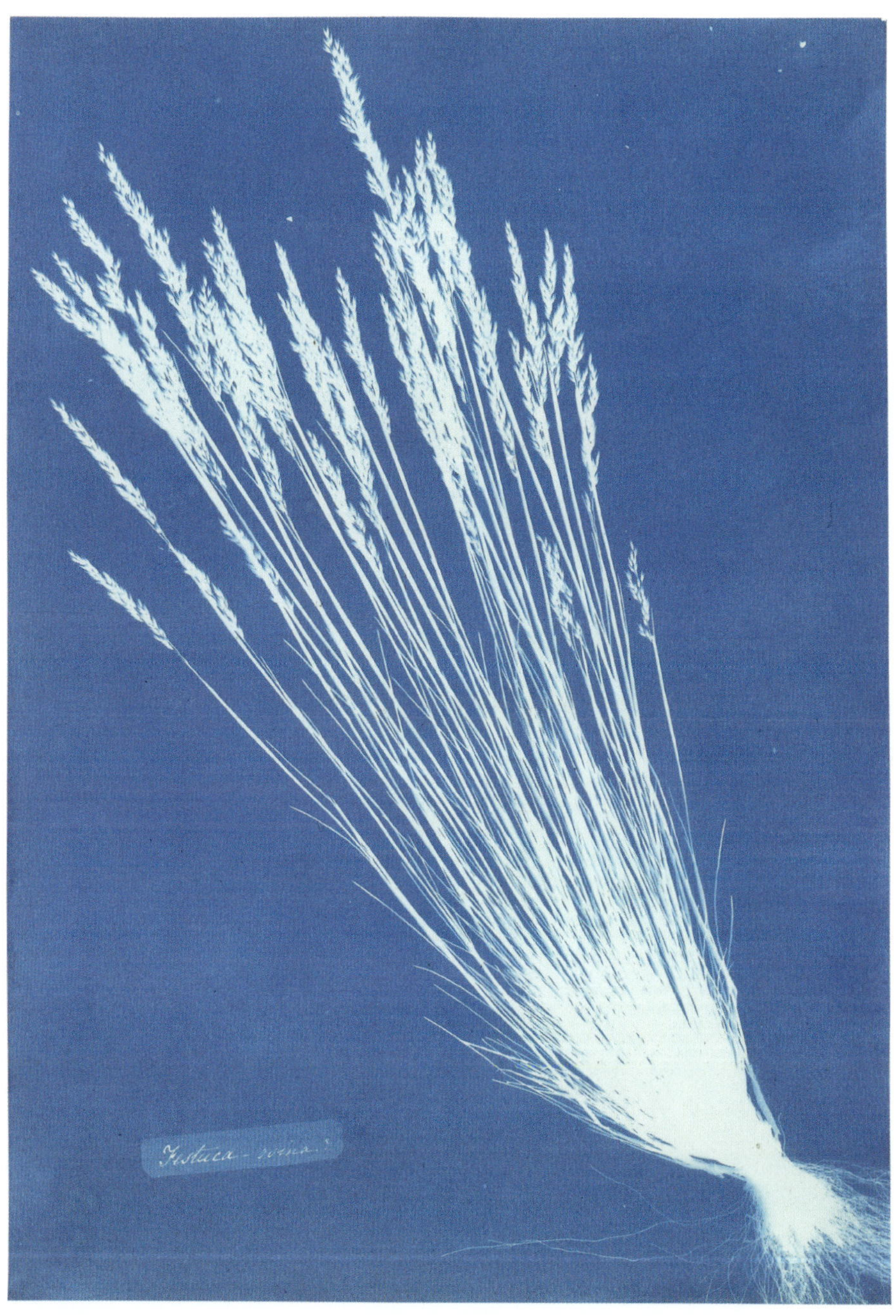

Anna Atkins (1799–1871)

Festuca Ovina (Fescue Grasses)

from *British and Foreign Flowering Plants and Ferns*
*c.*1854

Cyanotype
35 x 24.8 cm

Atkins was already a skilled technical illustrator by the time she took up the cyanotype photographic process invented by Sir John Herschel in 1842. A sheet of paper was brushed with iron salt solutions and dried in the dark. After exposing an object on the paper in sunlight for a few minutes the paper was washed in water. Oxidation produced a white image on a brilliant blue, or cyan, background.

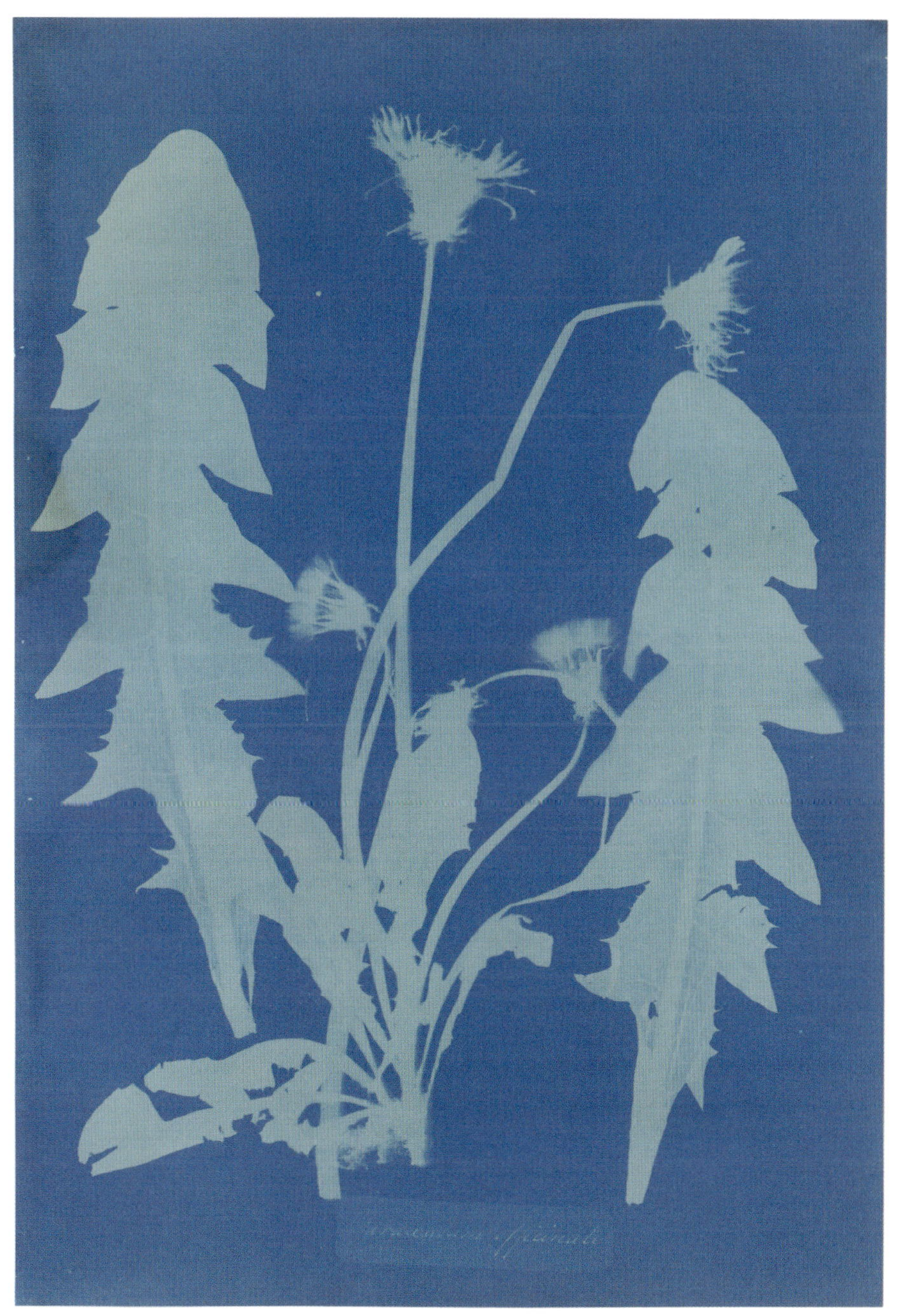

Anna Atkins (1799–1871)

Dandelion (*Taraxacum Officinale*)
from *British and Foreign Flowering Plants and Ferns*
*c.*1854

Cyanotype
35 x 24.8 cm

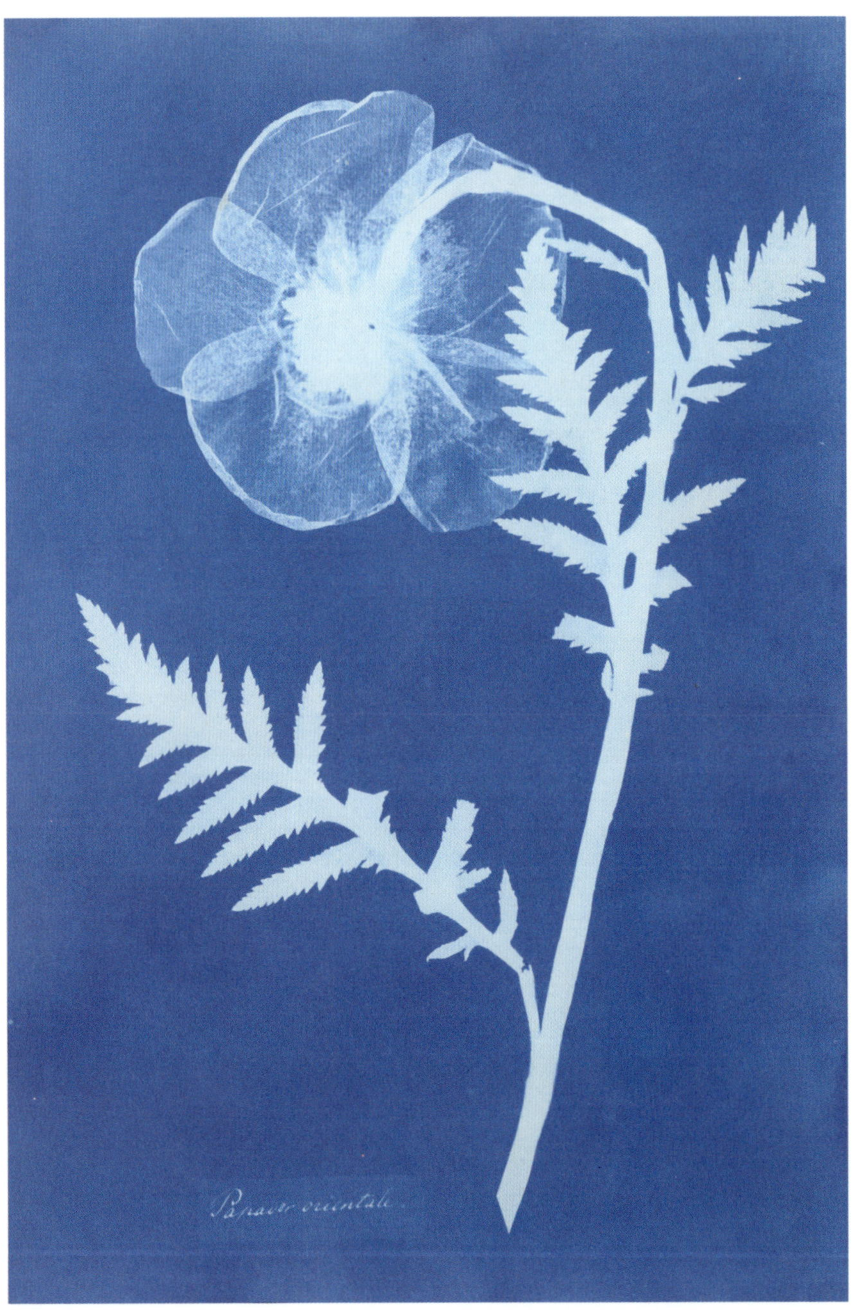

Anna Atkins (1799–1871)

Papaver Orientale

from *British and Foreign Flowering Plants and Ferns*
c.1854

Cyanotype
35 x 24.8 cm

At the time of its invention, the cyanotype process was little used, except for printing what are now described as photograms, like this example. From the 1880s it was used for copying engineering and architectural drawings, giving rise to the term 'blueprint'.

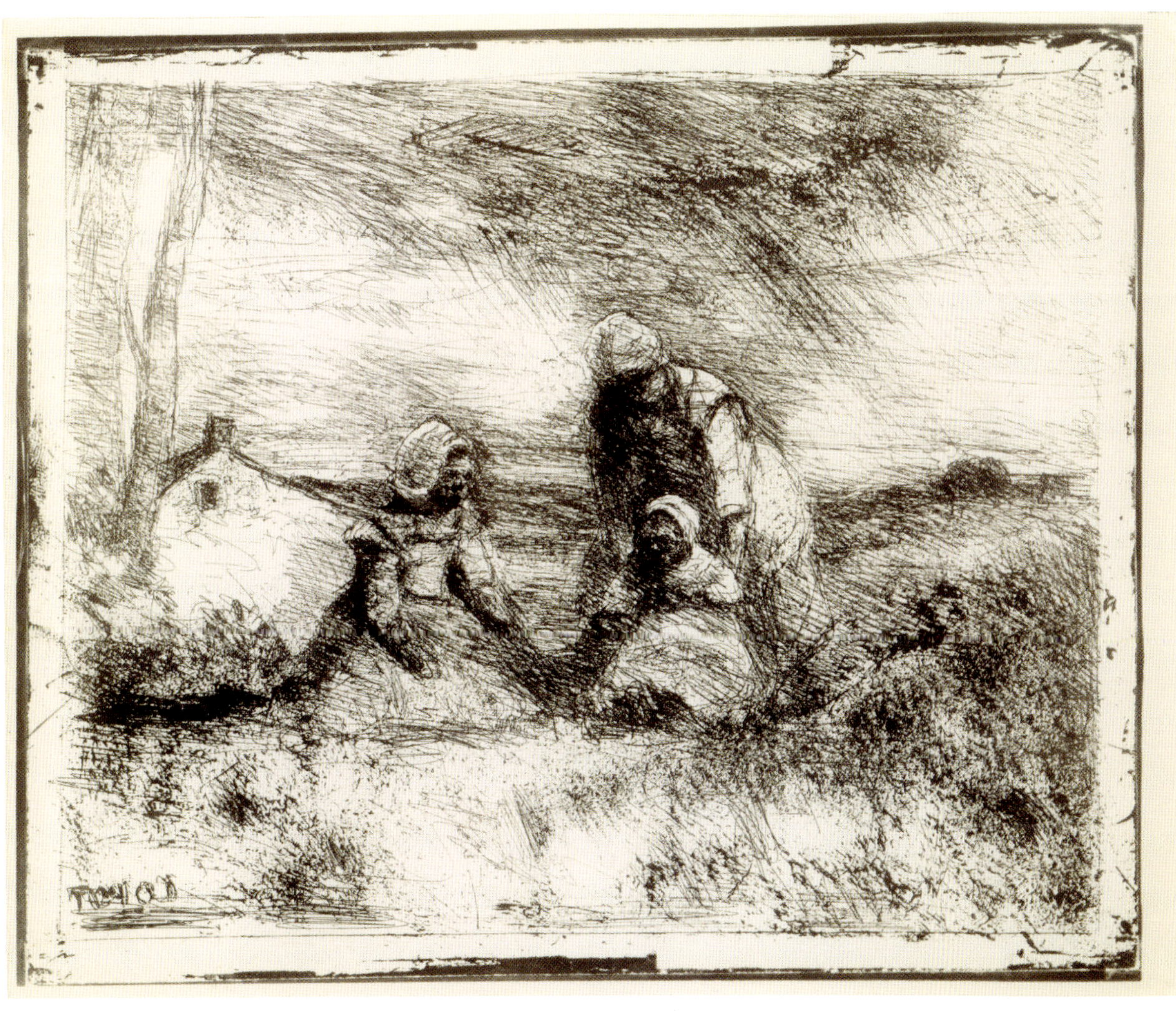

Jean-Baptiste-Camille Corot (1796–1875)

The Little Sister
1854

Cliché-verre on albumen paper
17.2 x 21.3 cm

A *cliché-verre* is a photograph made from a hand-drawn negative. The design is scratched onto a piece of smoked glass, which is placed on a sheet of sensitized paper and exposed to light. The blackened area of the glass acts as a stencil, protecting the sheet below from the light and thus creating black lines on the paper. Corot was a painter, but he also made many works using the *cliché-verre* technique.

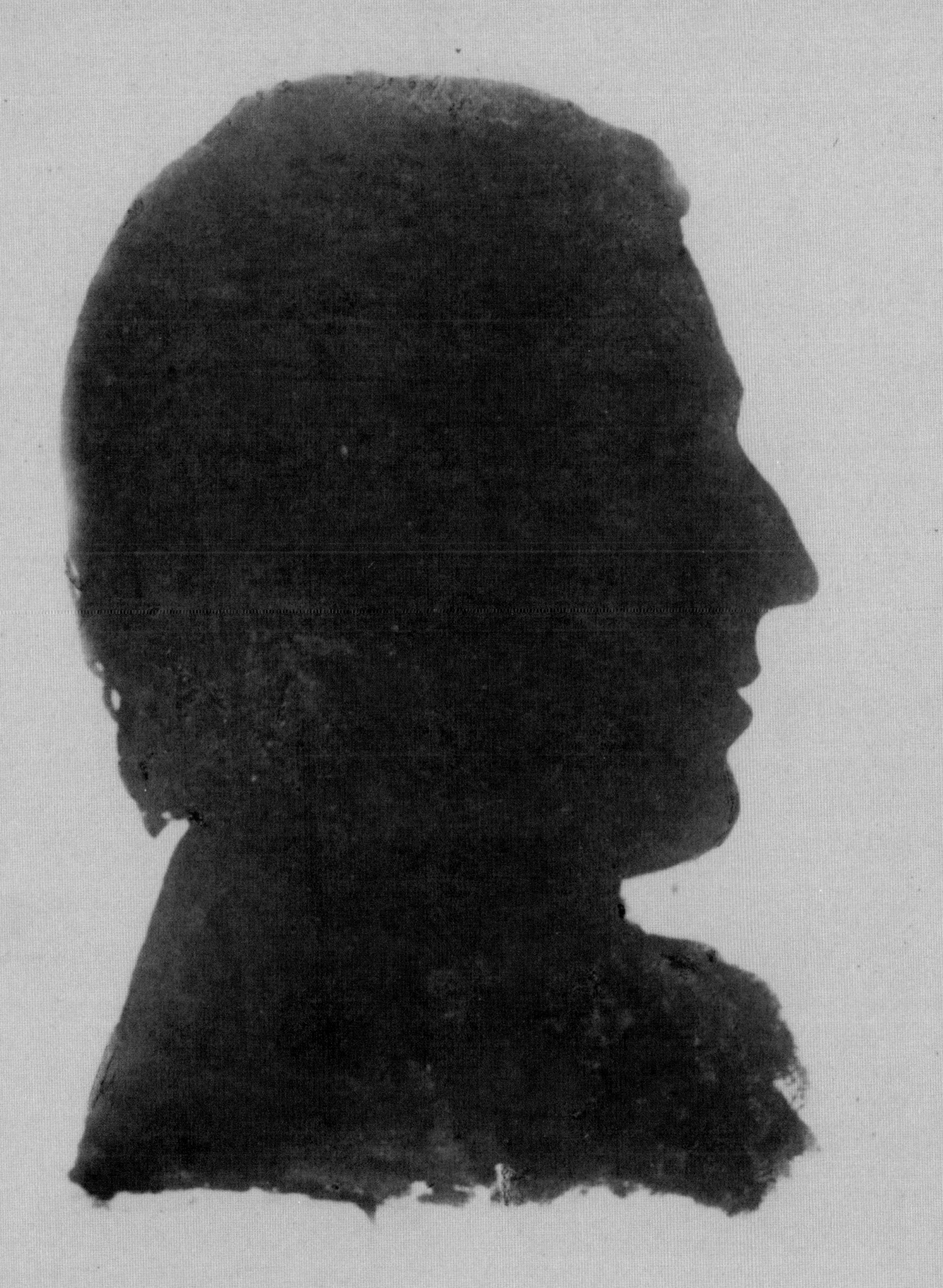

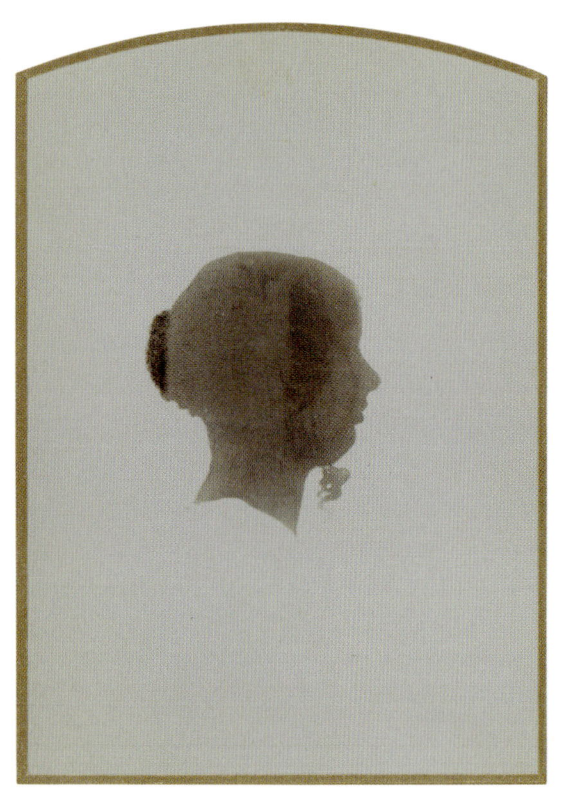

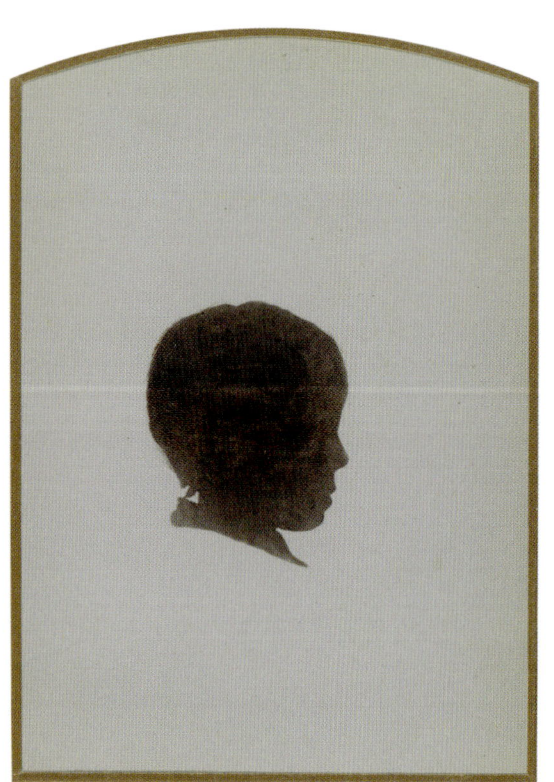

E. & J. Baldwin Photographic Portrait Studio (fl.1880s)

Silhouettes

from the album *Hurstbourne in the Forties*
silhouettes 1840s; photographs *c.*1880

Carbon prints
20.5 x 16.5 cm each

(detail p.47)

These photographs were collected in an album inscribed: 'The originals of these (life size) were done by outlining the shadows on a wall and then filled in with black – they were in my possession.' Probably owned by a member of the Fellowes family, the photographs record the proto-photographic silhouettes and represent an intersection of two closely related methods of portraiture.

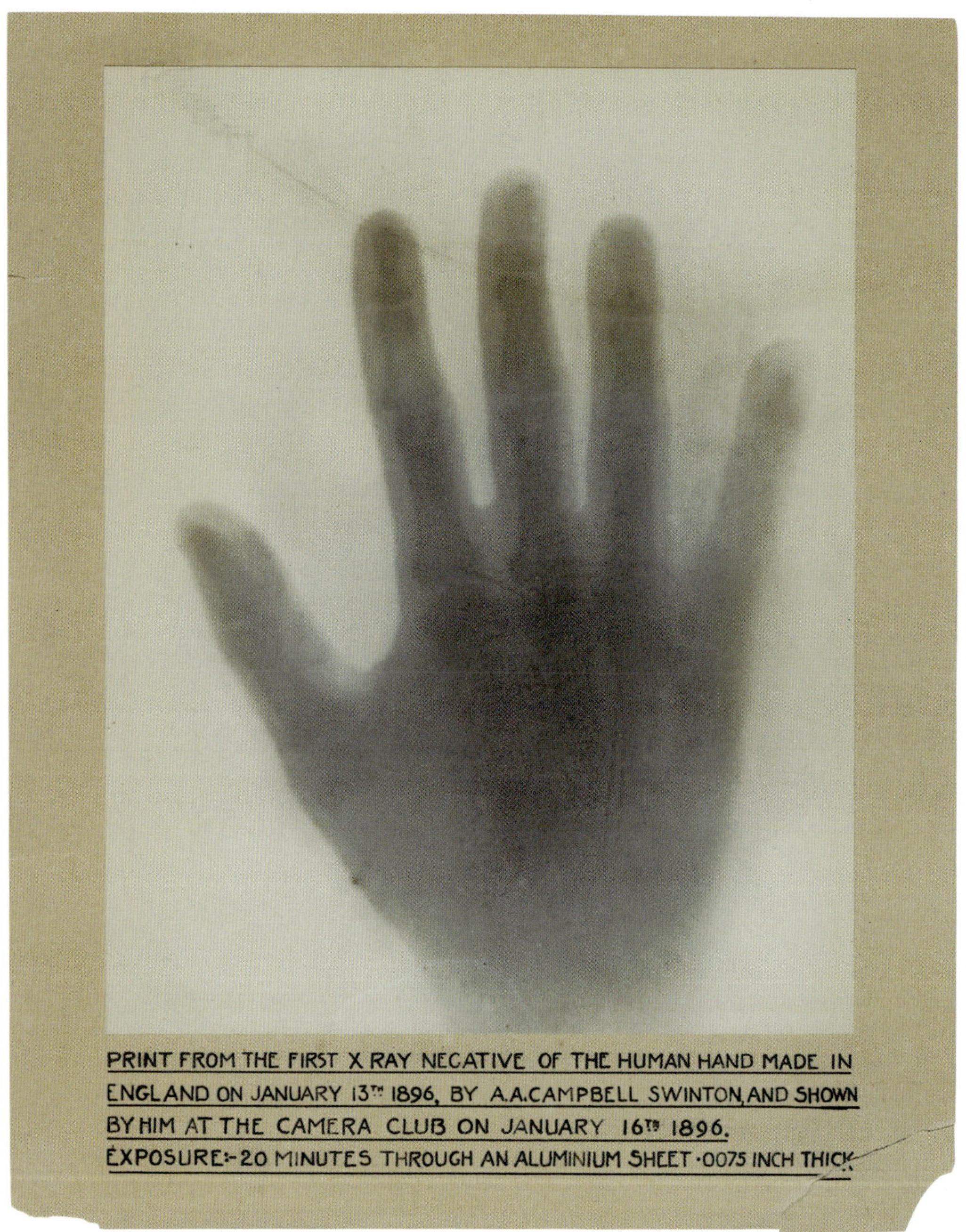

Alan Archibald Campbell-Swinton (1863–1930)

X-ray Negative of the Human Hand
13 January 1896

Gelatin silver print
30.5 x 24 cm

The first X-ray images were made in Germany by Wilhelm Röntgen in late 1895 and immediately caused a sensation. Electrical engineer Campbell-Swinton produced his own in England just weeks later. He was a pioneer in testing the new discovery for medical applications, opening the first radiographic laboratory in Britain in 1896. His experiments in imaging continued, and in 1908 he published an explanation of 'Distant Electric Vision' – what we now know as television.

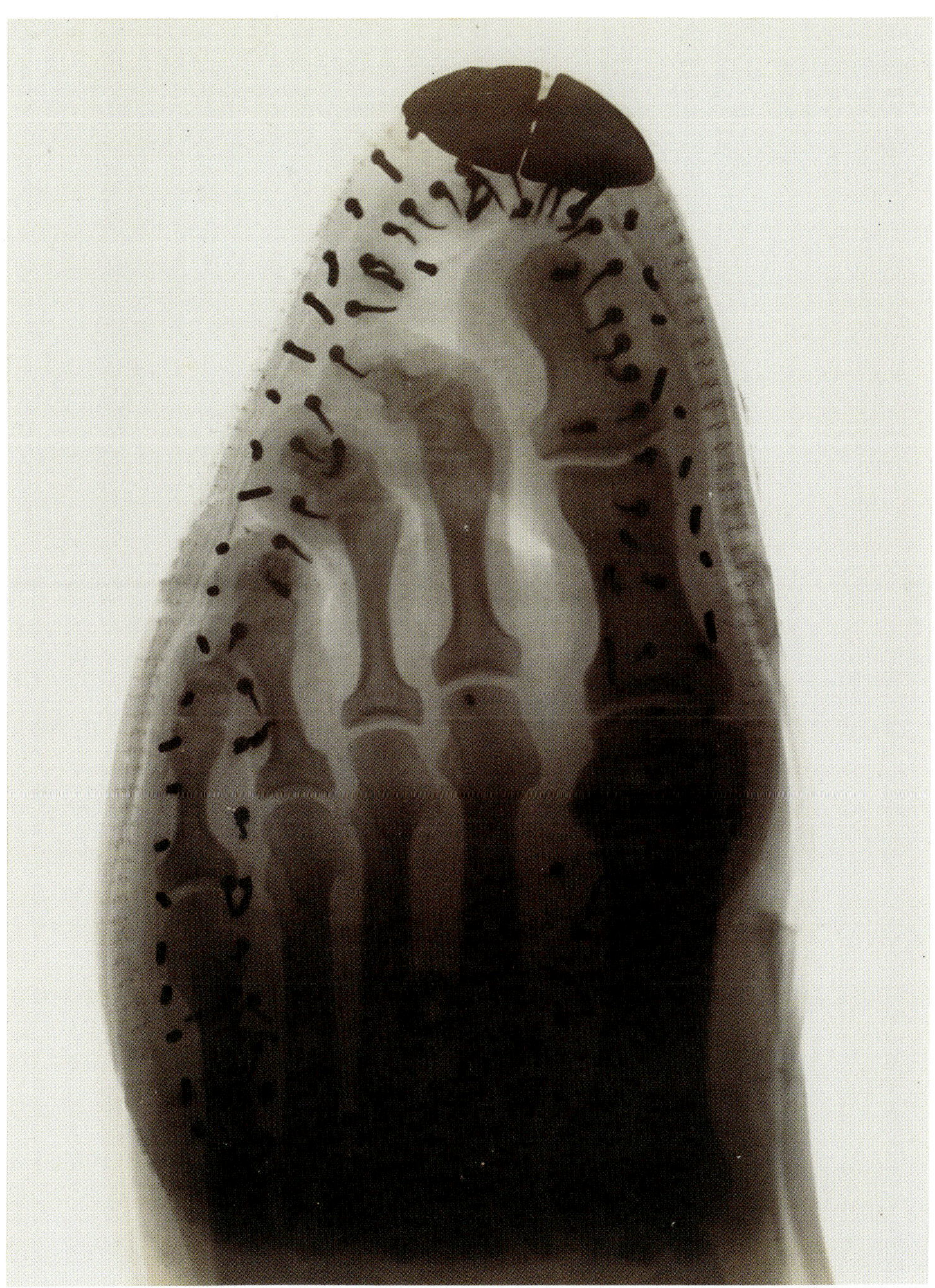

Ernest Payne (1862–early 20th century)

X-ray photograph of a foot in a shoe
*c.*1896

Gelatin silver print
20 x 15 cm

Radiography is the imaging technique using X-rays that pass through an object and are captured directly behind it on photographic film. Early examples like this captivated medical practitioners and the popular imagination. Payne's amateur interest led to an offer from Leicester Royal Infirmary, where he eventually headed the department in 'sciagraphy', as radiography was then known.

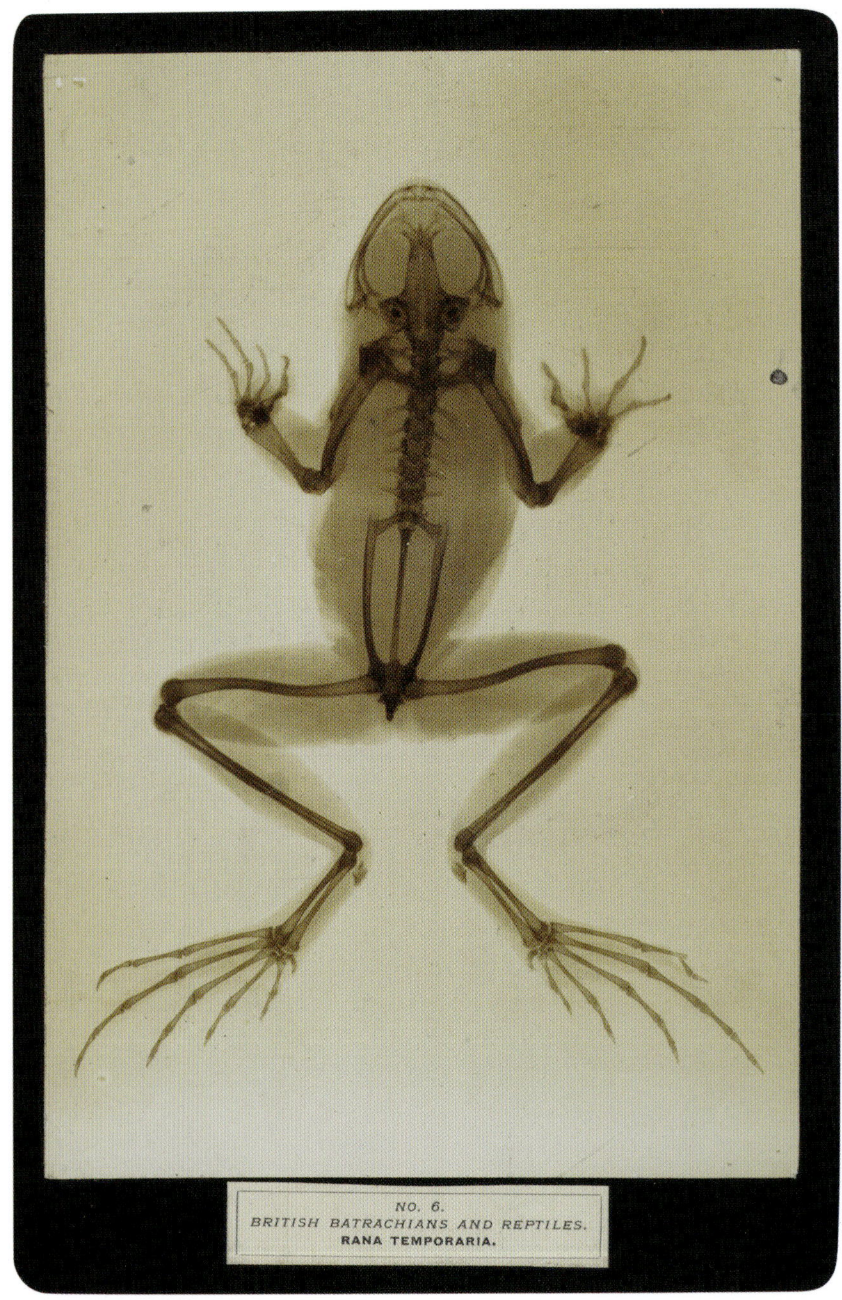

James Green and James H. Gardiner (fl.1890s)

No. 6 Rana Temporaria

from *Sciagraphs of British Batrachians and Reptiles*
c.1896

Gelatin silver print
16.2 x 10.8 cm

Toads and frogs have long been the subject of scientific observation, and images of them are a common trope in scientific photography. This X-ray of a common frog appears in a boxed set of individual images mounted on cards showing various amphibians and reptiles.

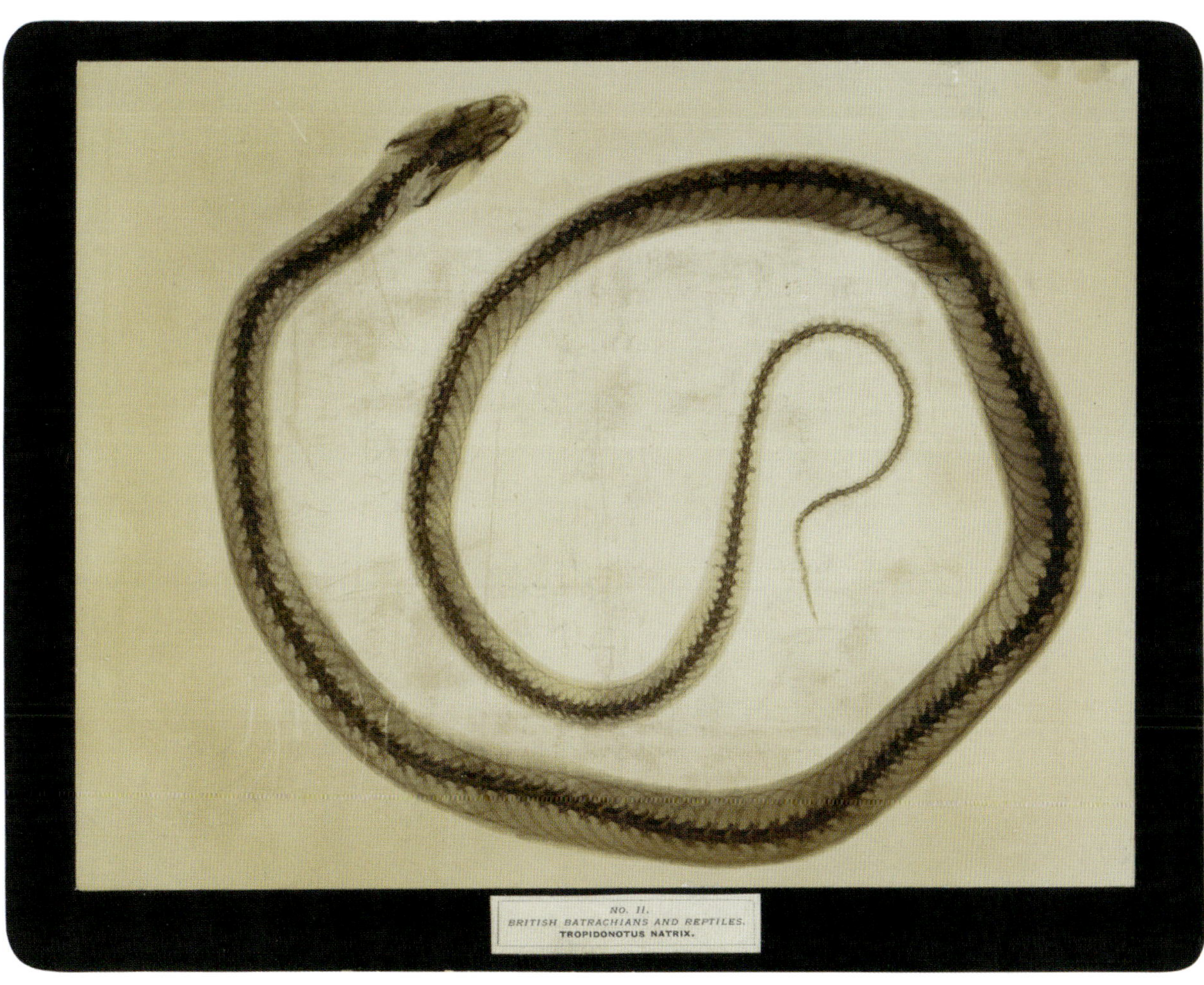

James Green and James H. Gardiner (fl.1890s)

No. 11 Tropidonotus Natrix

from *Sciagraphs of British Batrachians and Reptiles*
c.1896

Gelatin silver print
17 x 22.2 cm

The *Proceedings of the Linnaean Society* (5 November 1896) note: 'James Green and J.H. Gardiner exhibited a series of sciagraphs ... in which the details of the skeleton were very sharply defined, and its relation to the external outline well shown.' In addition to its scientific value, this image of a coiled grass snake, a predator of the common frog in the previous plate, has a strong graphic quality.

László Moholy-Nagy (1895–1946)

Photogram IV
1925–8, printed 1929

Gelatin silver print
39.5 x 30 cm

Moholy-Nagy began making cameraless photographs in 1922, adopting the term 'photogram' in 1925. He saw this as the artistic equivalent of the X-ray. In 1932, he wrote, 'The photogram ... which embodies the unique nature of the photographic process, is the real key to photography. It allows us to capture the patterned interplay of light on a sheet of sensitized paper without recourse to any apparatus.'

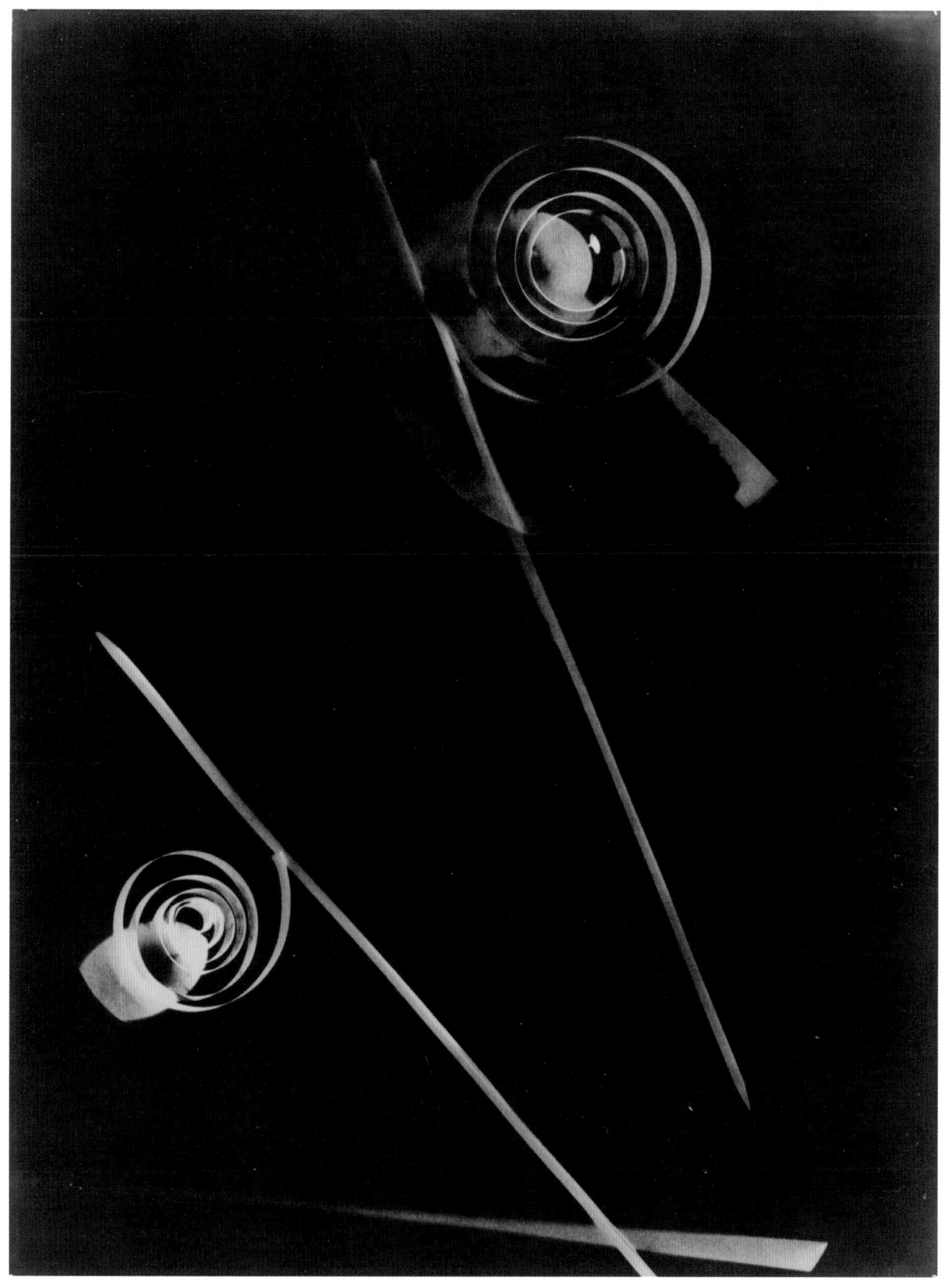

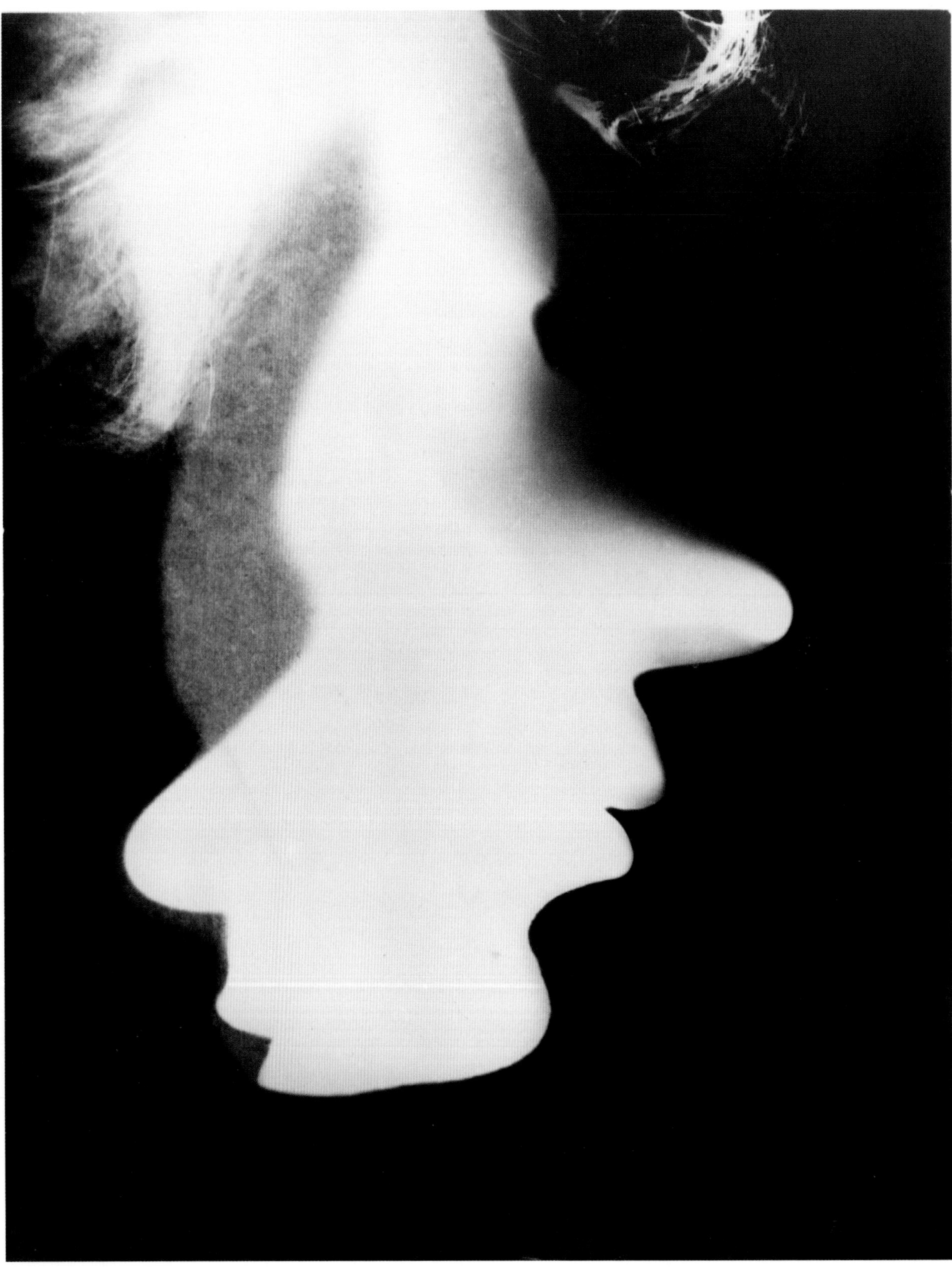

László Moholy-Nagy (1895–1946)

Untitled
1926, printed 1973

Gelatin silver print
35 x 26.2 cm

This two-faced figure is a double portrait showing the artist on the right and the photographer Lucia Moholy, his first wife, on the left. Taking it in turns to lay their heads on the photographic paper, they created this image among several others that are thought to be the earliest surviving self-portrait photograms.

Curtis Moffat (1887–1949)

Abstract Compositions
c.1925

Gelatin silver prints
59 36.5 x 29 cm
60 36.6 x 28.7 cm
61 37.2 x 29.4 cm
62 29.1 x 24.5 cm

Moffat began experimenting with photogram techniques in collaboration with Man Ray in Paris from 1923. He titled his works *Abstract Compositions* and exhibited them in the showrooms of his London interior design emporium, Curtis Moffat Ltd, seeing them as an element within a decorative scheme. Yet he also described them as 'painting with light' and showed them as artworks in their own right. Besides the photogram, Moffat's *Abstract Compositions* employed other cameraless techniques. In one image, an insect's body – a grasshopper, locust or cricket – is used in place of a photographic negative. In another (p.62), Moffat appears to have painted directly on the paper, perhaps with photographic chemicals.

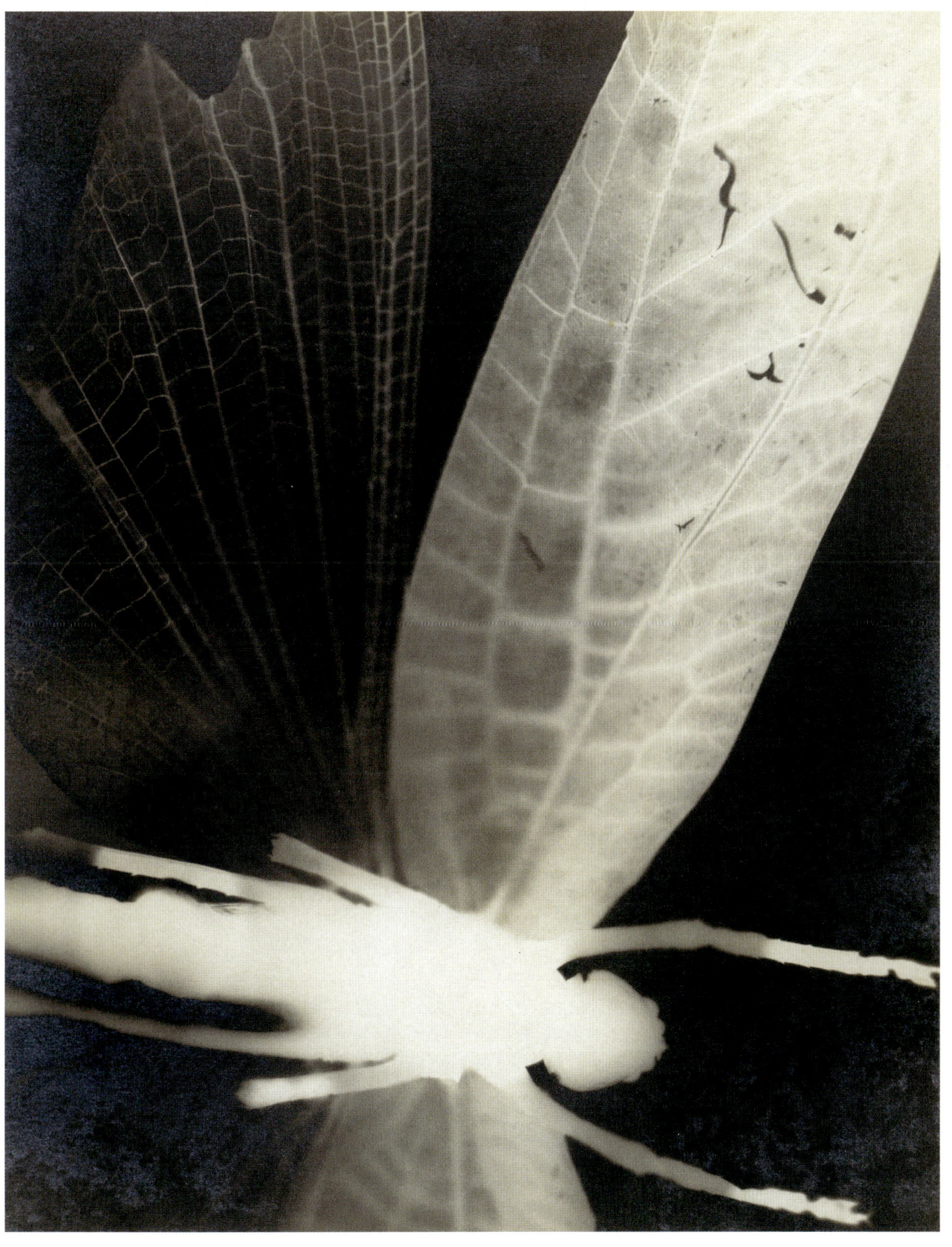

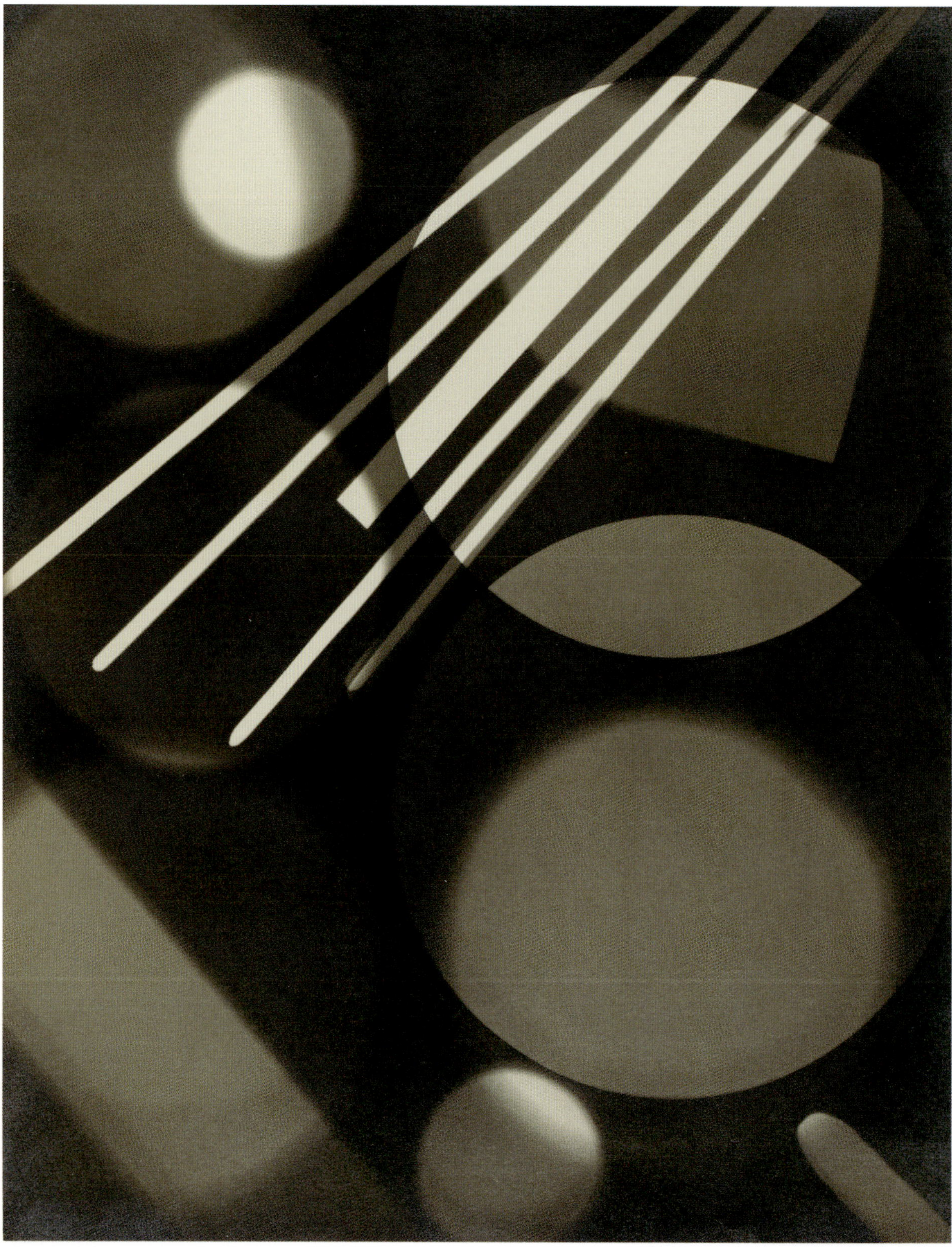

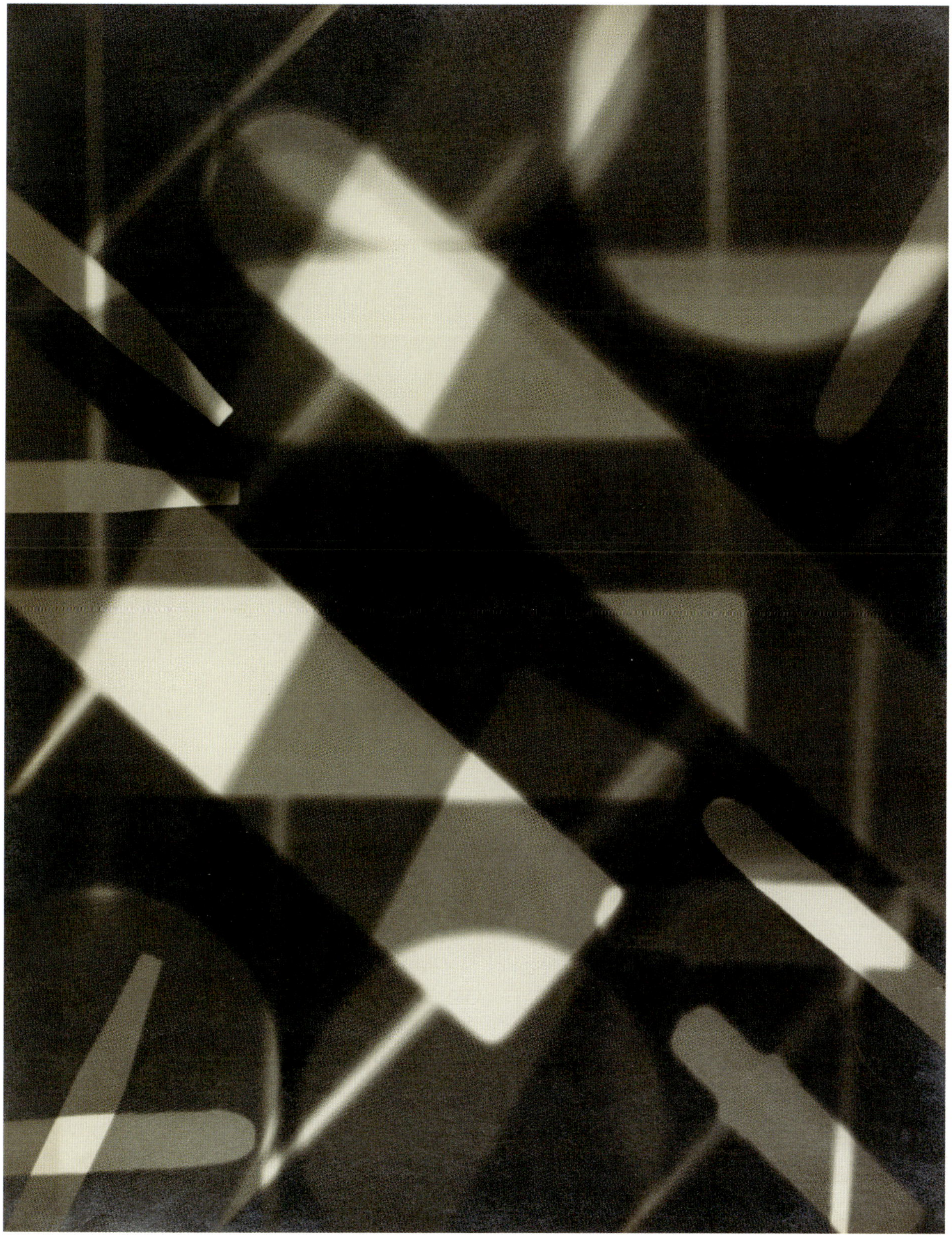

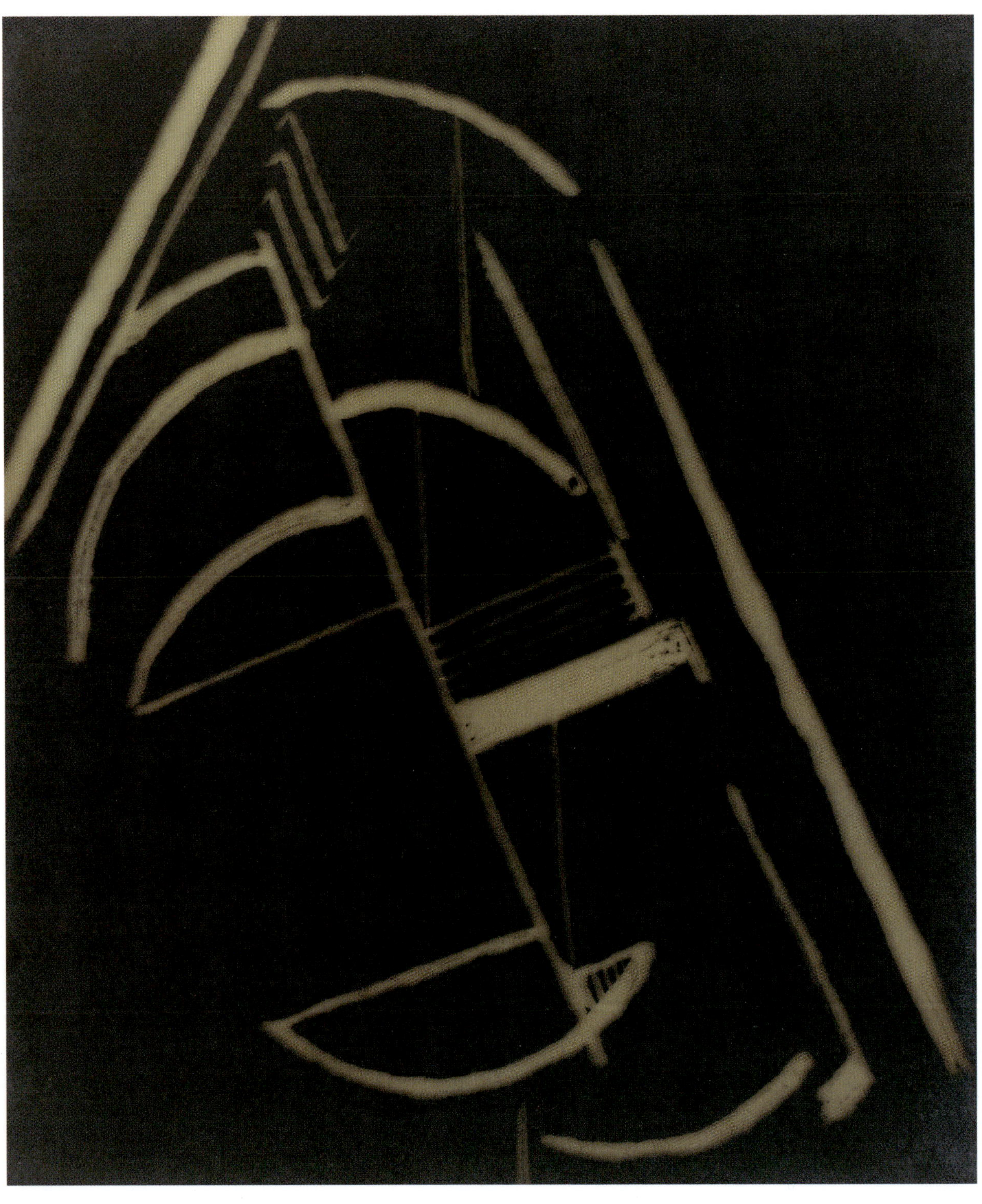

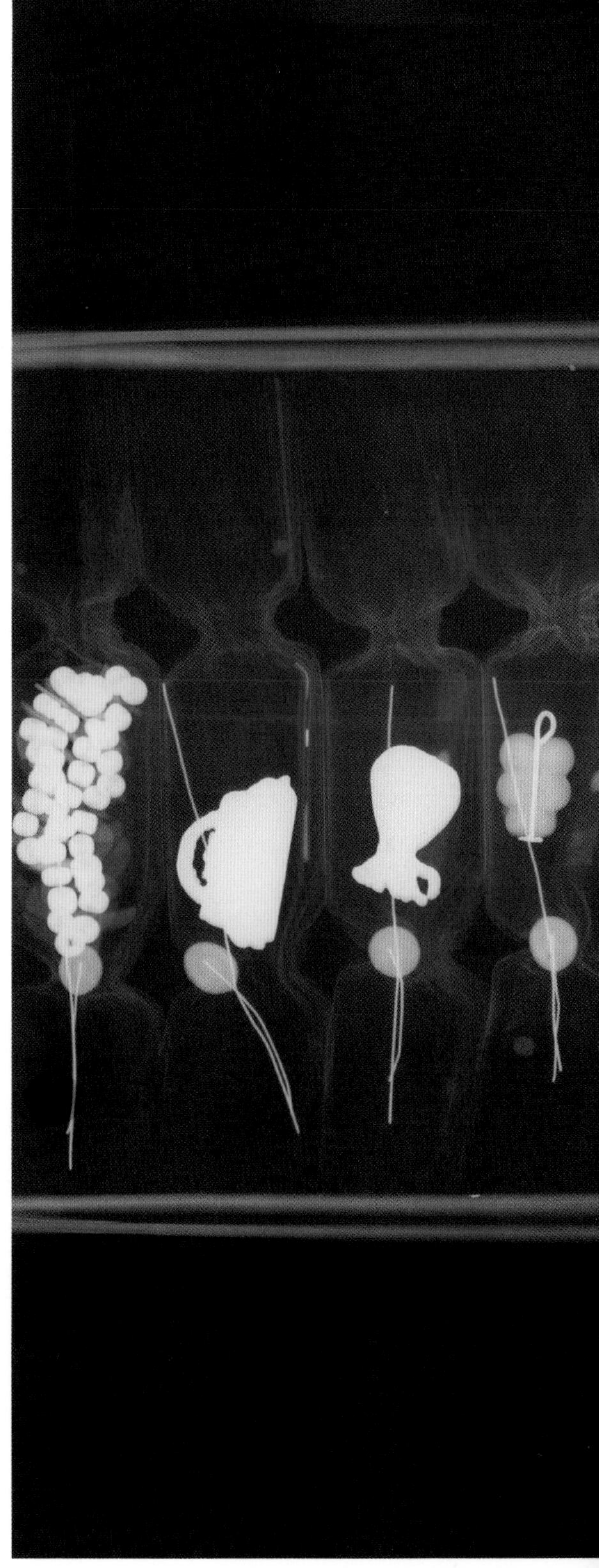

Bart's Hospital X-ray Unit

Box of Christmas crackers
1930

X-ray negative
20 x 25 cm

The capacity of radiographs to reveal objects hidden within objects is playfully explored in this example made by the X-ray unit of London's venerable St Bartholomew's (or Bart's) Hospital. It is presumably a test – light, festive relief for the radiography staff – deliberately spoiling the traditional surprise of the gift trinkets within the cracker.

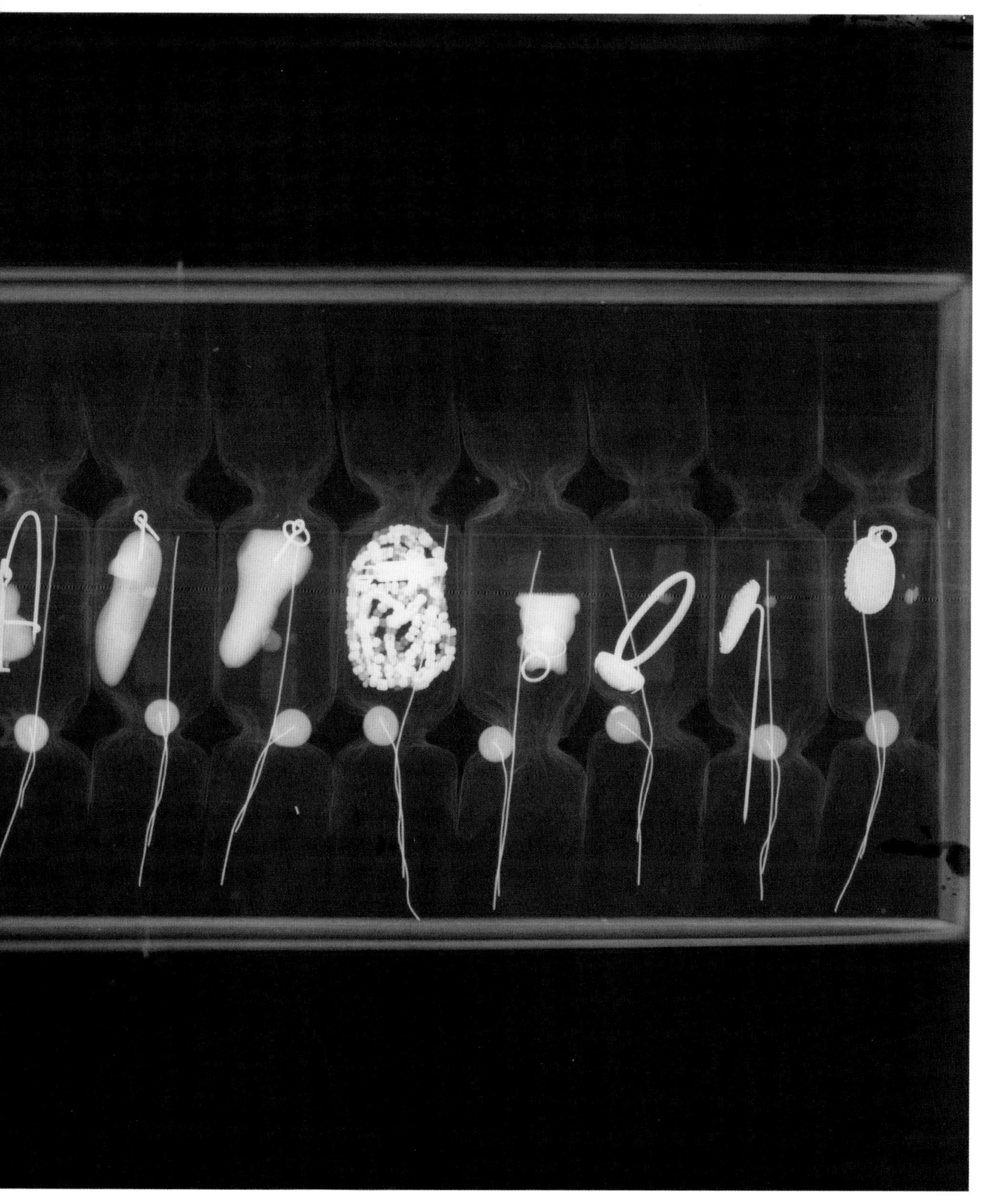

Man Ray (1890–1976)

La Maison, Salle à Manger, Lingerie and *Le Souffle*
from the portfolio *Électricité*
1931

Photogravures from photograms
26 x 20.3 cm each

Man Ray's images from his *Électricité* portfolio are some of the best examples of the graphic and commercial use of the photogram, or what he called the 'rayograph' after his own name. Commissioned by a French energy company for its shareholders, the set of ten images showed the range of modern innovations that depended on electricity. Some incorporated camera-made with cameraless techniques. The four selected here – showing a light shade and bulbs, a toaster, a hand with an iron, and a fan – are purely cameraless.

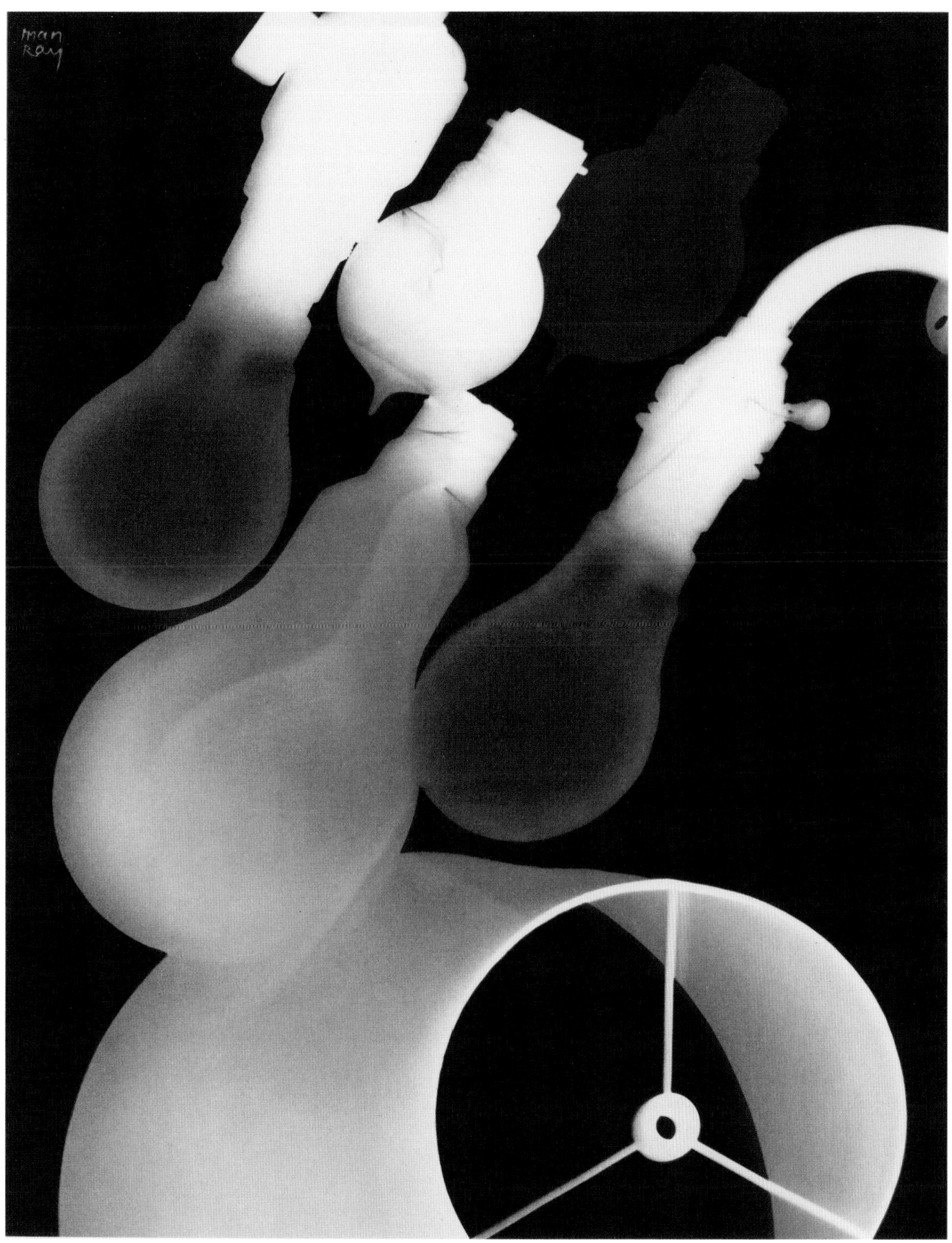
man
Ray

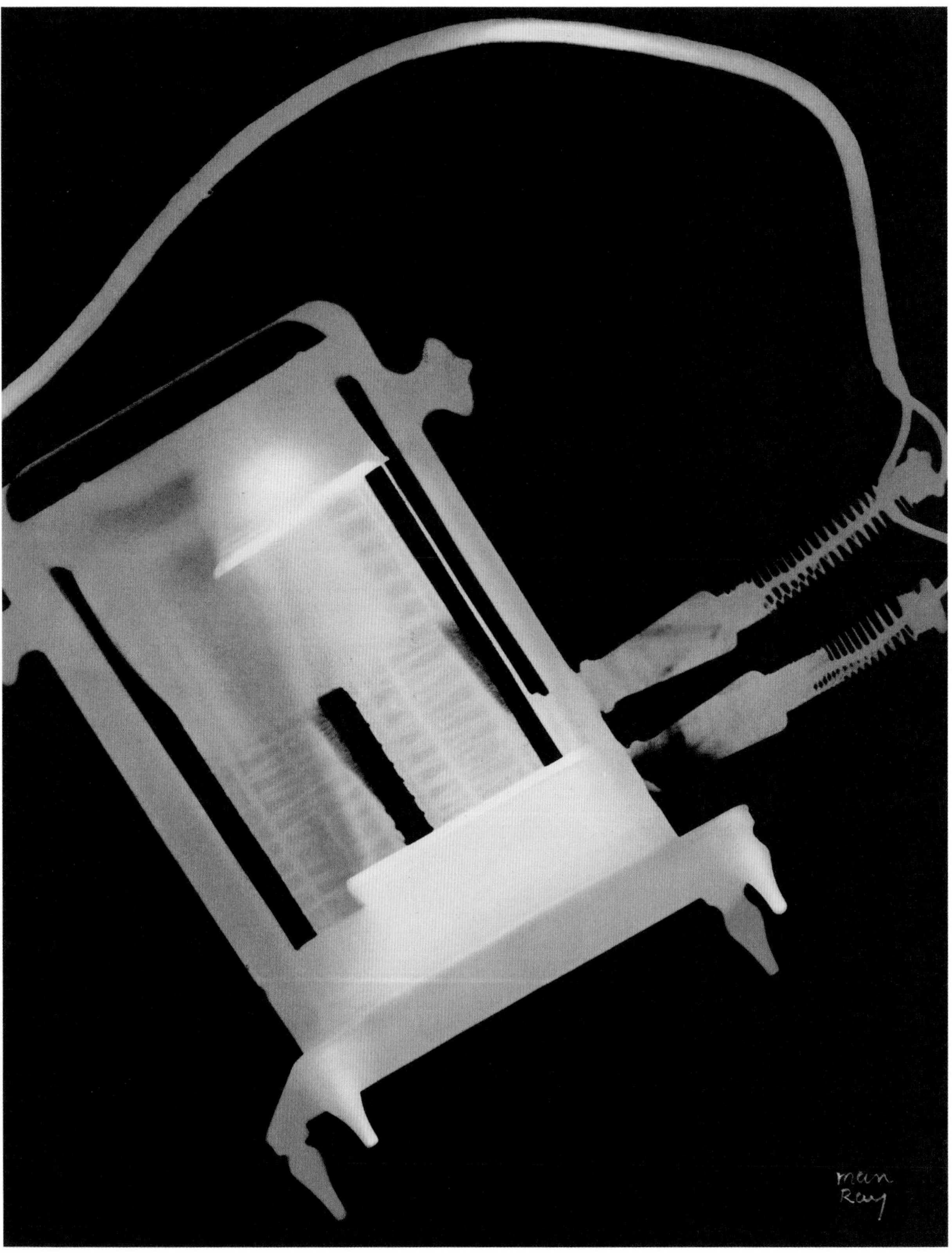
man
Ray

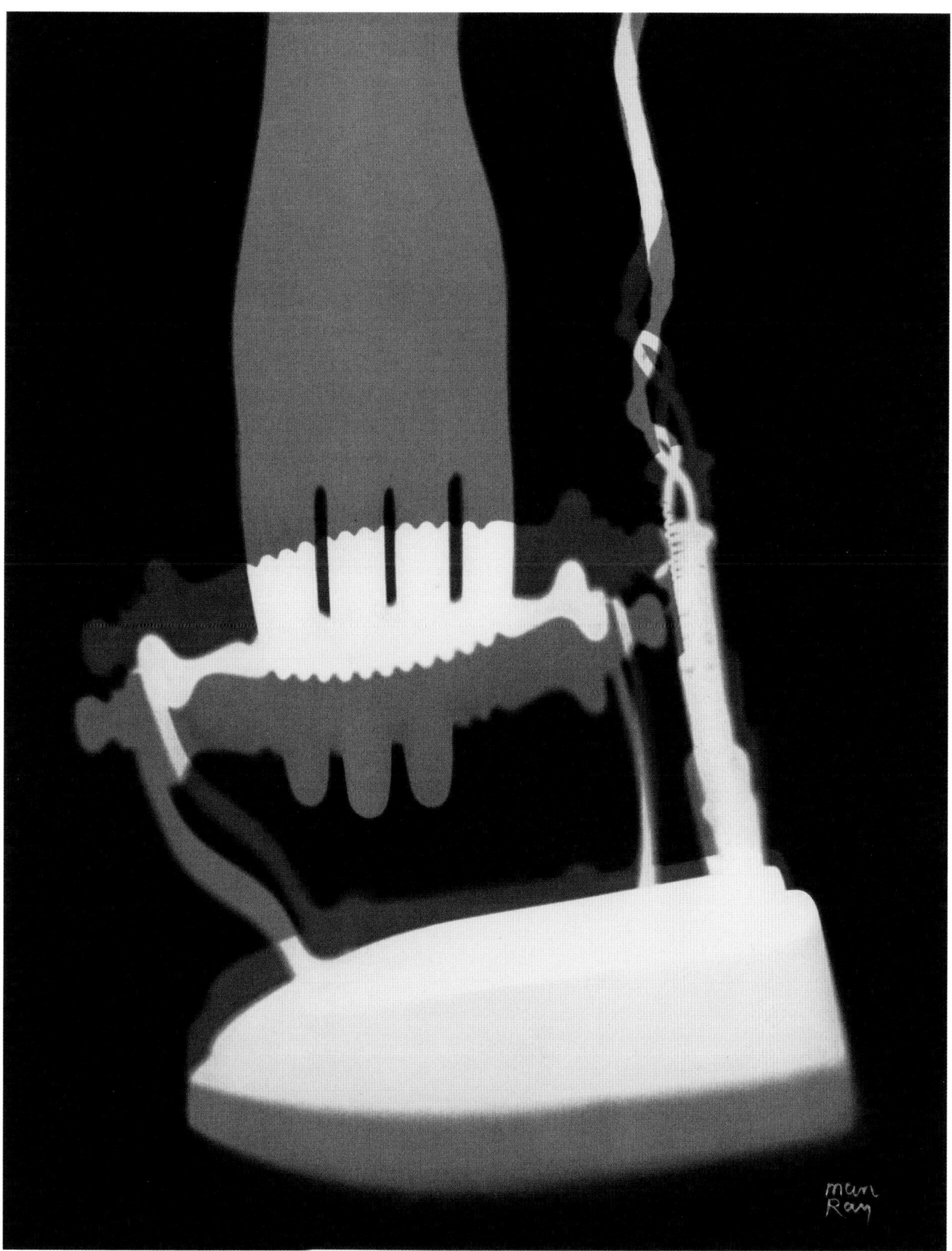
man
Ray

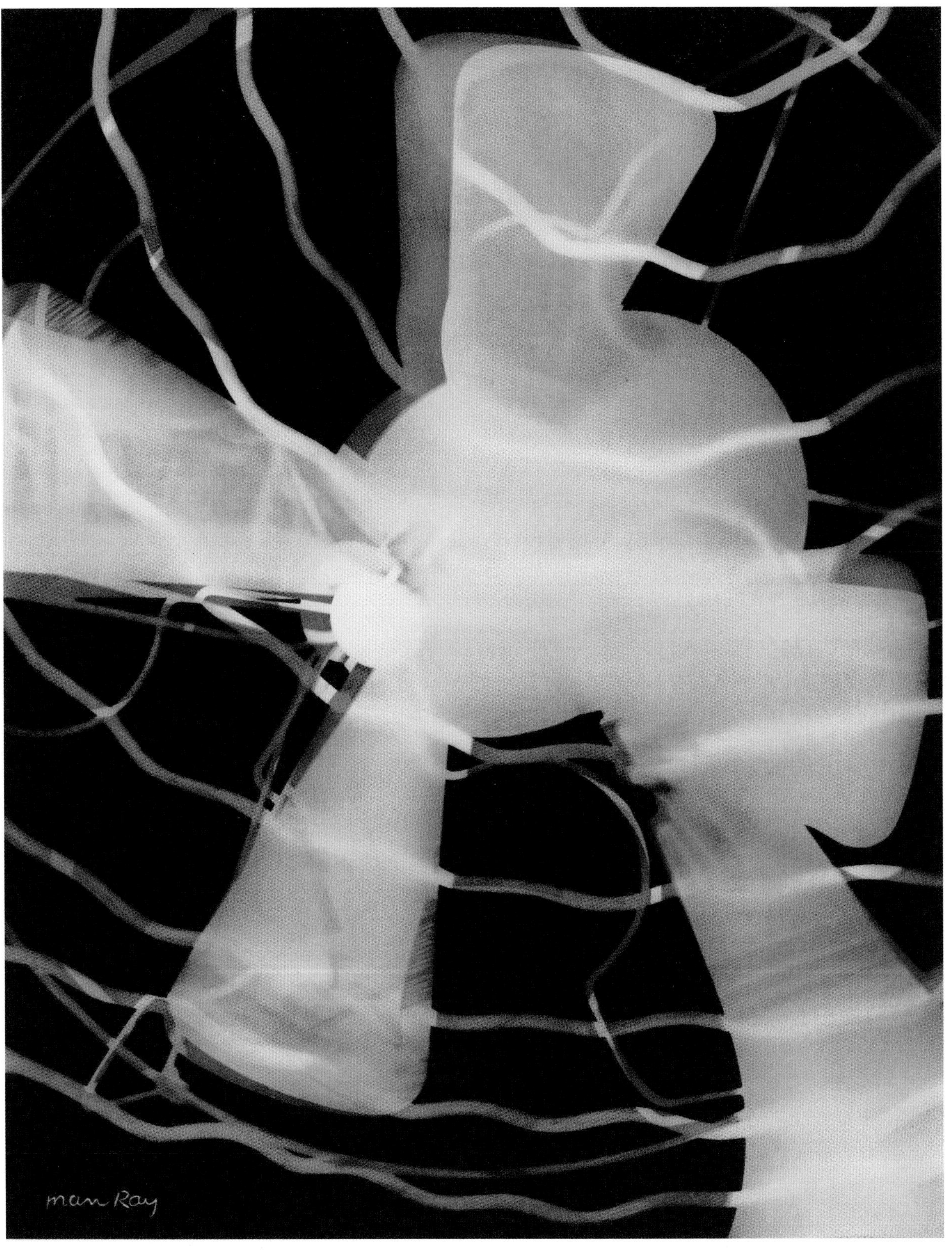
man Ray

John Arthur Fairfax Fozzard (1905–1993)

Macacus Rhesus in Uterus
1937

Gelatin silver print from X-ray
15 x 11 cm

This image of a rhesus macaque monkey in the womb is one of many meticulous and artistically composed radiographs by Fozzard that form part of the Royal Photographic Society's 'Medical Group' collection. Fozzard was in charge of photography and radiography in the Anatomy School at the University of Cambridge, where he was involved in medical research for over forty years.

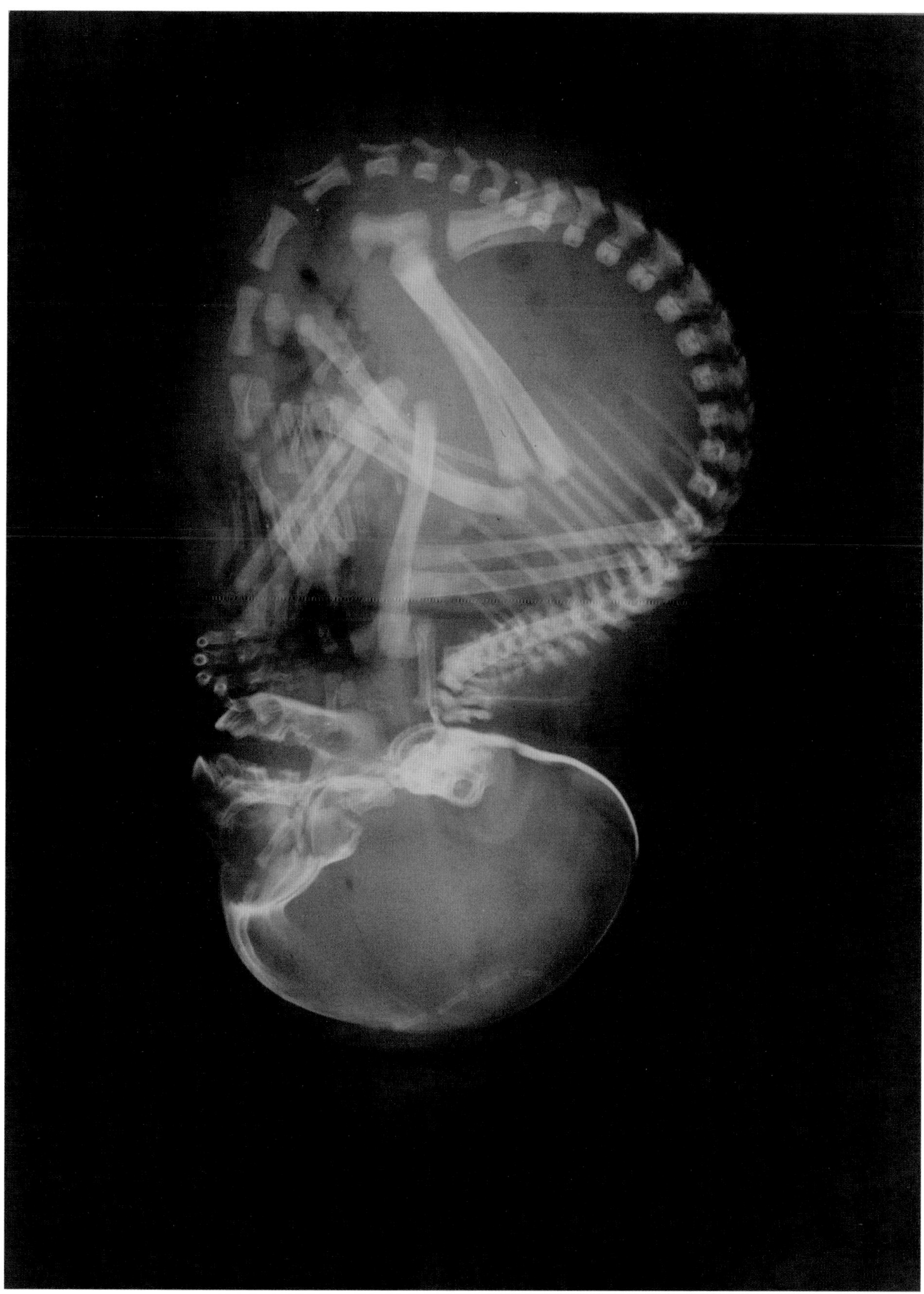

Franciszka and Stefan Themerson
(1907–1988 and 1910–1988)

Photogram in Motion
from the film *The Eye and the Ear*
1944–5

Gelatin silver print, printed 1983
15 x 20 cm

The Themersons adapted photograms to moving film. They placed objects onto a sheet of translucent paper on a glass table top. With lights above, the images were shot frame by frame from below. This image is a still from a section of their film *The Eye and the Ear*, which synchronizes the music of Polish composer Karol Szymanowski (1883–1937) to songs by Julian Tuwim (1894–1953), with changing geometric shapes representing orchestral instruments.

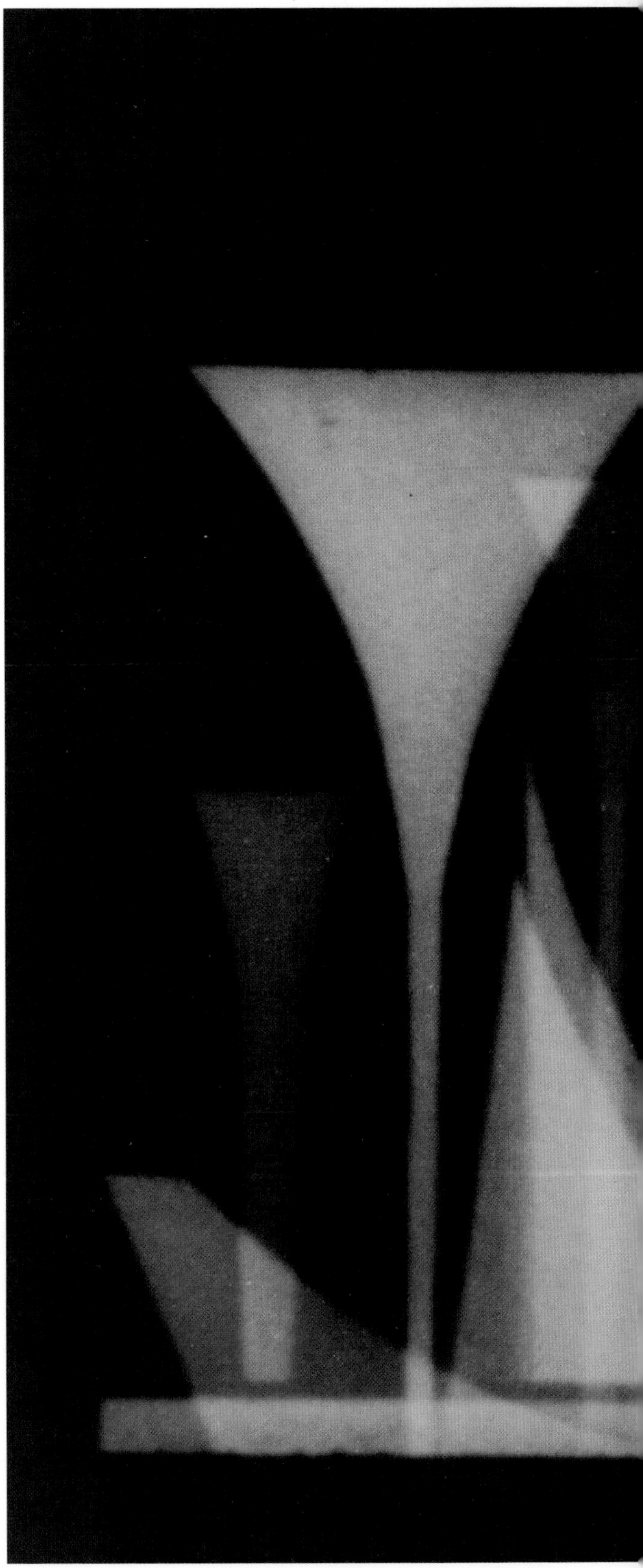

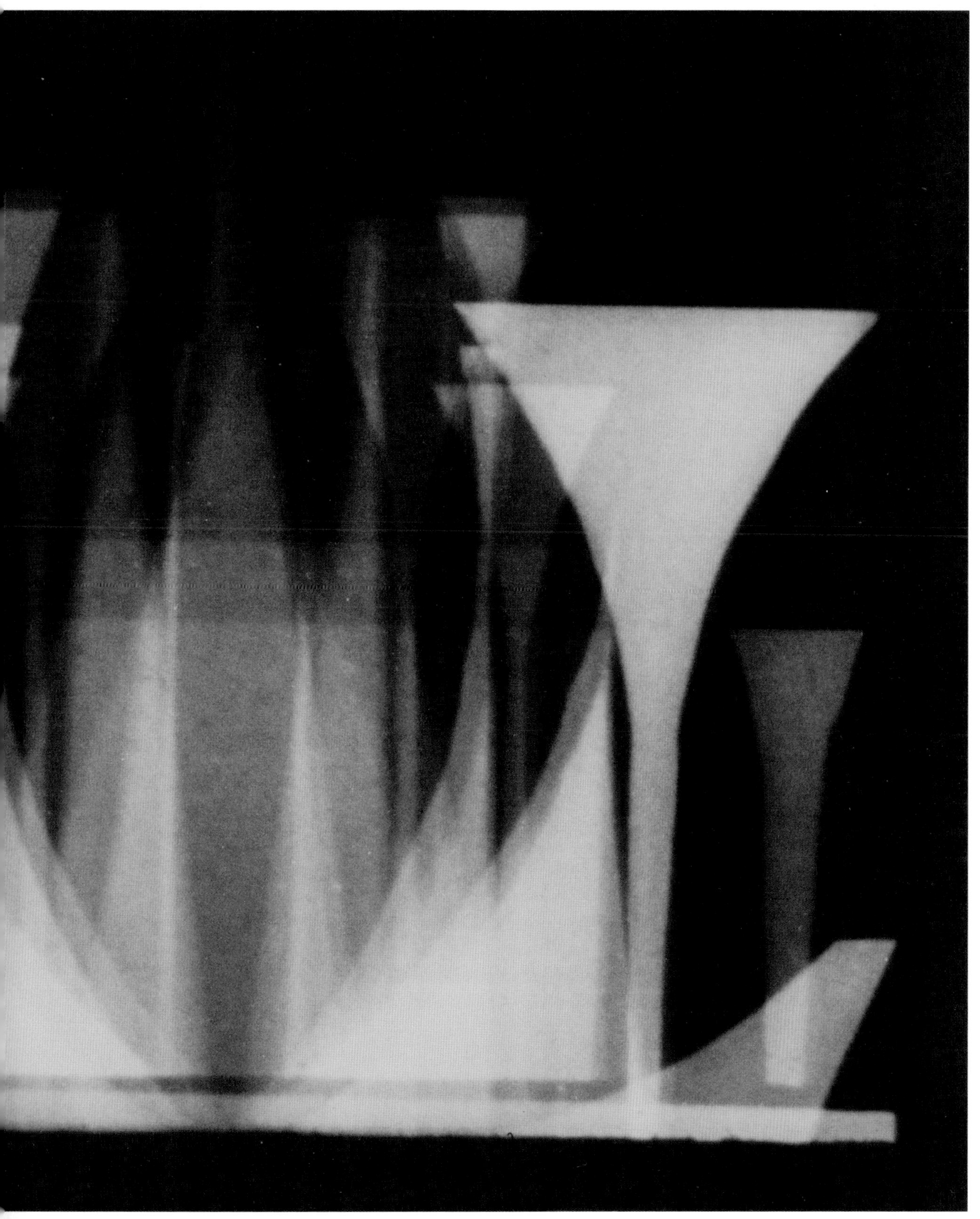

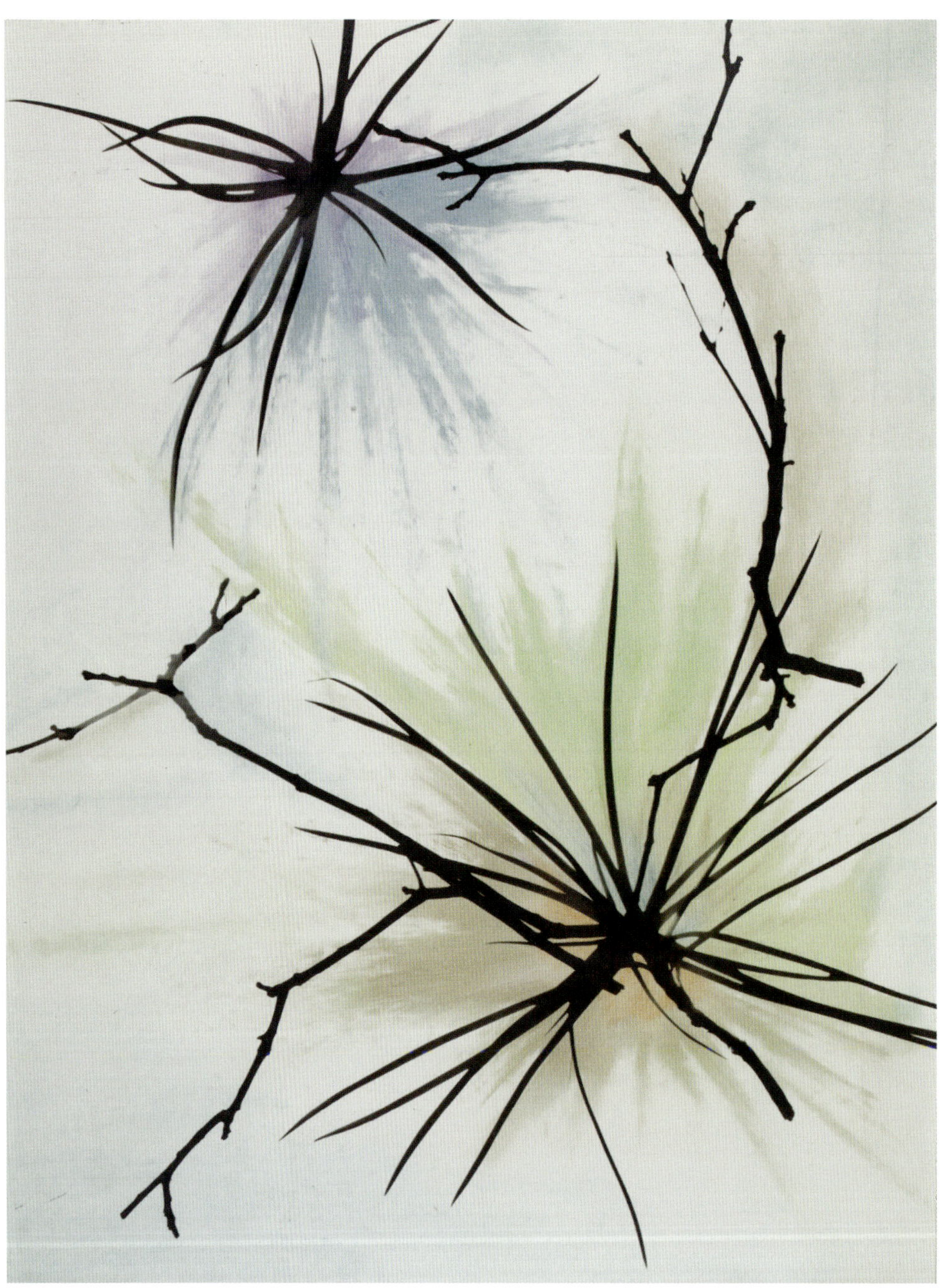

Josef Breitenbach (1896–1984)

Untitled
1948

Gelatin silver print, hand-coloured
34.2 x 25.5 cm

Breitenbach fled Europe for New York in 1941. Though not officially a Surrealist, he shared the movement's interest in dreams and the unconscious mind. In this fusion of photogram and hand-painted surface, the floating shapes of twigs and other organic forms are reminiscent of biological synaptic images.

Henry Holmes Smith (1909–1986)

79 *Mother and Son*
1951, printed 1973

80 *Giant*
1949, printed 1973

81 *Growing Up I*
1952, printed 1973

Gelatin silver prints
30 x 23 cm each

In 1937, Smith met László Moholy-Nagy, who responded positively to his work and invited him to teach at the New Bauhaus in Chicago. Smith made photograms by applying thick syrup onto a glass sheet and adding water to refract the light. The abstracted shapes are often suggestive of figures. He typically gave the works metaphorical titles, emphasizing their expressive and imaginative potential.

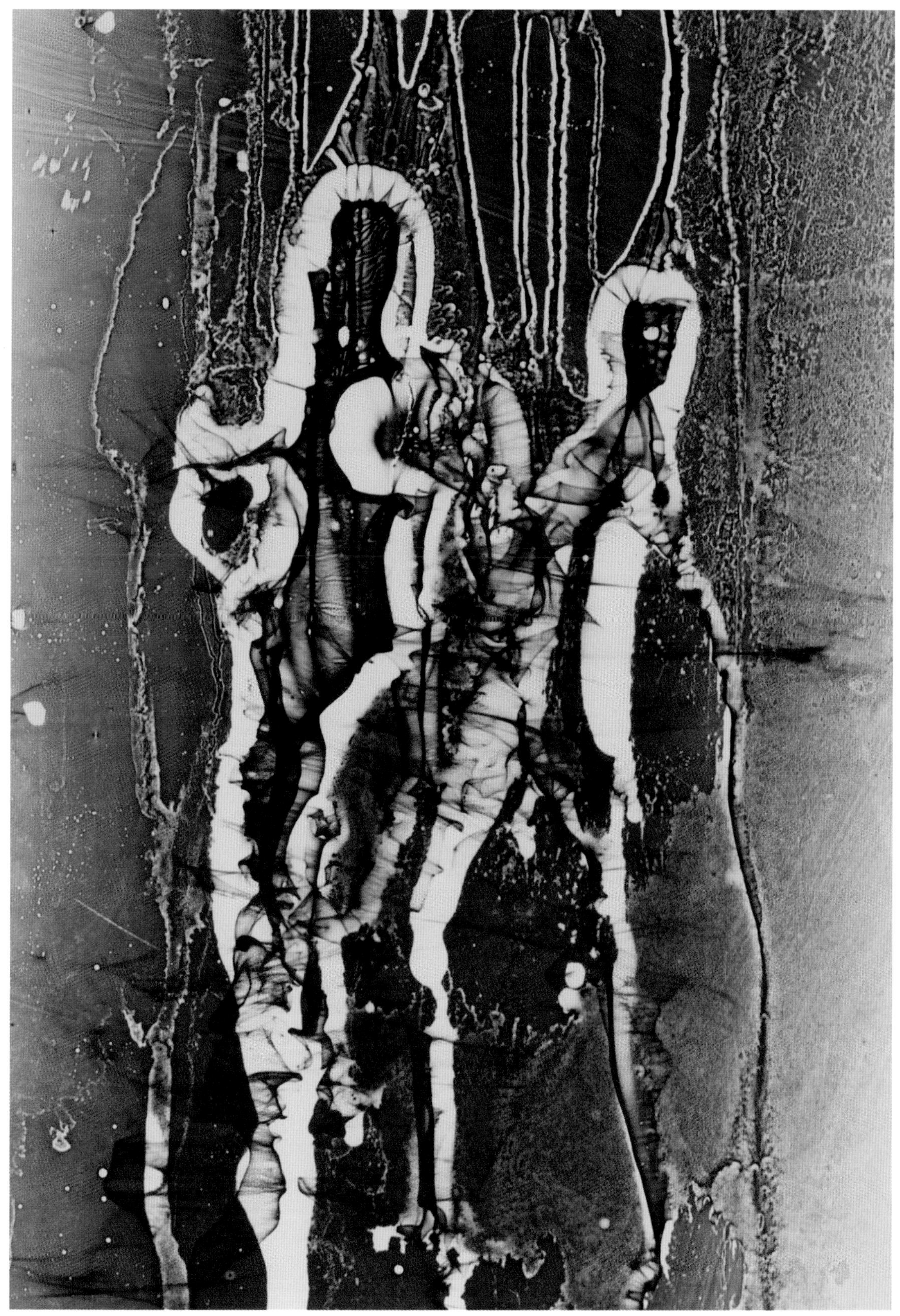

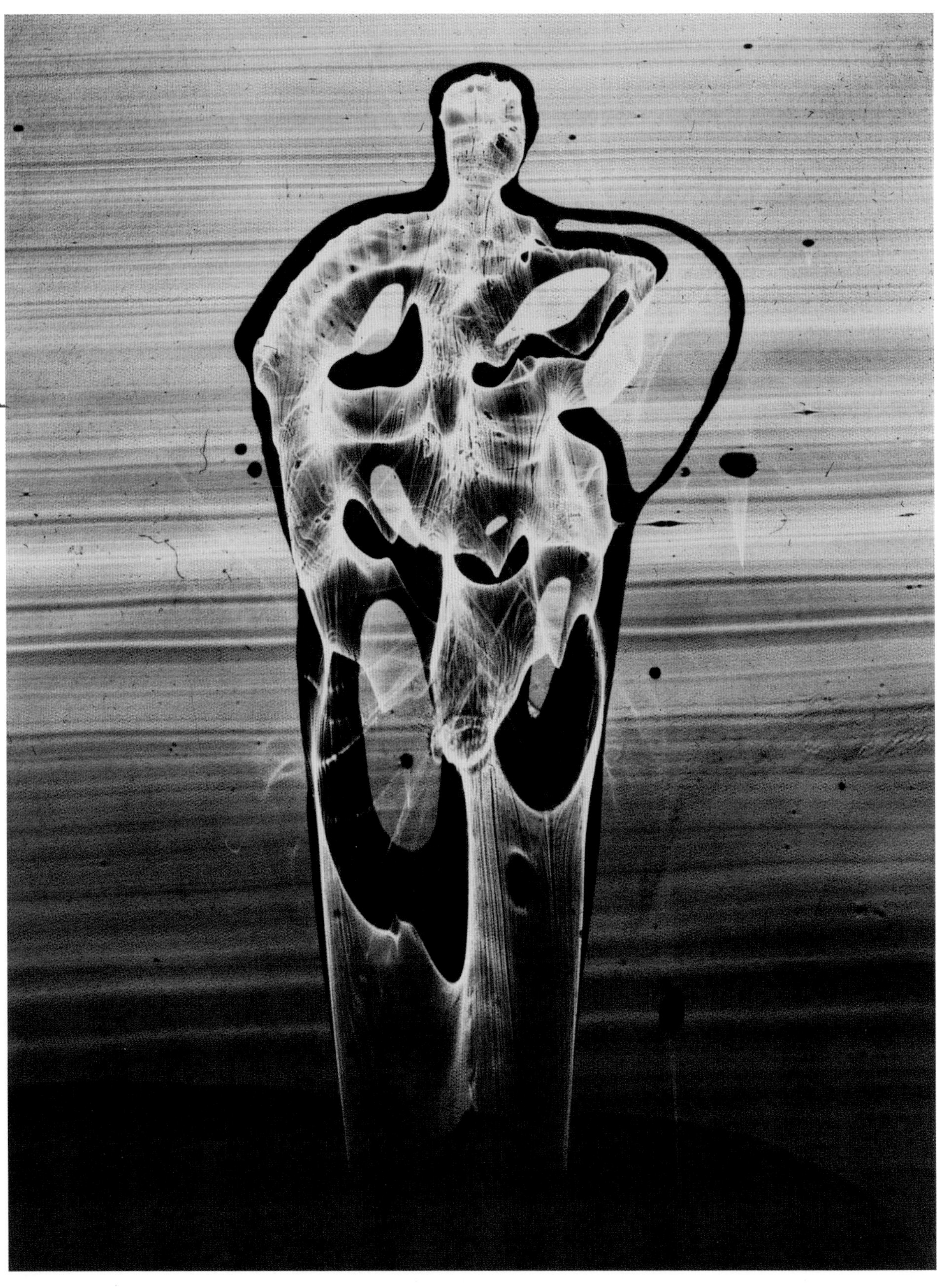

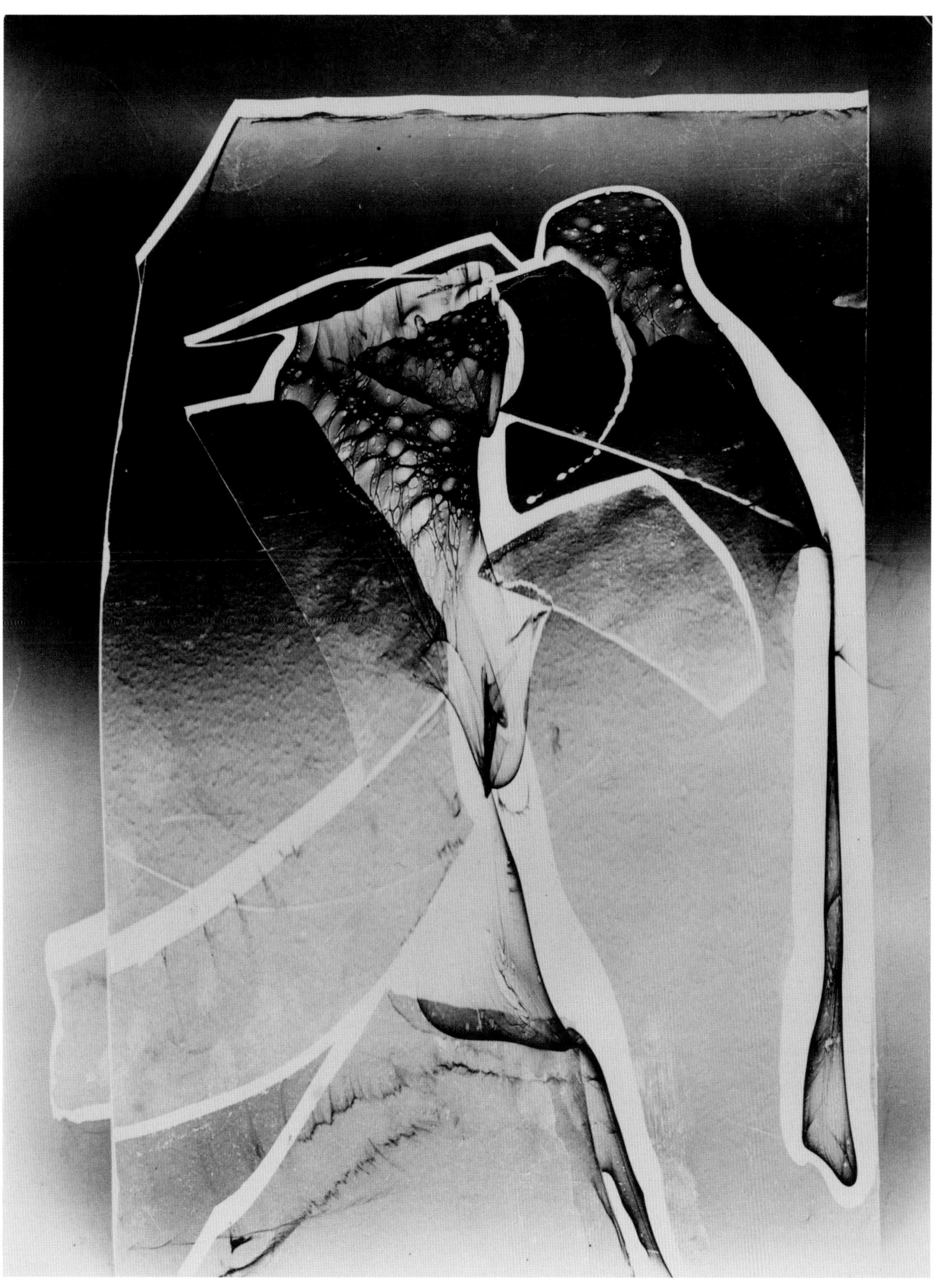

Frederick Sommer (1905–1999)

Paracelsus
1959

Gelatin silver print
33.8 x 25.6 cm

In 1957, Sommer began to make photographs using 'synthetic' or cameraless negatives. He created these by applying smoke or paint to cellophane and glass. For the *Paracelsus* 'negative', he manipulated oil paint between two pieces of cellophane, then pulled them apart to reveal a textured shape. The result bears an uncanny resemblance to a human torso and led Sommer to name the photograph after Paracelsus, the sixteenth-century Swiss doctor, alchemist and philosopher.

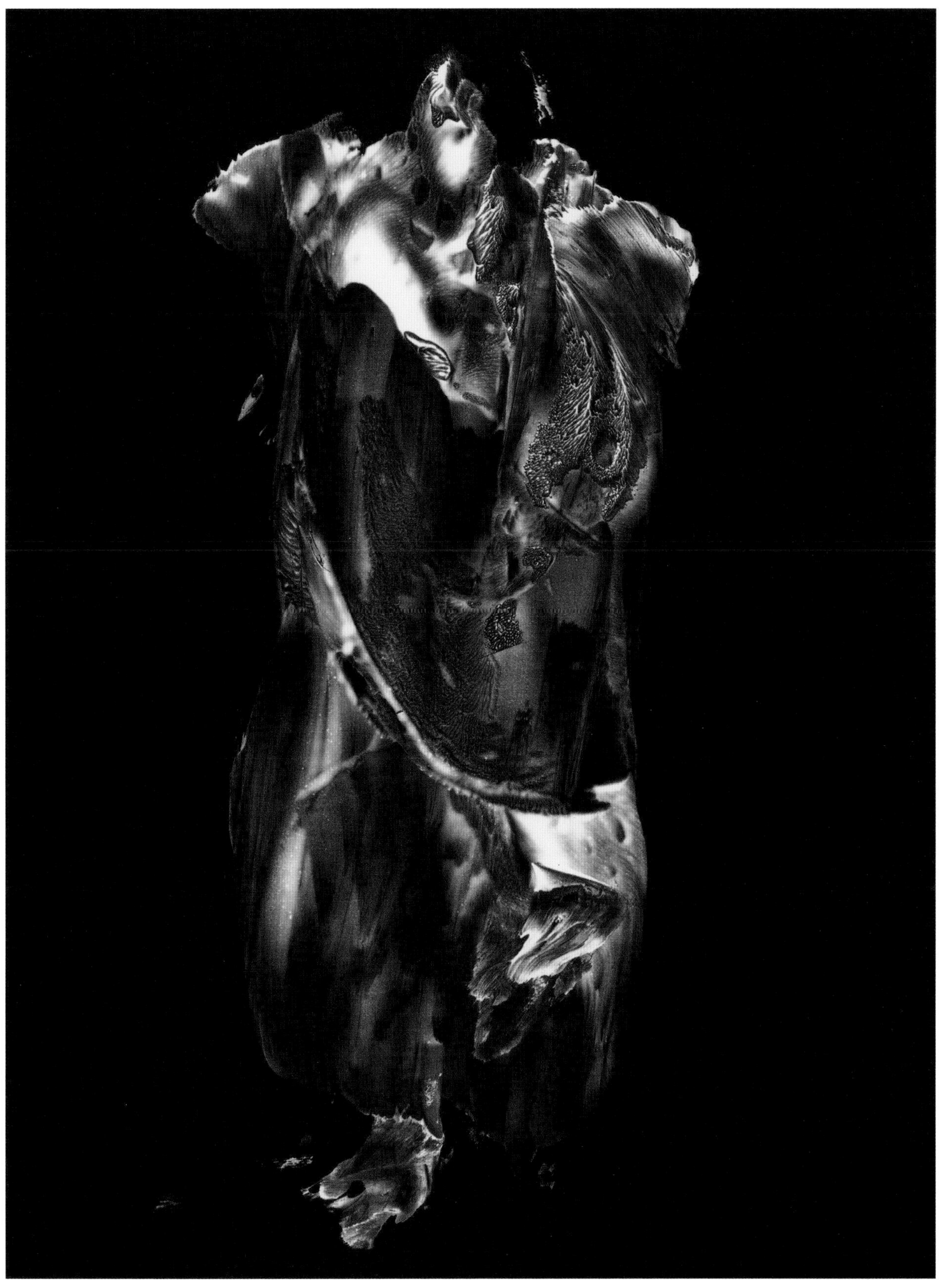

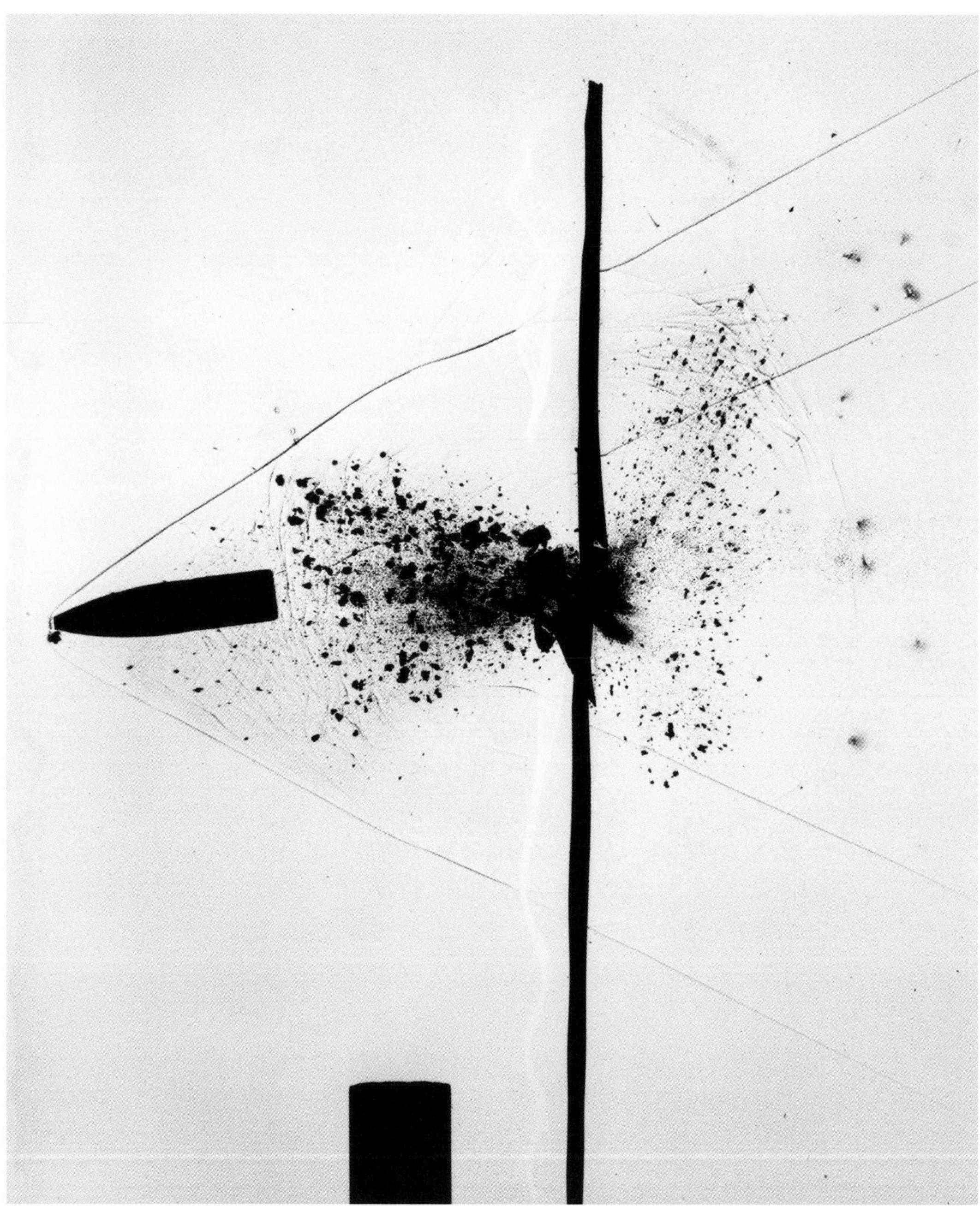

Harold Edgerton (1903–1990)

Bullet Through Plexiglas
1963, printed 1970–89

Gelatin silver print
44 x 37 cm

(detail p.1)

Edgerton was an electrical engineer who invented the strobe light. He used it mostly to capture rapid motion with camera-made photographs that recorded his experiments. Here, however, the exposure of less than one microsecond was made directly onto a sheet of film. It records the silhouette of the bullet shattering the Plexiglas, shockwaves and hot gasses, and marks where Plexiglas shards punctured the film.

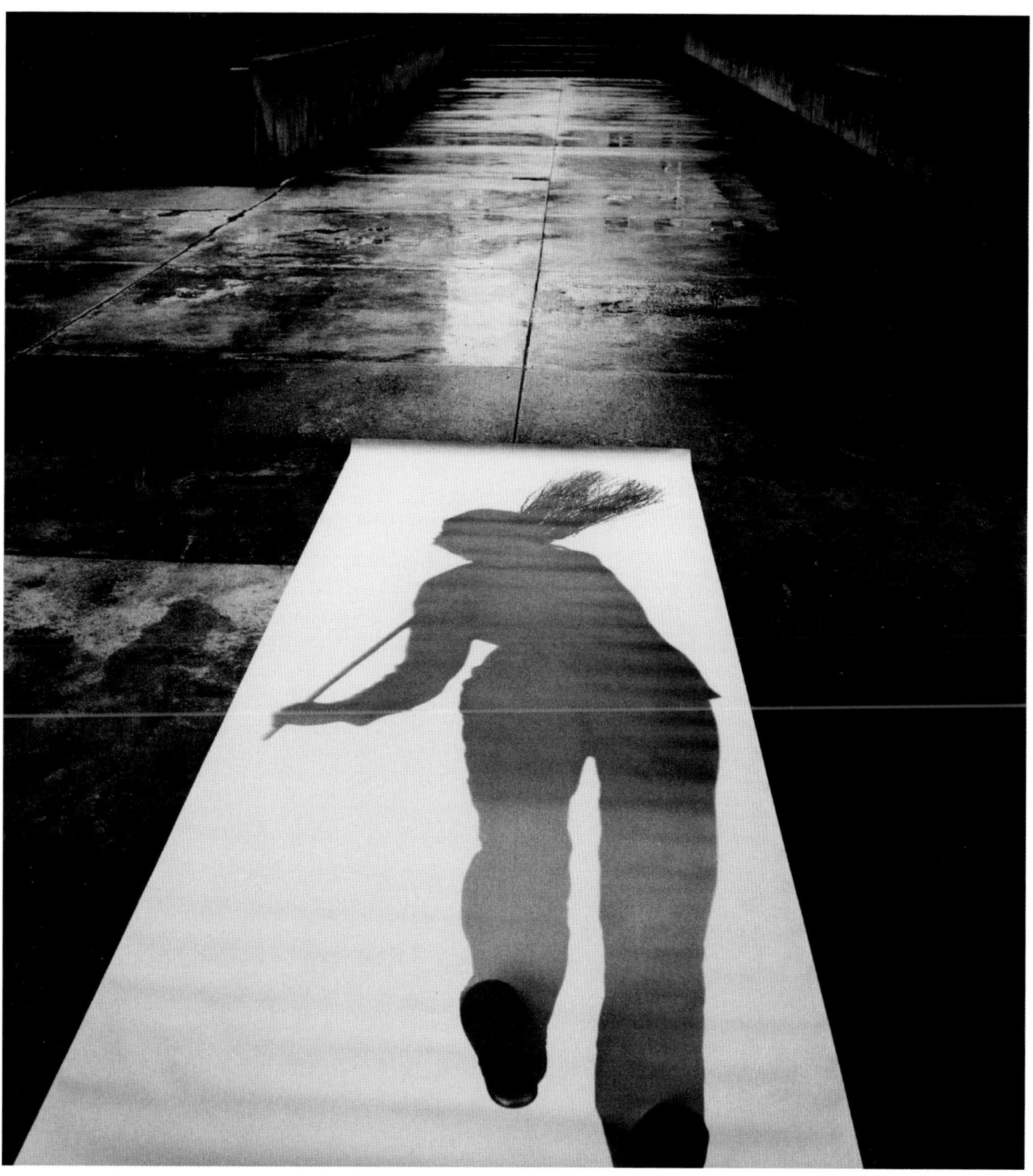

Floris Neusüss (b.1937)

Schattenfenger (Shadow Sweeper)
1983

Gelatin silver print
24.5 x 22.5 cm

Life-sized photograms of figures sometimes appear as installation pieces in Neusüss's work. Here, a photogram is transplanted from the darkroom where it was created to an urban setting and the scene documented in a regular photograph. The photogram creates the illusion of a shadow with a life of its own – magically detached and somehow remaining in place after the sweeping figure that created it has departed.

Floris Neusüss and Renate Heyne
(b.1937 and 1947)

The Naked Dress
1972
Photogram printed on linen
150 x 92 cm

The Naked Dress (record photographs)
c.1972
Gelatin silver prints
24 x 18 cm each

Neusüss worked in collaboration with his wife Renate Heyne to create this unique photogram dress, which she wore on several occasions. The abstracted shape of Heyne's body, front and reverse, is captured on the corresponding sides of the linen. It is a clever play on the idea that a garment might both reveal and conceal its wearer.

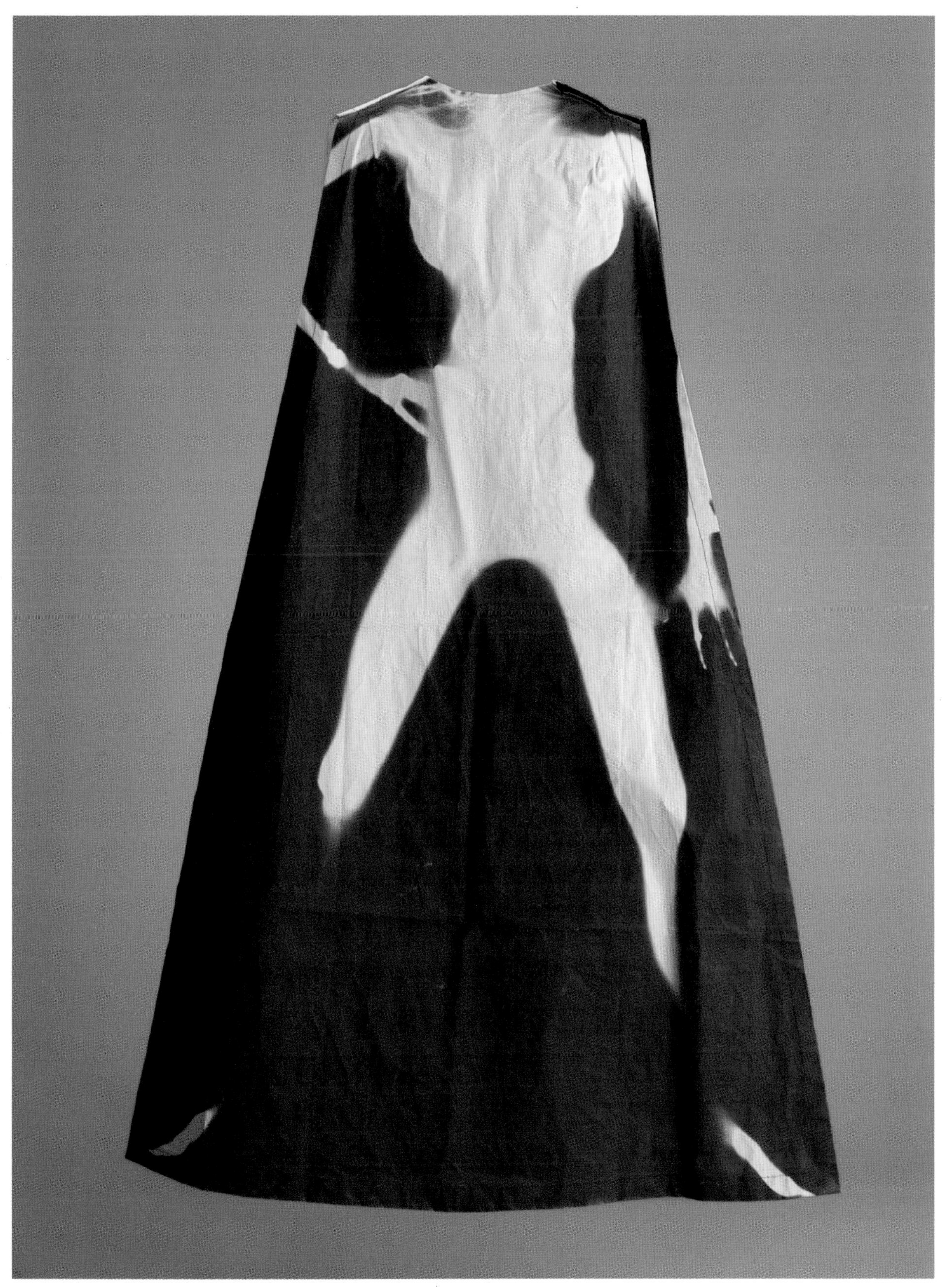

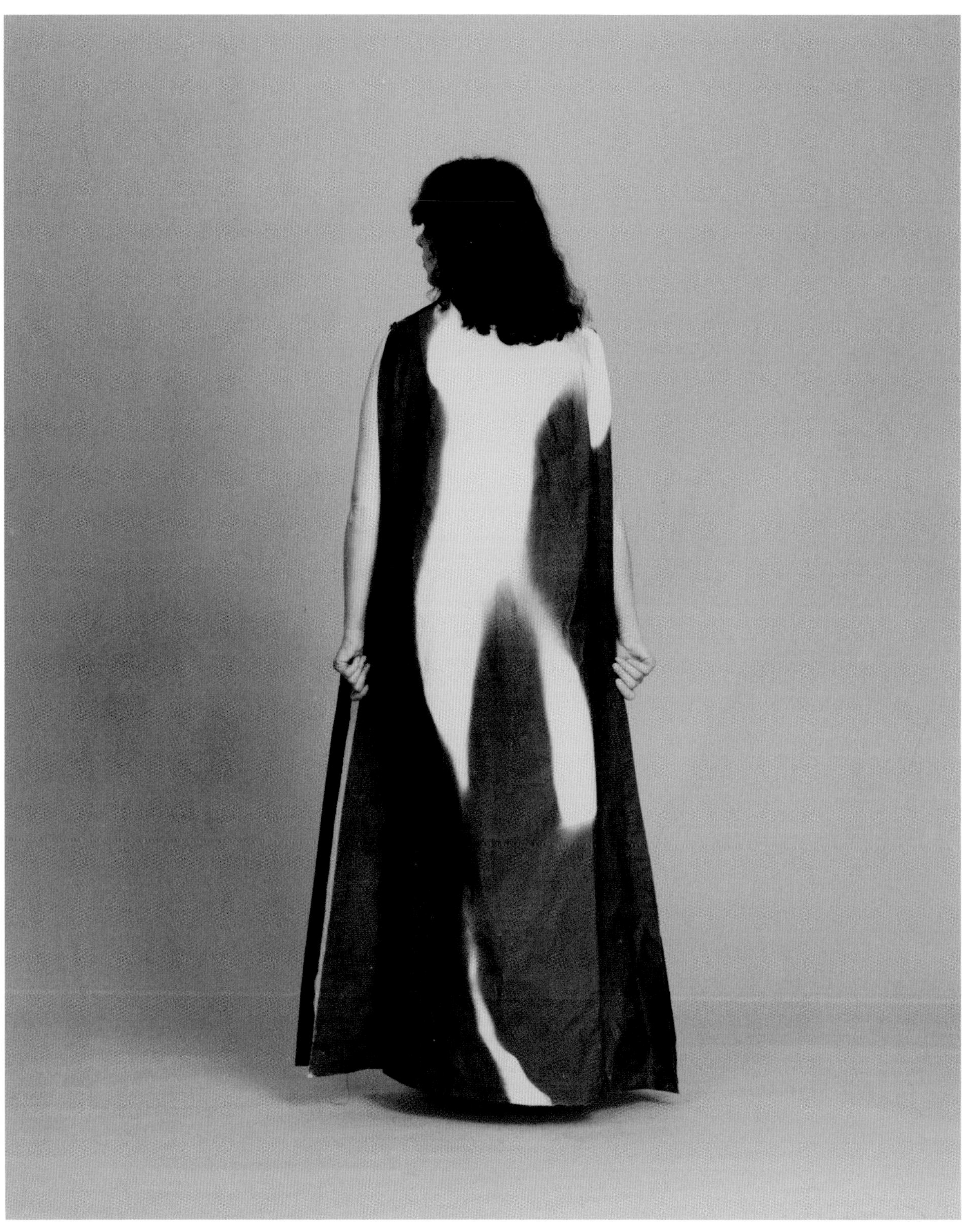

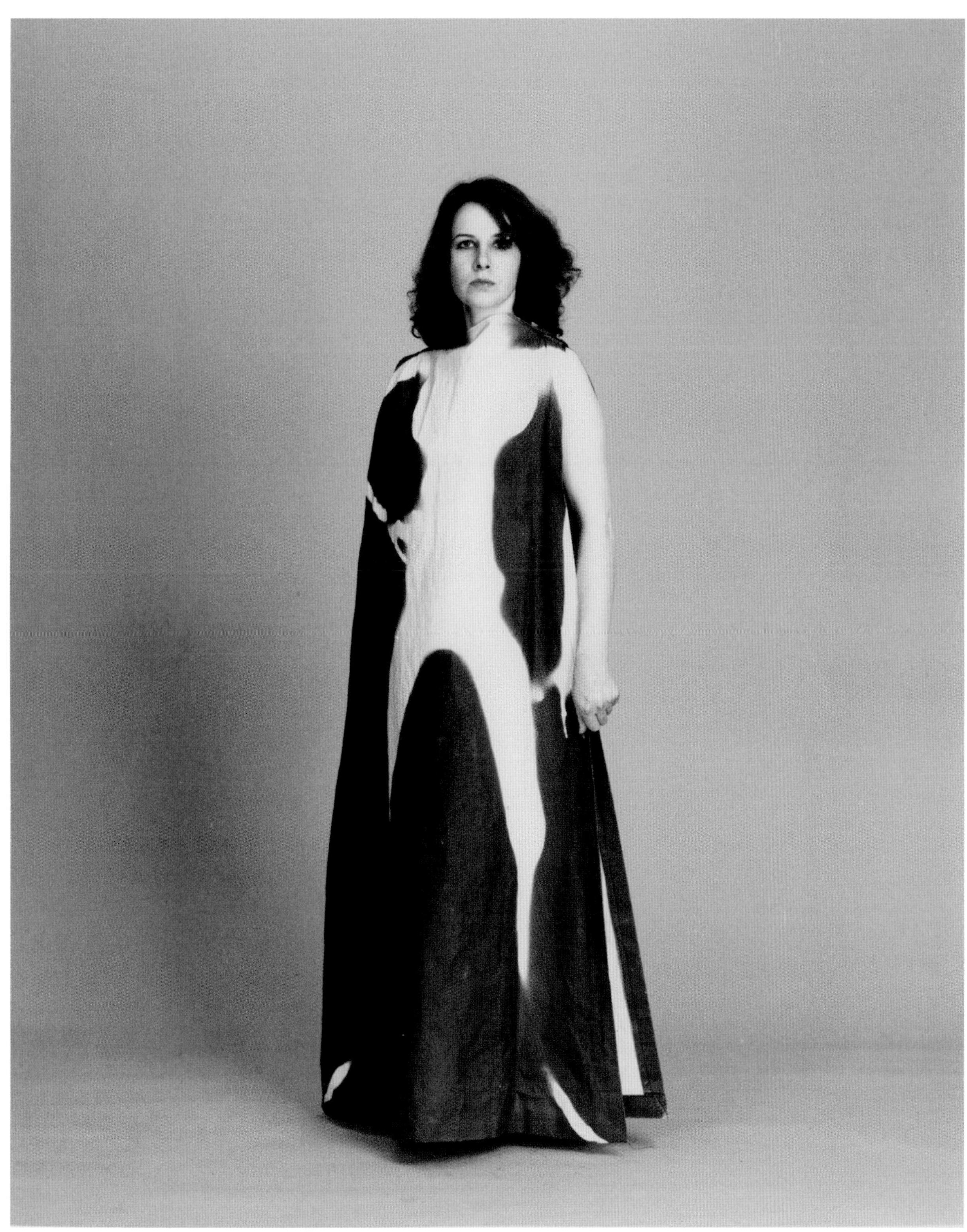

Floris Neusüss and Renate Heyne
(b.1937 and 1947)

The Latticed Window
2010

Dye destruction prints
322 x 277 cm (framed)

This window at Lacock Abbey, Wiltshire, was the subject of the earliest surviving photographic negative, made by William Henry Fox Talbot in 1835. Neusüss and Heyne, after covering the interior of the window with photographic paper at night, exposed the paper by shining a light from outside. The resulting photogram recreates the subject of Talbot's original small negative, but life-size.

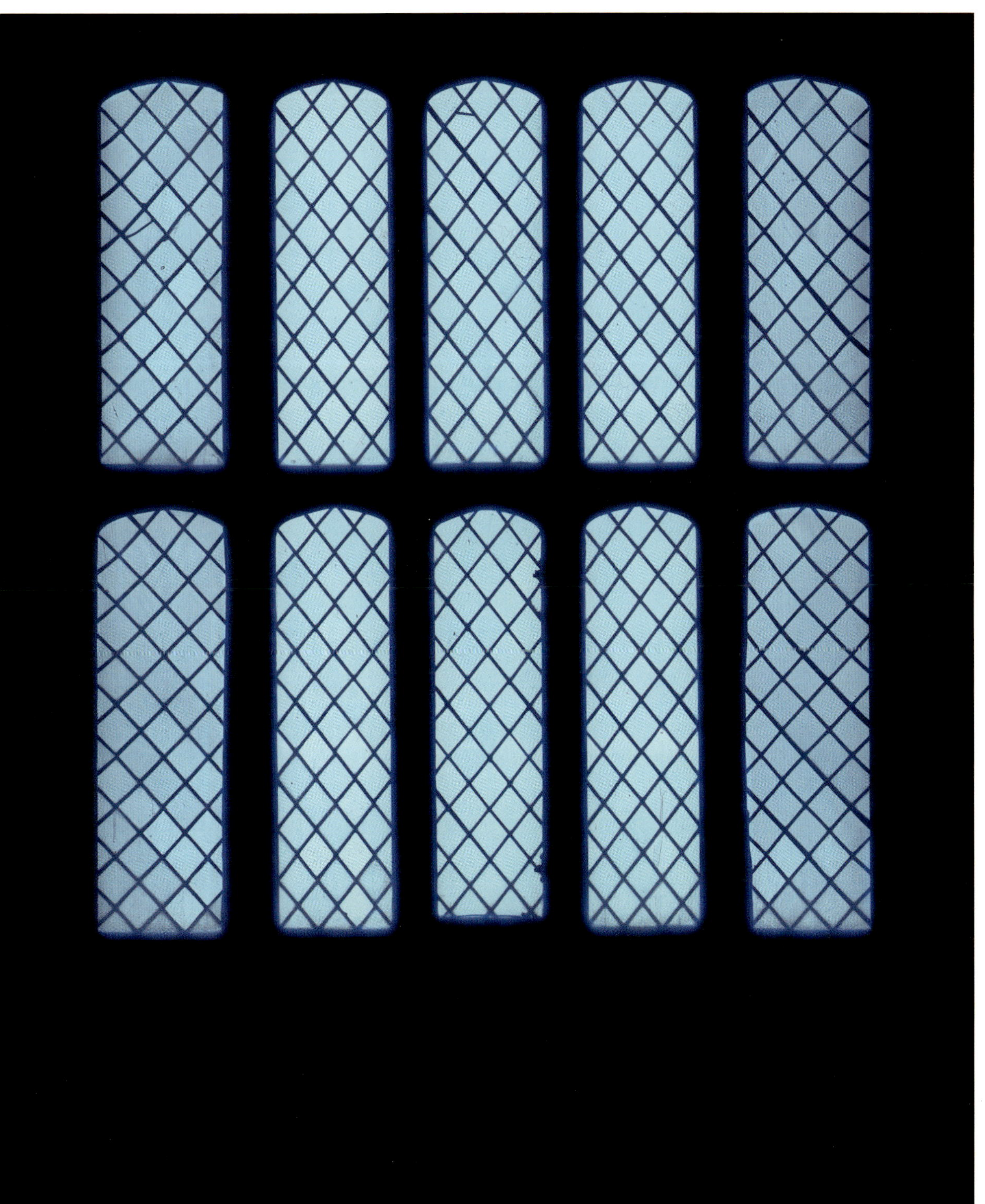

Robert Heinecken (1931–2006)

from the portfolio *Are You Rea*
1968

Lithographs from photograms
93 27.3 x 20 cm
94 22.9 x 19.1 cm
95 27.8 x 15.7 cm
96 27.4 x 16.8 cm
97 20.5 x 15.9 cm

Titled as a truncation of the headline 'Are You Real?', this selection, from a total set of twenty-five, is a satirical comment on the media explosion of the 1960s. Believing that too many photographic images already existed, Heinecken turned to sources of 'found images' such as newspapers and product packaging. Images and texts from the front and back of printed pages overlap, creating new accidental compositions. The layers explore notions of consumer culture.

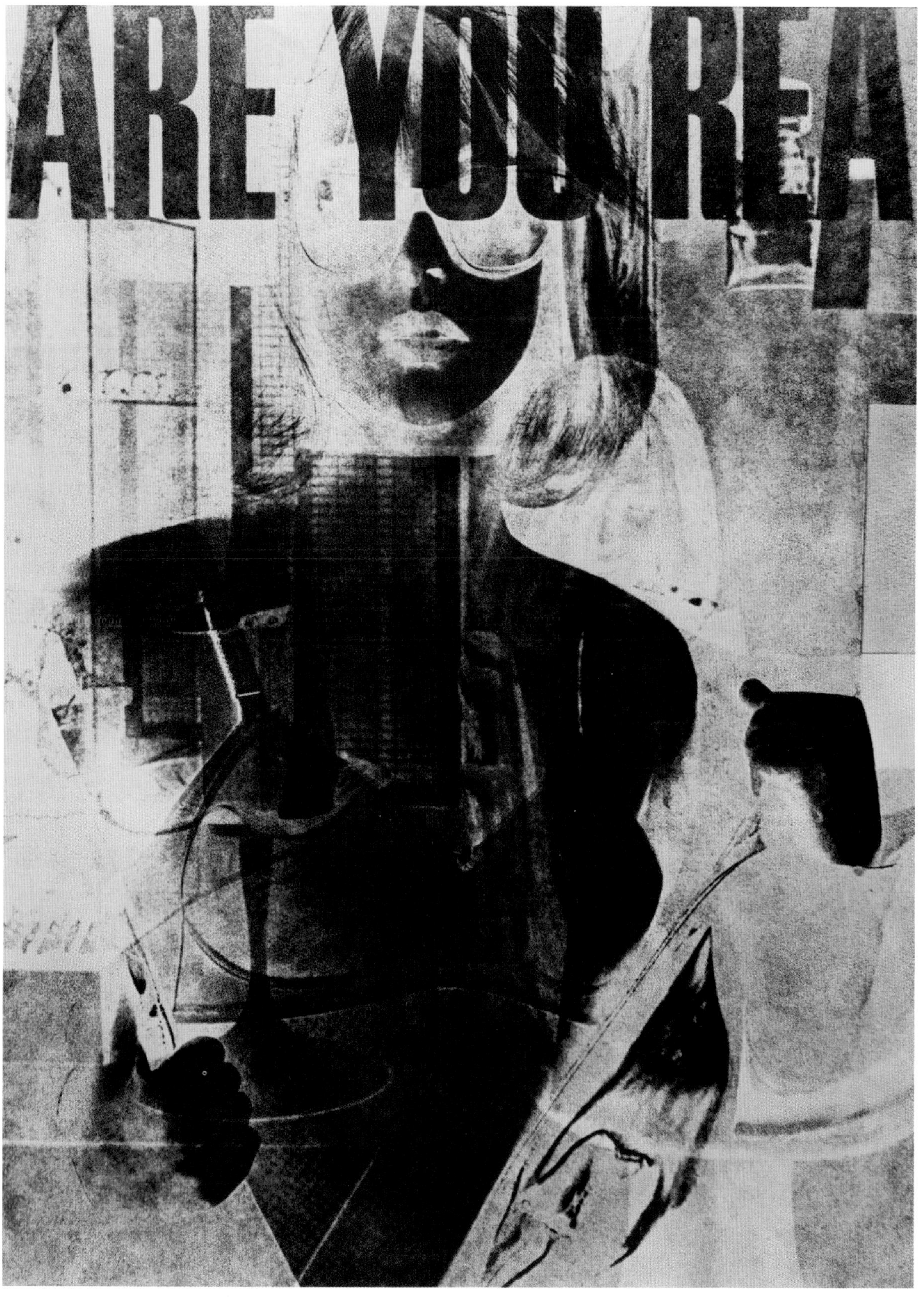
ARE YOU REA

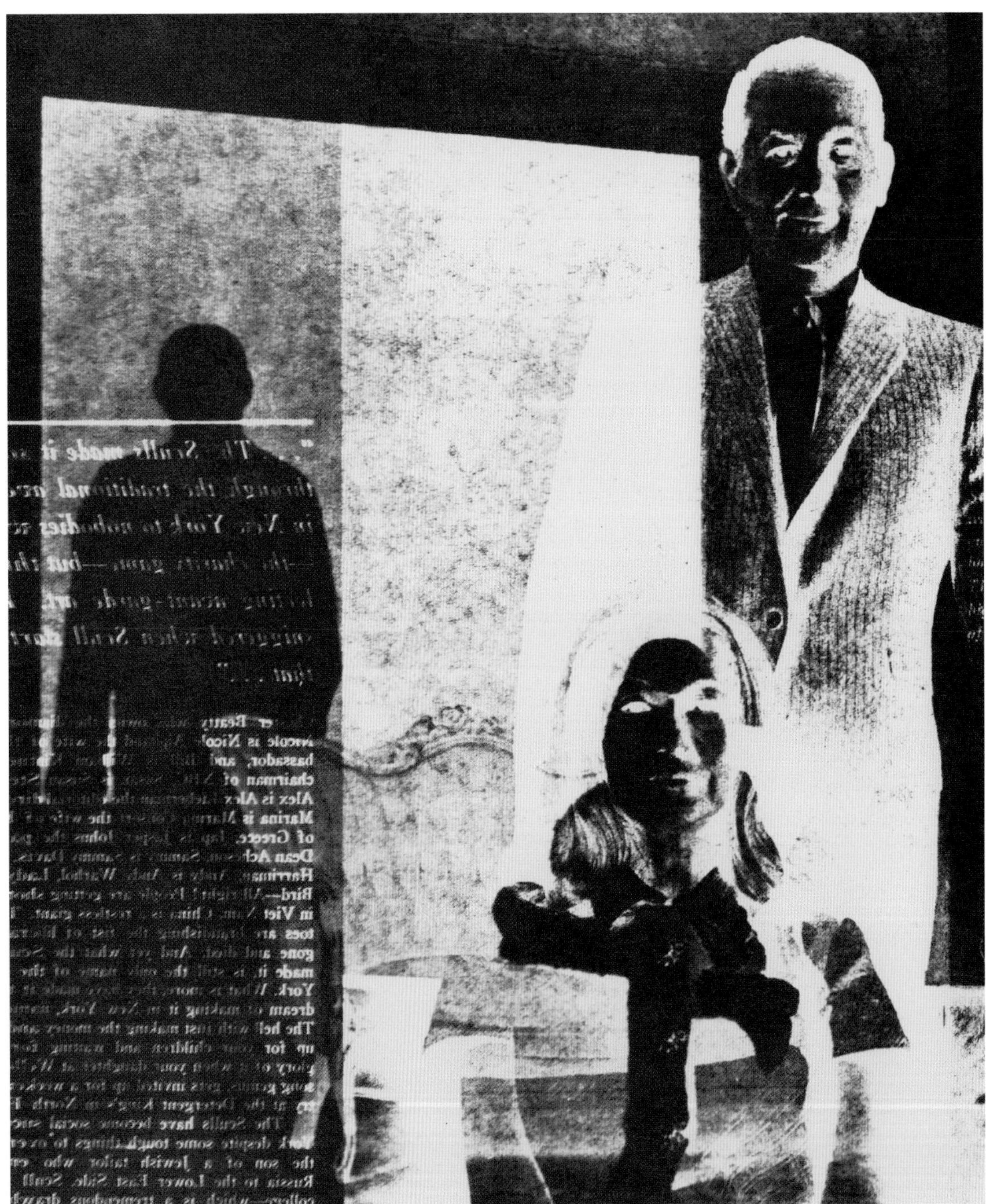

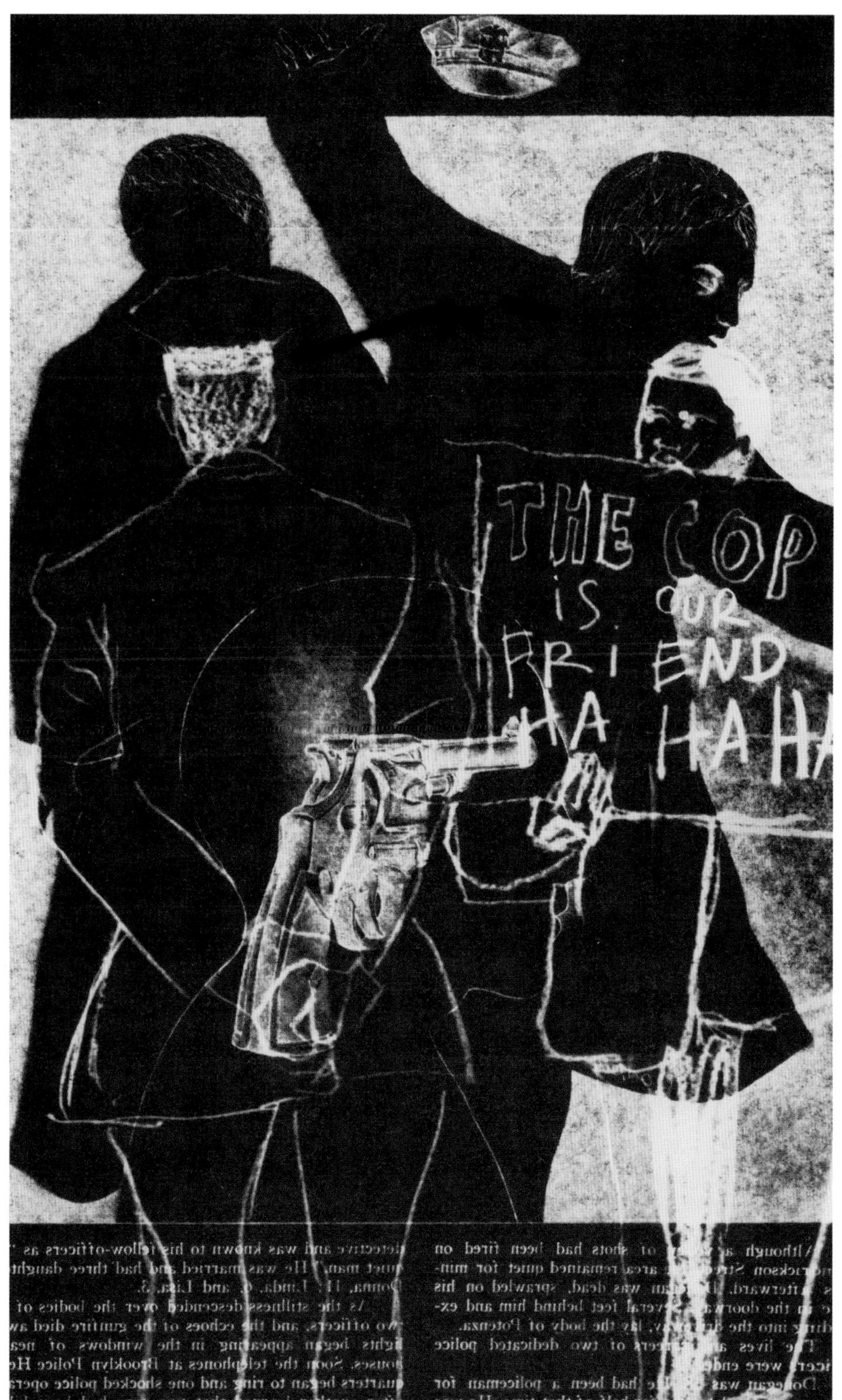
THE COP
IS OUR
FRIEND
HA HAHA

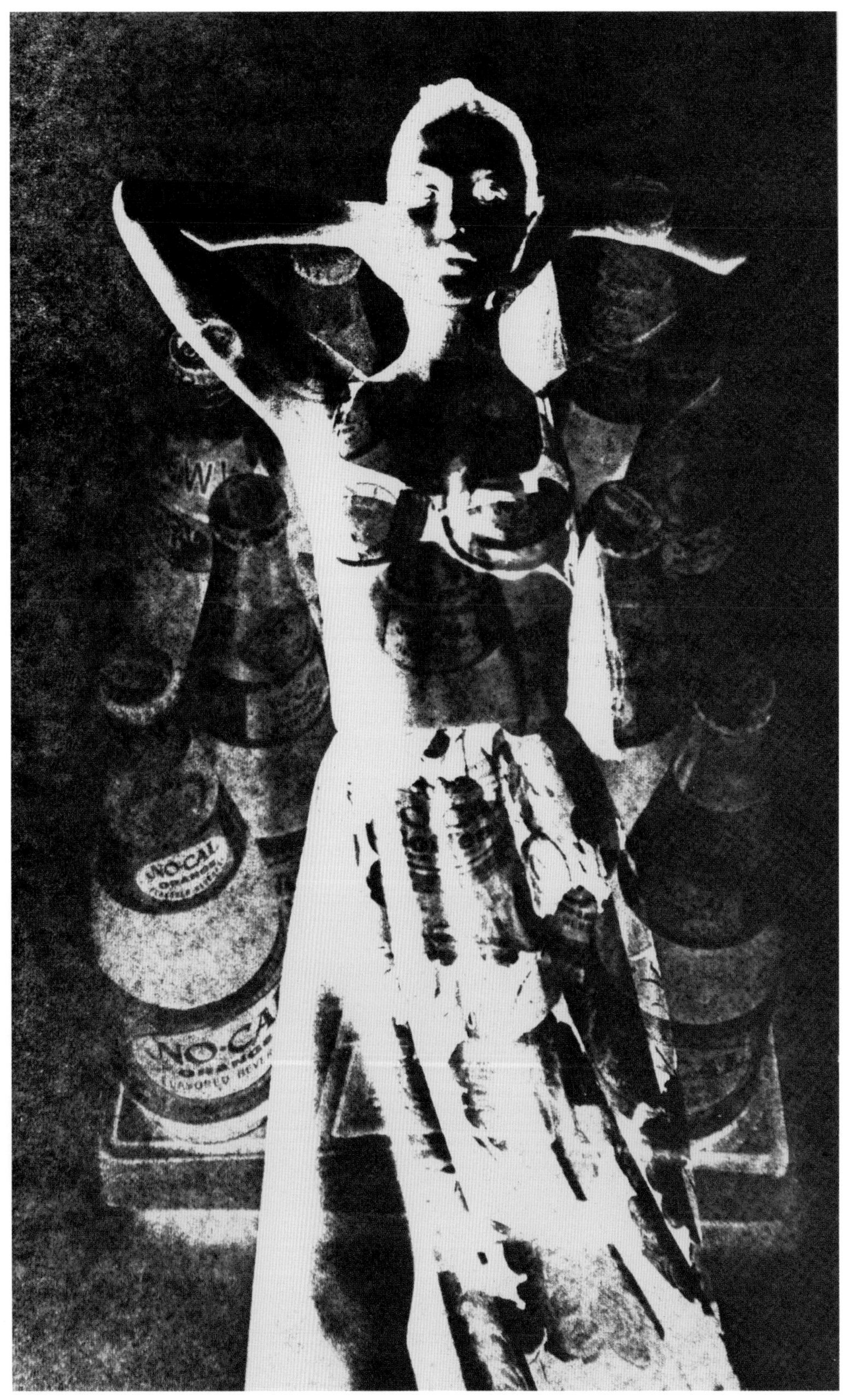
NO-CAL
ORANGE
NO-CAL

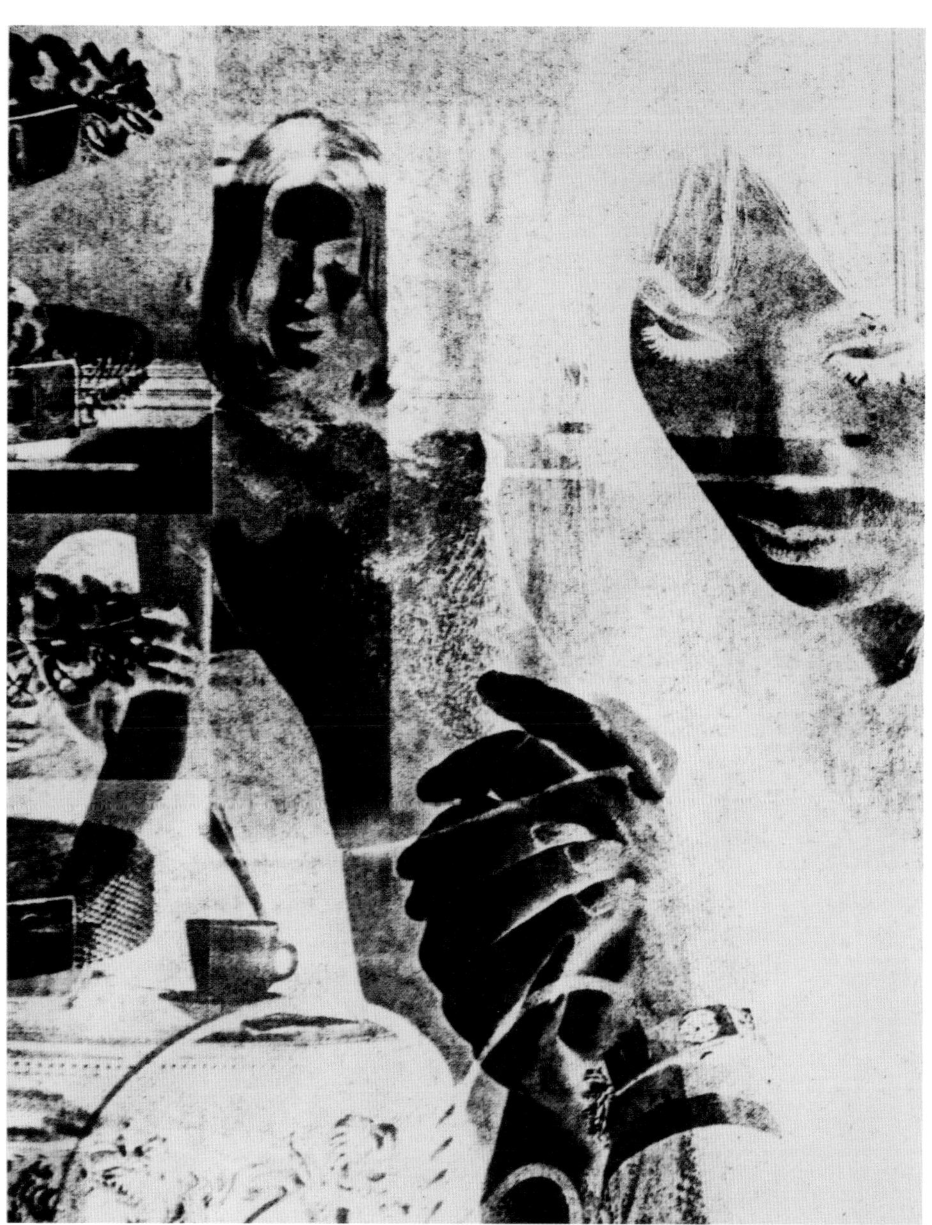

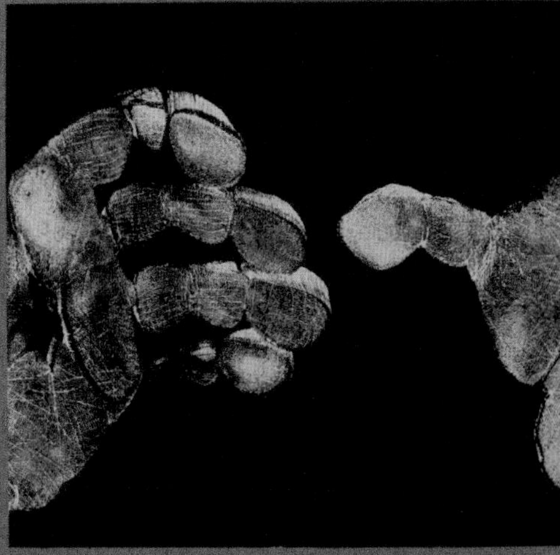

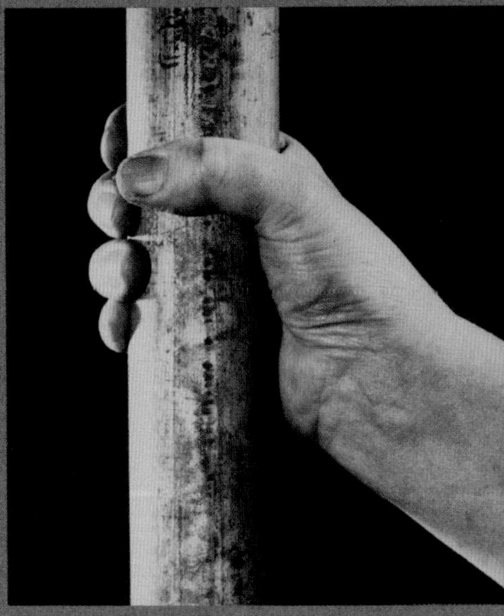

Frances Ellis (fl.1960s)

Power Grips
1968

Gelatin silver prints mounted to board
55.5 x 64 cm

This instructional panel, possibly made for teaching purposes, was produced by a member of the photographic department at the Royal Free Hospital, London. It reveals patterns of hand grips through the simple use of the chemigram. A text on the panel explains: 'The prints were taken with the printing paper wrapped closely round the objects.'

POWER GRIPS

Gripping a 2·5cm. diam. rod: large palmar area in contact for transmission of torque.

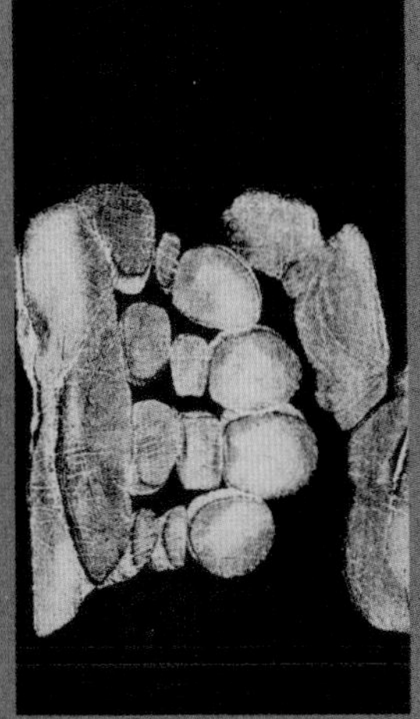

Holding a hammer: large area in contact for exerting torque, pads of fingers and thumb in contact for manipulative control.

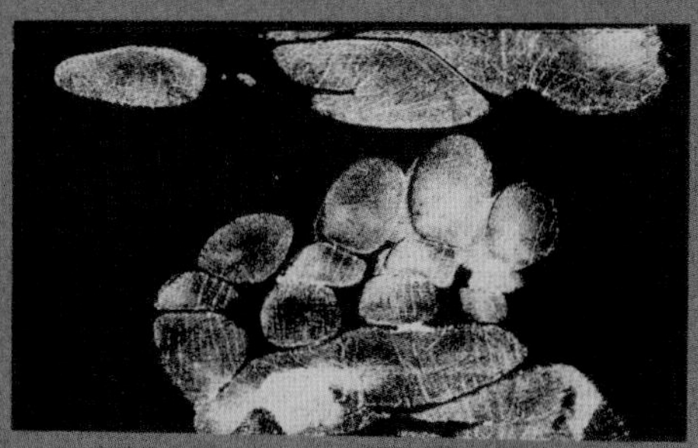

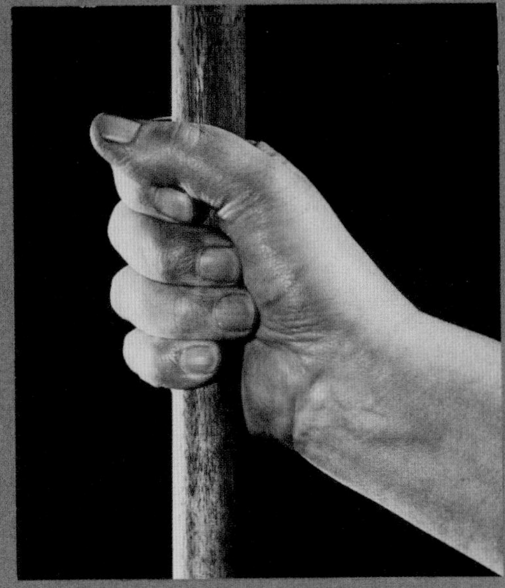

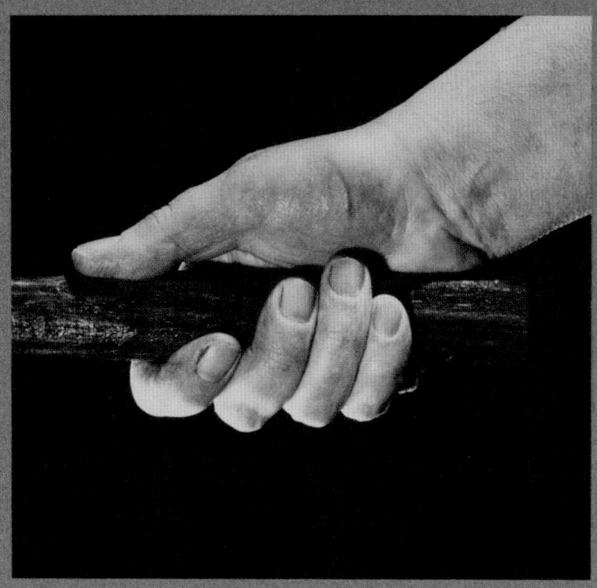

'RAPPED CLOSELY ROUND THE OBJECTS, THE JOINS OF PAPER BEING BETWEEN THE FOREFINGER AND THUMB.
PHOTOGRAPHS AND PALMAR PRINTS IS A FEMALE, AGED 57.

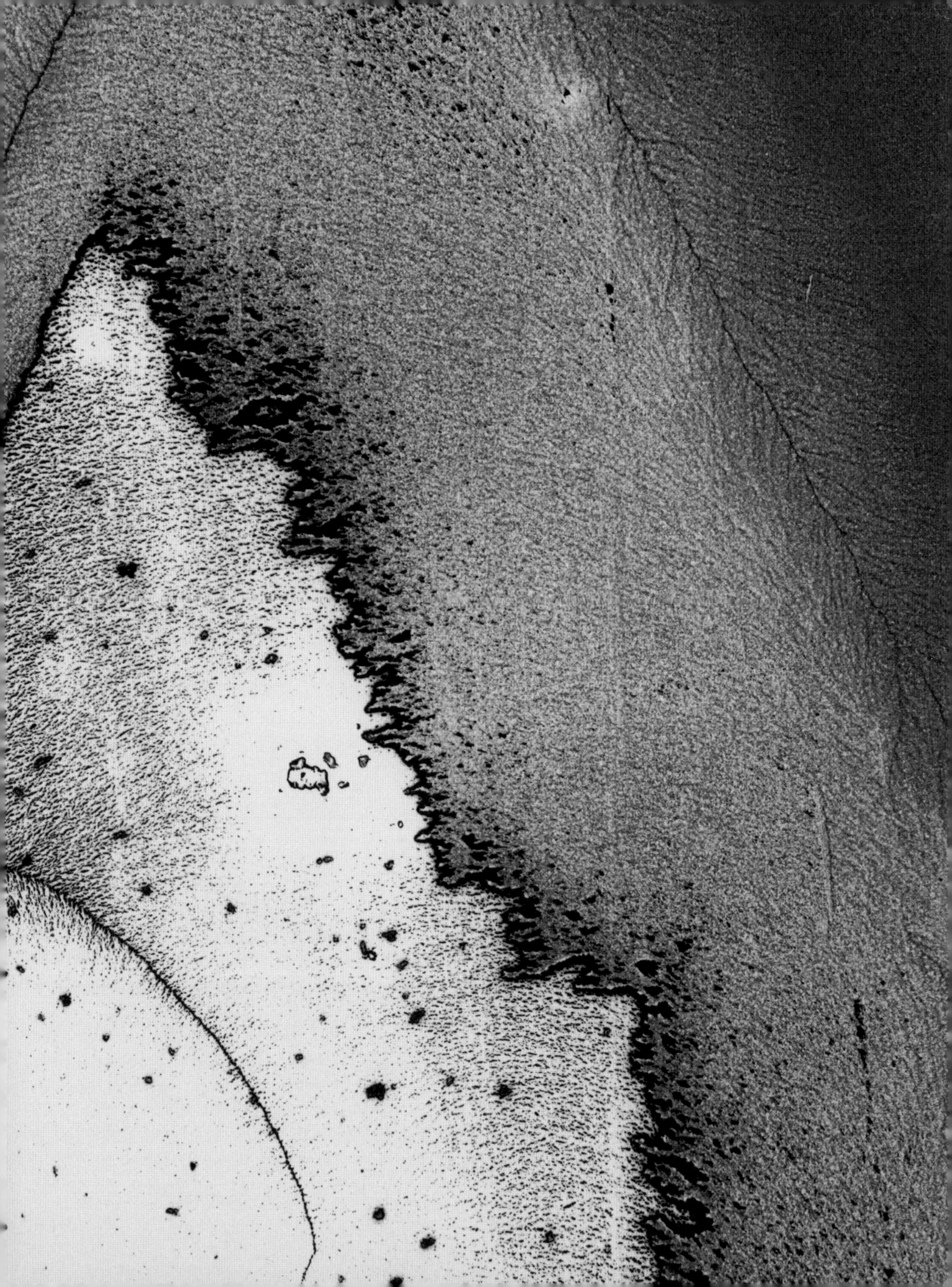

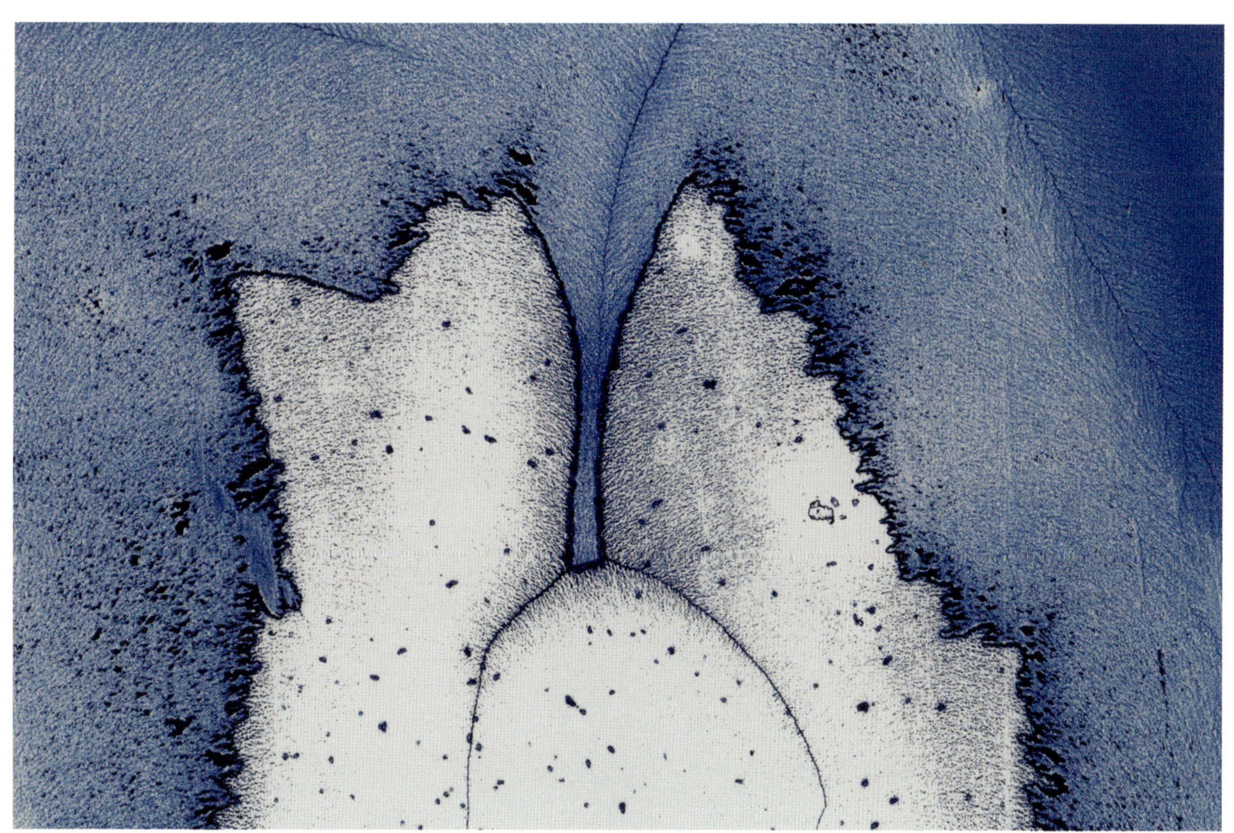

Jean-Pierre Sudre (1921–1977)

Untitled
1972

Gelatin silver print, toned
19.7 x 30.2 cm

(detail p.101)

Sudre created abstracted natural patterns by forming crystals on glass plates, which he would then use as a 'negative' for cameraless photographs, in the same manner as *cliché-verre*. He often printed them using a technique known as 'mordançage', also known as 'etch-bleach', a process using metal toning and etching that gives the image a shimmering appearance.

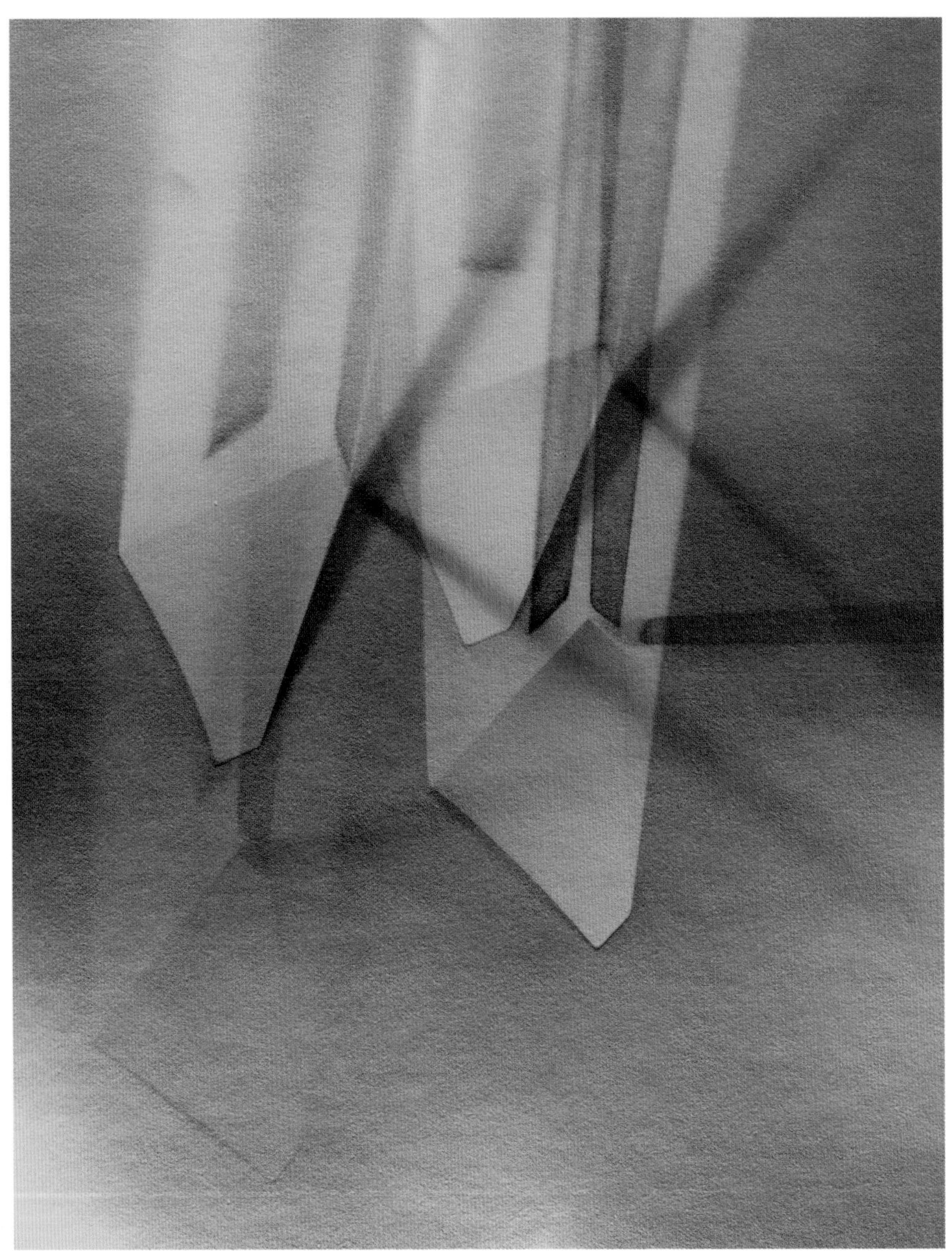

Arnold M. Gilbert (1921–2001)

Untitled
1979

Gelatin silver print
32.7 x 25.4 cm

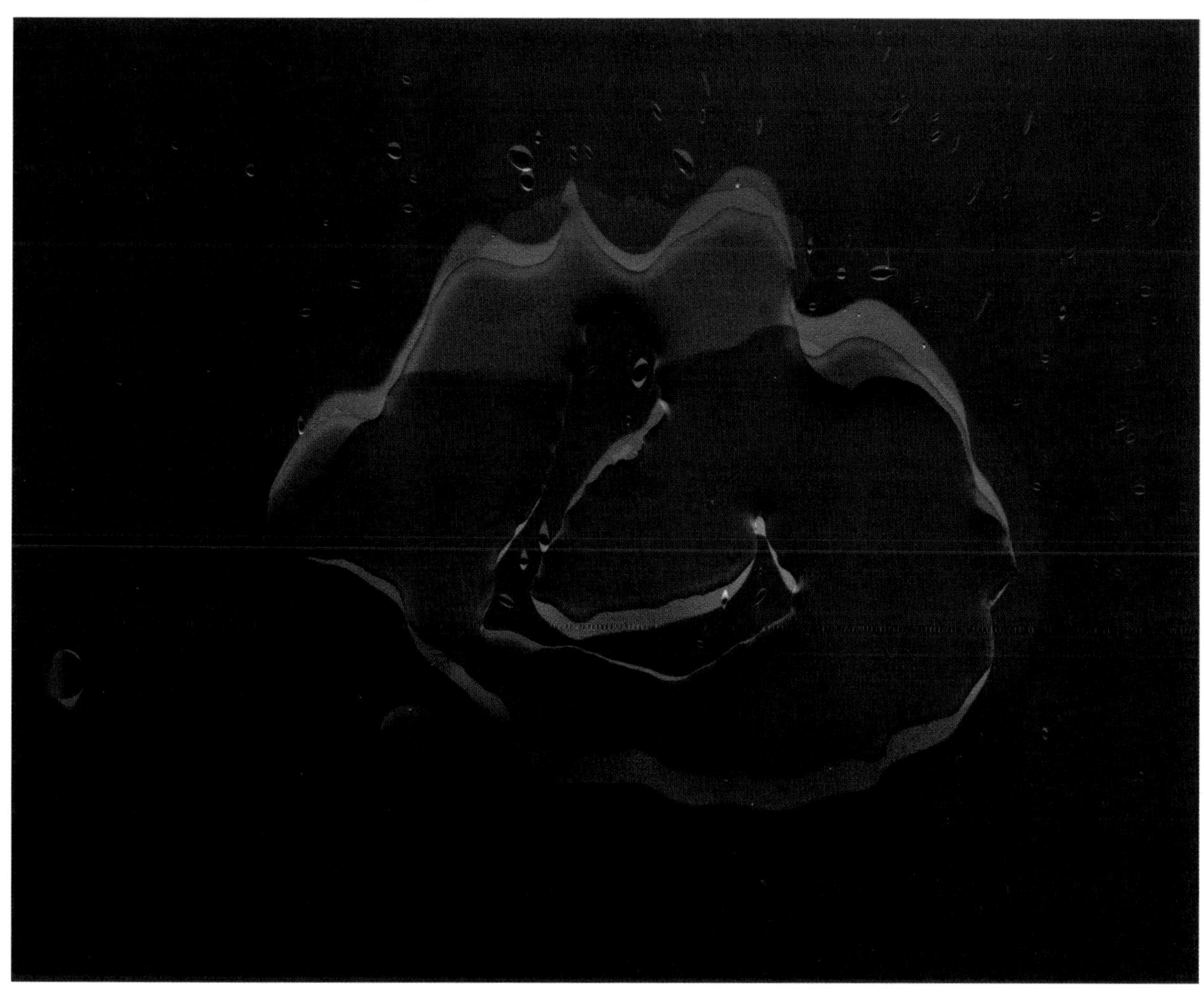

Arnold M. Gilbert (1921–2001)

Untitled
1980

Gelatin silver print
26.1 x 33.2 cm

Gilbert was a Chicago-based artist and collector, and a founding benefactor of the city's Museum of Contemporary Photography. The enduring influence of László Moholy-Nagy, alongside that of his followers at the New Bauhaus in Chicago, can be traced in Gilbert's work. His photograms explore a range of textures and forms, from light and shadow to liquid, rendered with delicacy and a subtle tonal range.

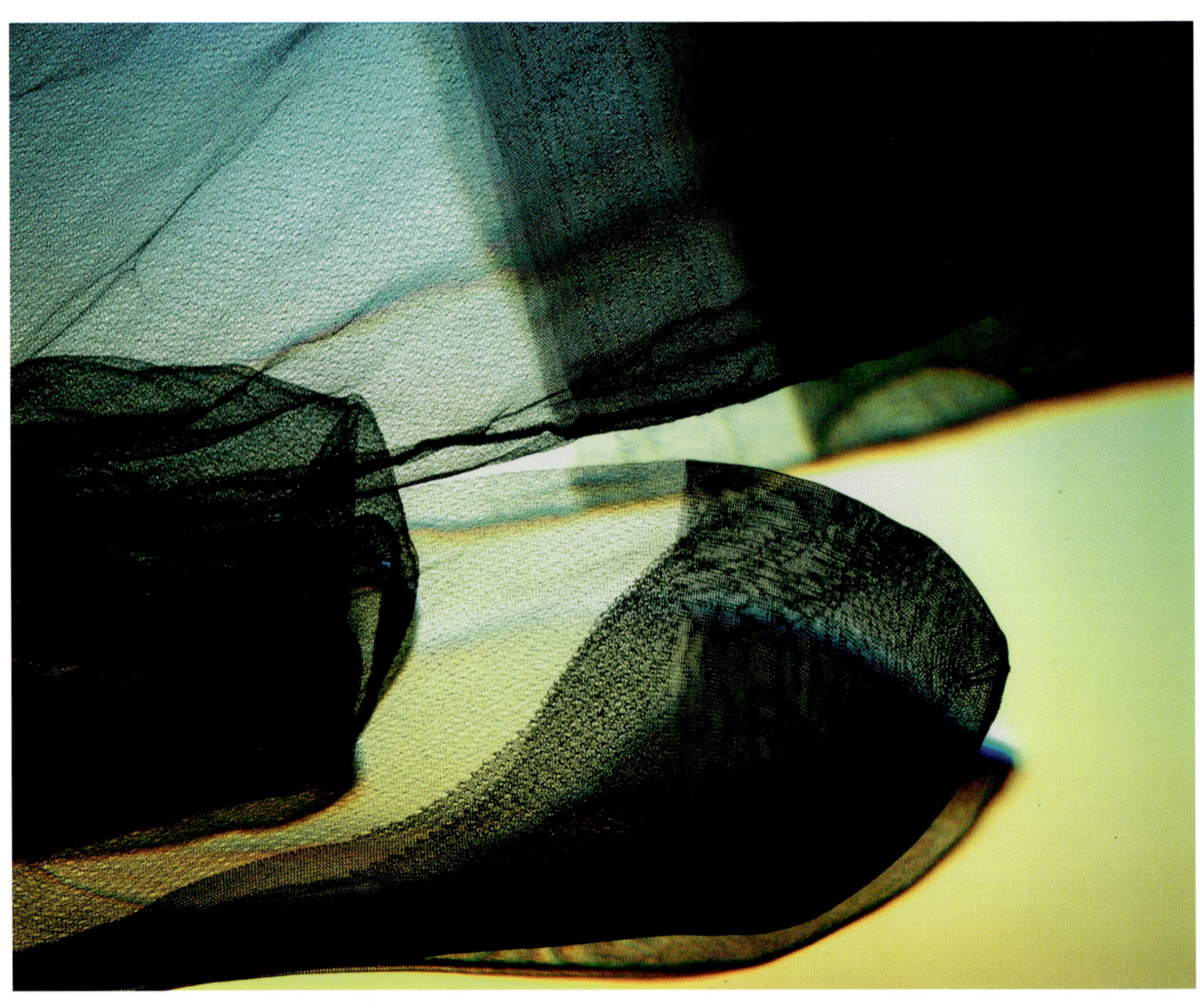

Susan Gamble (b.1957)

Stockings
from the series *The Body in Question*
1982

Transmission hologram
20.3 x 25.4 cm

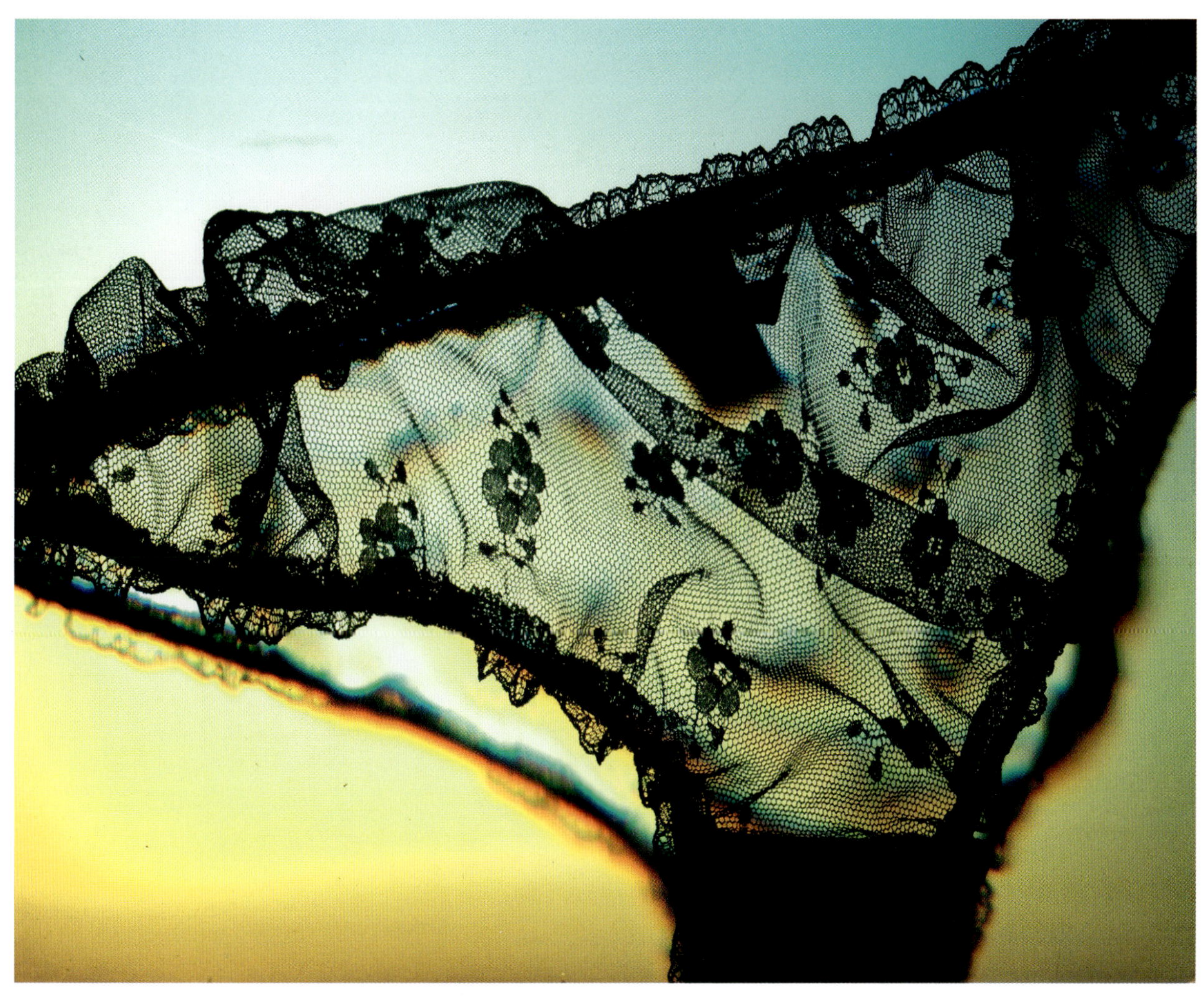

Susan Gamble (b.1957)

Knickers
from the series *The Body in Question*
1982

Transmission hologram
20.3 x 25.4 cm

Gamble pioneered the use of holography as fine art during a period of innovation and acceptance for the medium in the 1980s. To make these images, she playfully 'dressed' the hologram plates with lingerie. The laser used to expose the plates imprints a sharp shadow and spectral colours, while moiré patterns appear between the different layers.

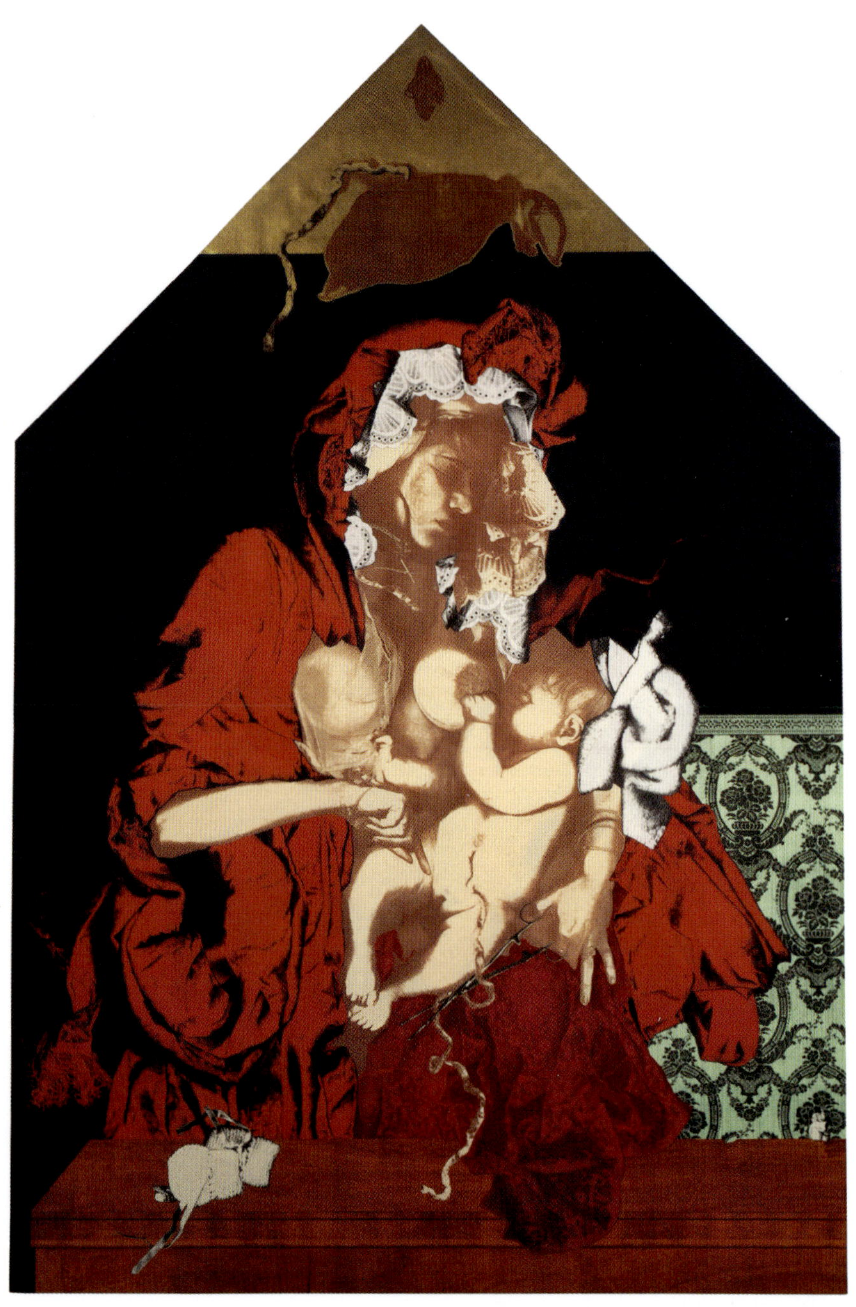

Helen Chadwick (1953–1996)

One Flesh
1985

Photocopy collage
160 x 106.7 cm

One Flesh represents a Renaissance Madonna-like figure, a female child and a placenta in a gilt-framed collage of toned photocopies from life. The photocopies make use of modern office machinery to revisit the past, and they liberated the artist from conventional photography. While photocopies – like photographs – are intended to replicate in quantity, Chadwick used them in this instance to assemble a unique work of art.

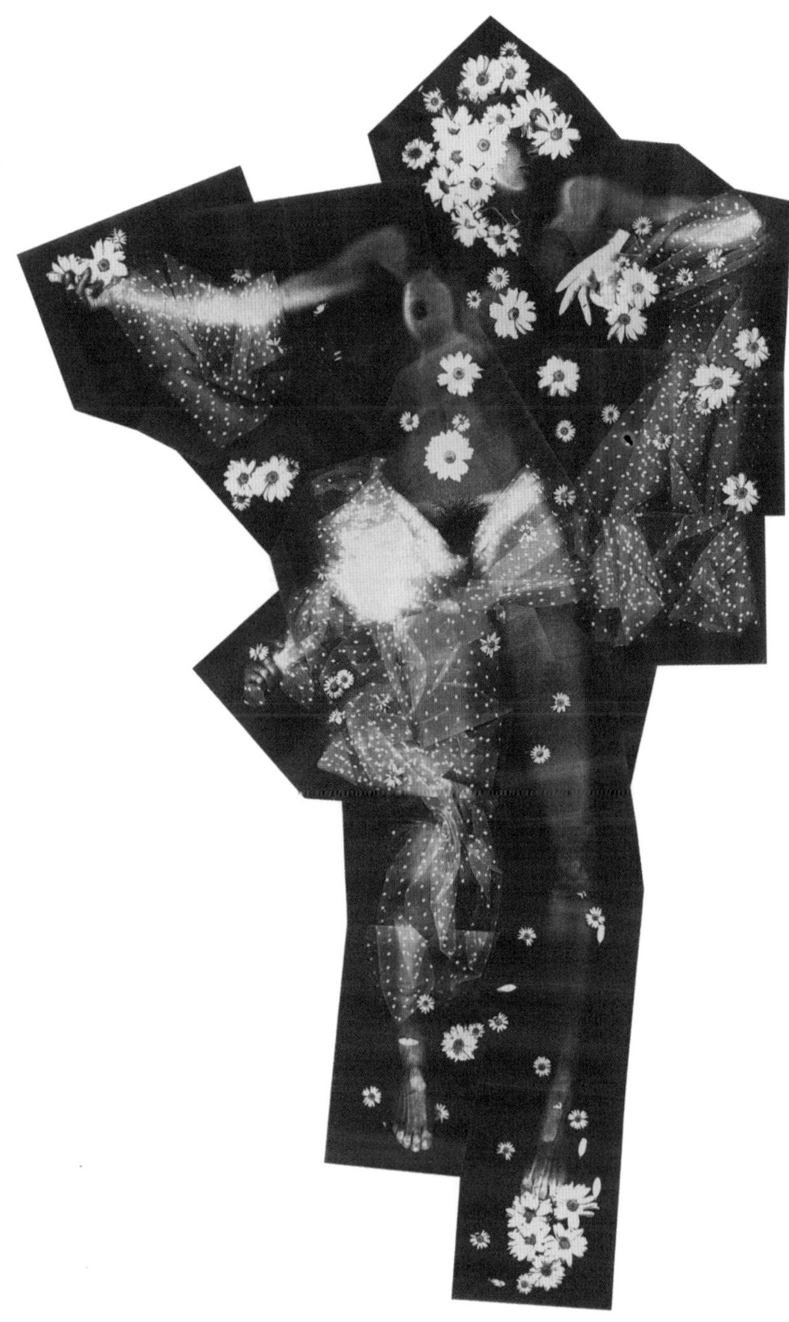

Helen Chadwick (1953–1996)

Study for *Of Mutability*
1986

Photocopy collage
147 x 90.7 cm

(detail p.12)

Chadwick's use of photocopy collage reached its height with her large installation, *Of Mutability*. Placing her own body and other objects on the copier, she created an ethereal world of figures appearing to float in a pool. The piece shown here is a test, including motifs of the body with flowers and fabric not seen in the final installation.

Christopher Bucklow (b.1957)

Sleeping Guest, 8.17 pm, 31 July 1996
1996

Dye destruction print
99 x 72 cm

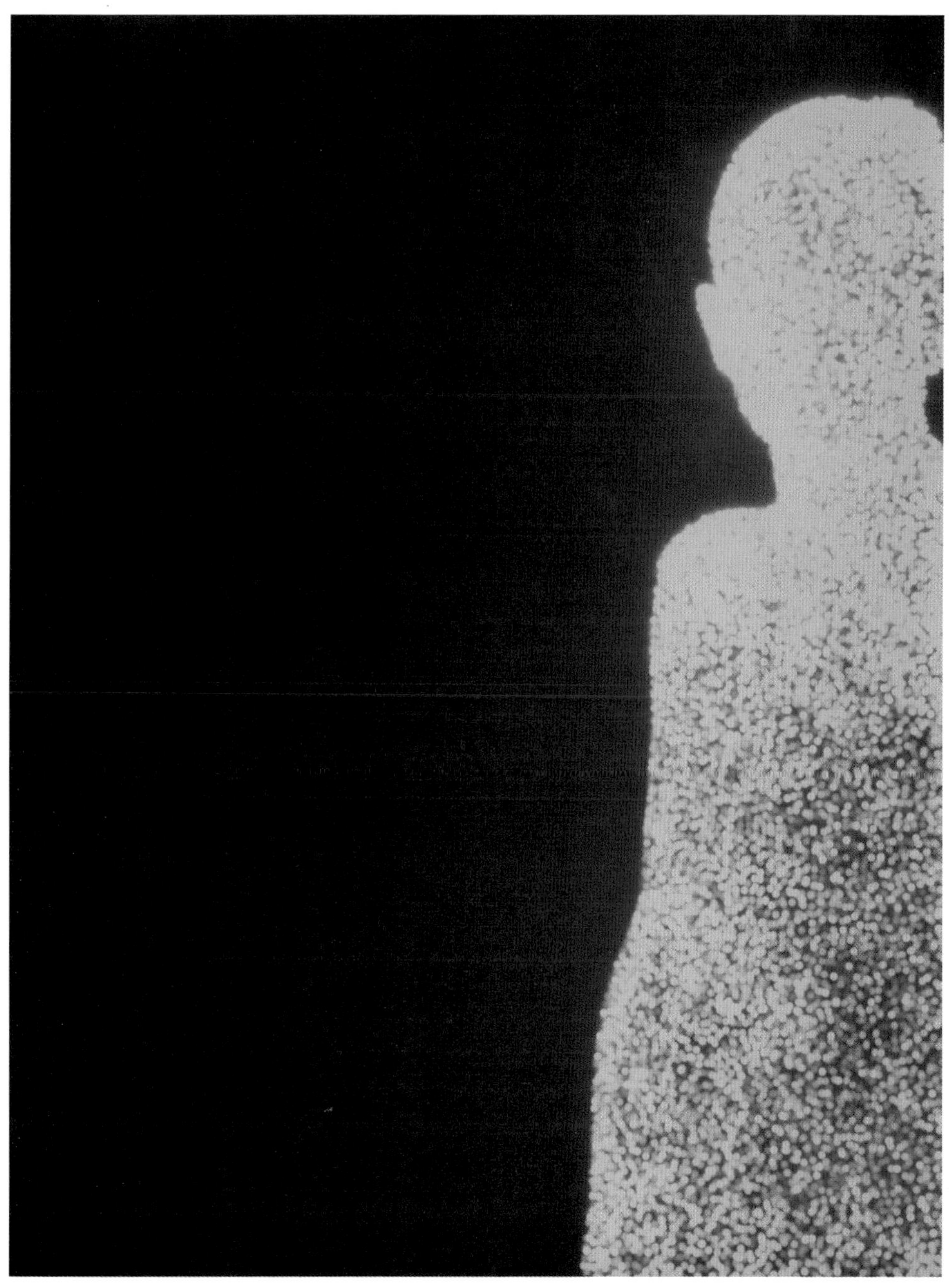

Christopher Bucklow (b.1957)

Guest, 1.56 pm, 4 November 1995
1995

Dye destruction print
99 x 72 cm

The people depicted in Bucklow's *Guest* series are mainly characters who have appeared in the artist's dreams. The images are created by drawing around a person's silhouette. Bucklow transfers the outline to foil and punctures this with thousands of pinholes. The foil is stretched over a box containing photographic paper which is exposed to the sky. Each hole focuses the sun onto the paper to create a glowing, otherworldly presence.

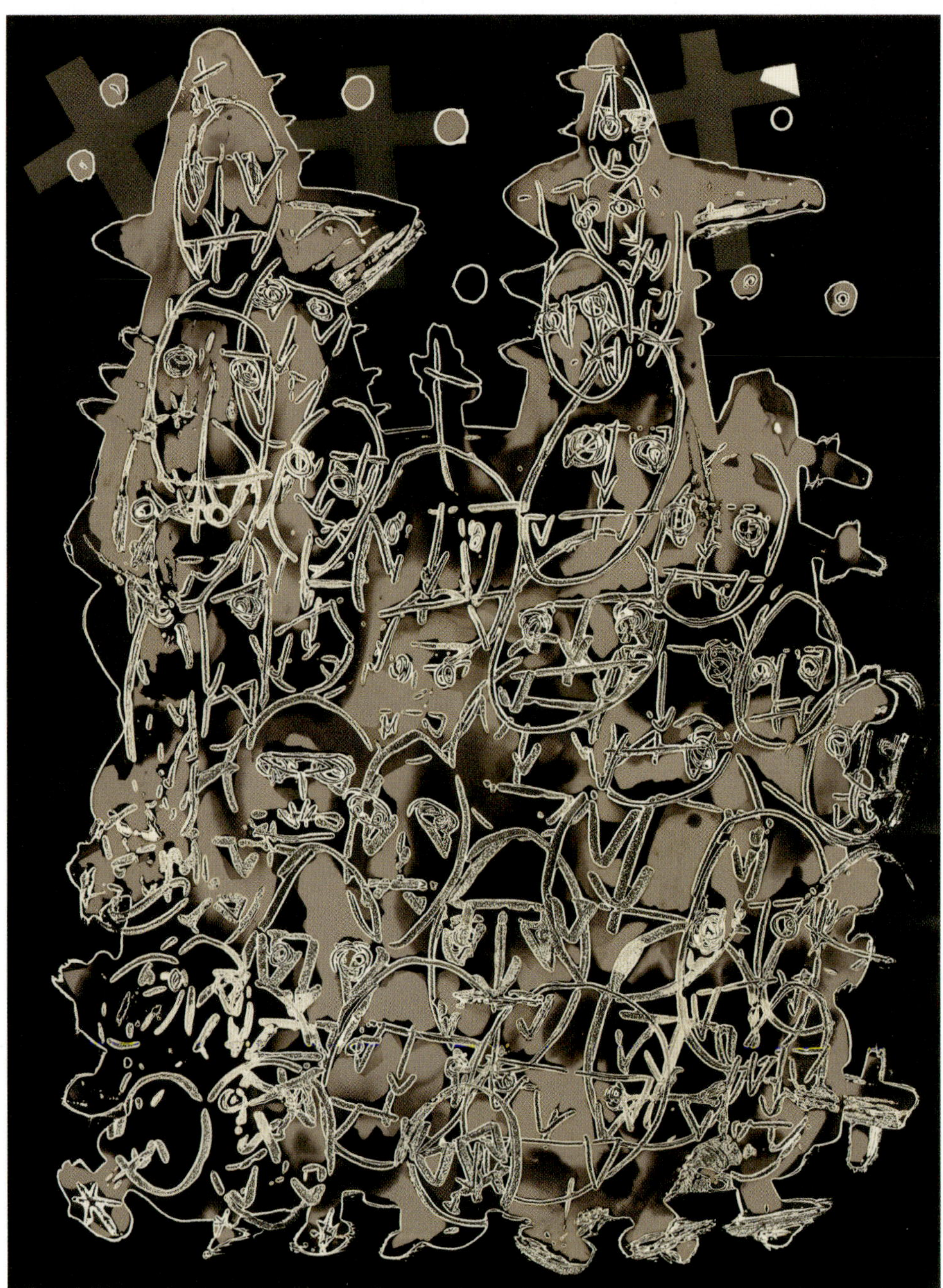

Pierre Cordier (b.1933)

Chemigram + Photogram 20/12/56
'La Révolution hongroise'
1956

Chemigram on gelatin silver paper
24.1 x 18.1 cm

Pierre Cordier discovered the chemigram process in 1956 and has systematically explored its potential ever since. Typically, he applies photographic developer to the paper to create dark areas and fixer for lighter tones. Further changes to shape and pattern are made with varnish, wax, glue, oil, egg and syrup. These protect the surface of the photographic emulsion or can be incised to create entrancing motifs. The processes usually take place in full light.

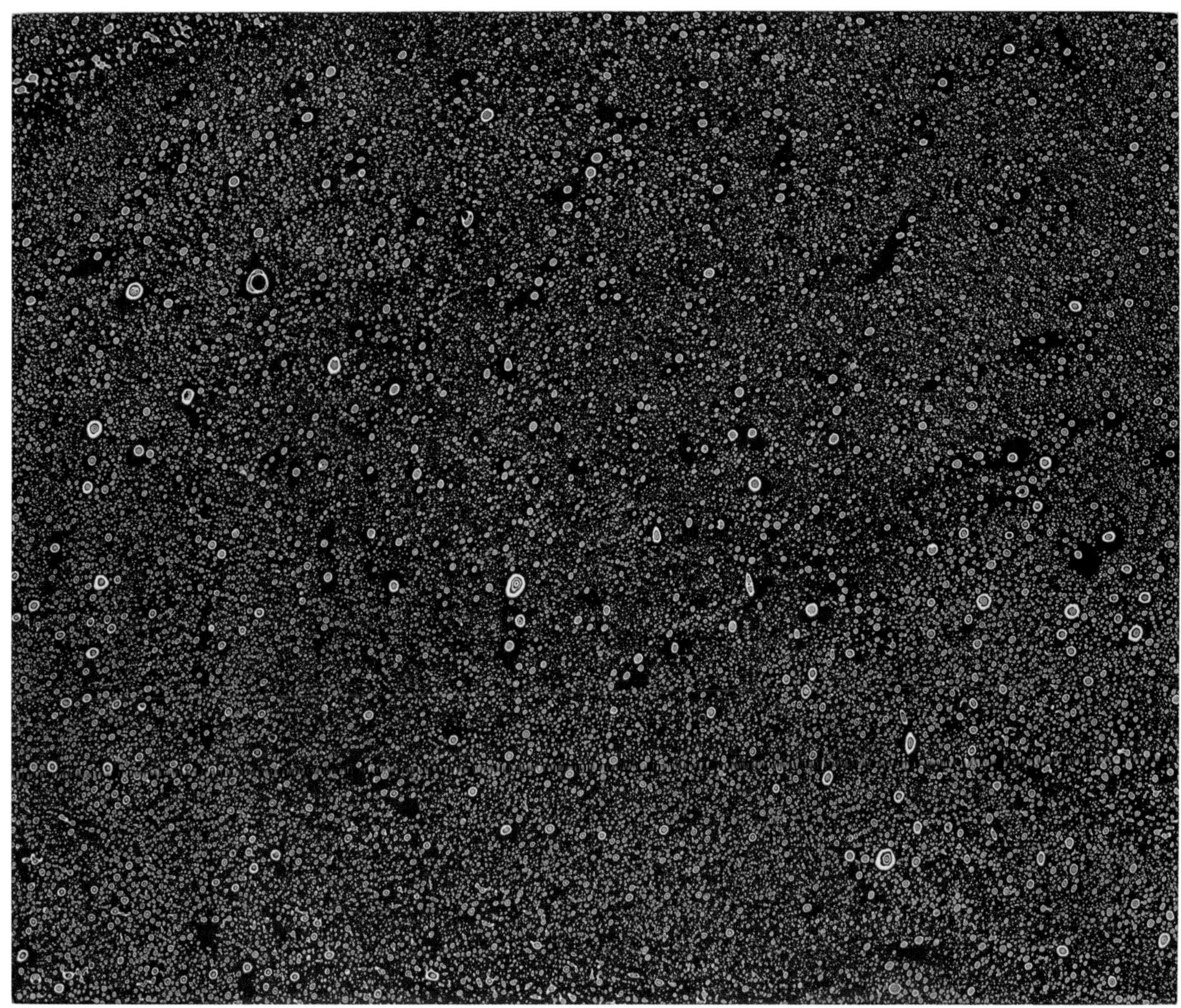

Pierre Cordier (b.1933)

Chemigram 9/1/61 III 'Big Bangram'
1961

Chemigram on gelatin silver paper
24.1 x 29.1 cm

(detail p.113)

Although he is not a scientist, science informs Cordier's work: the question of nanostructures, for instance, objects that exist on a molecular scale. 'To explore a chemigram,' he says, 'you often need eagle eyes, a magnifying glass or a microscope. Sometimes, a seemingly insignificant detail reveals a whole world. Like the messages hidden by spies in the dot of an i.'

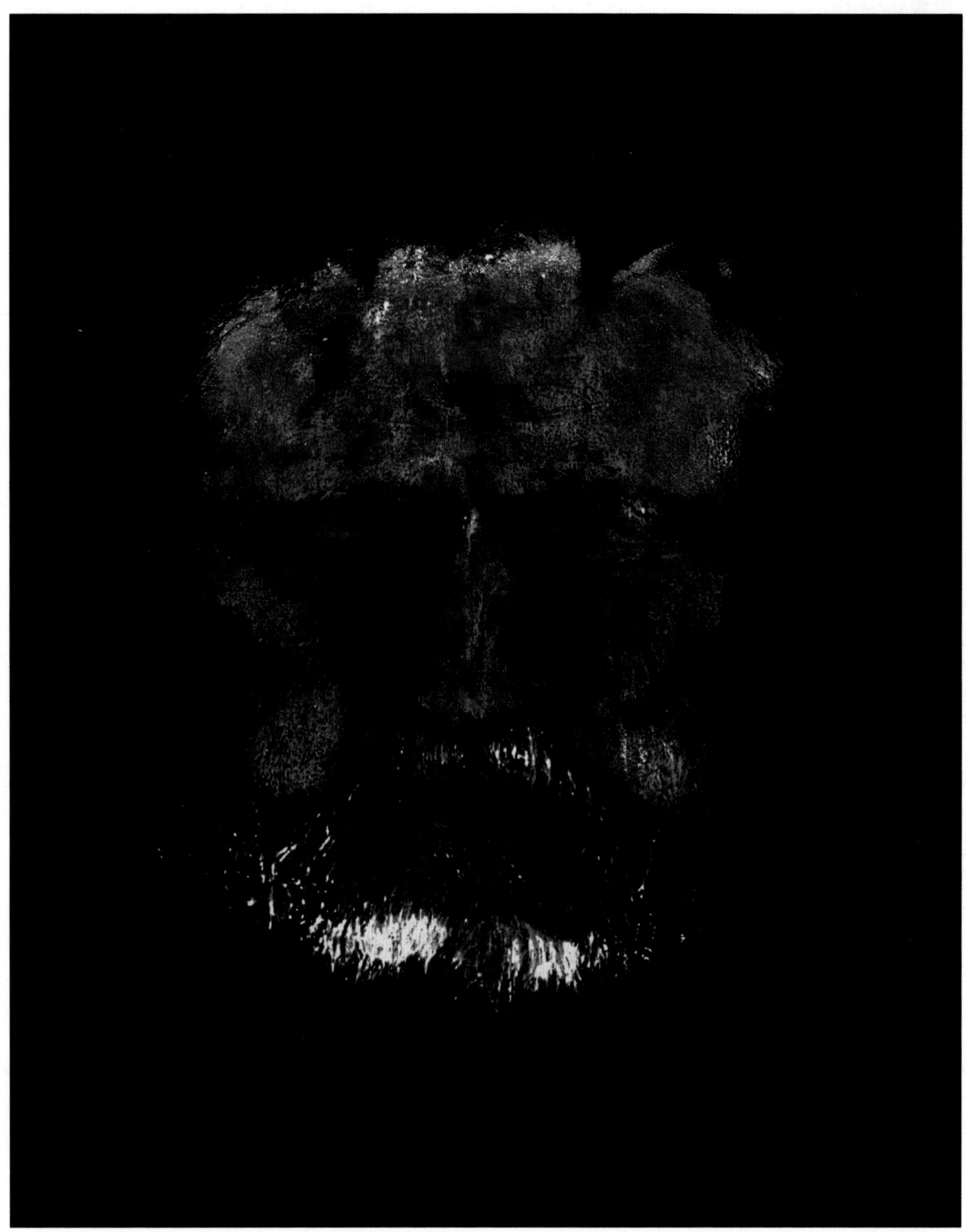

Pierre Cordier (b.1933)

Auto-Chemigram 10/2/81 / 'Pierre Cordier'
1981

Chemigram on gelatin silver paper
49 x 38 cm

Cordier made this self-portrait by coating his face in a thin layer of skin cream and pressing it into photographic paper. He then dipped the paper in developer, removed the cream and dipped it in fixer so that the face remained white. The results can be read as a kind of Veil of Veronica or Shroud of Turin.

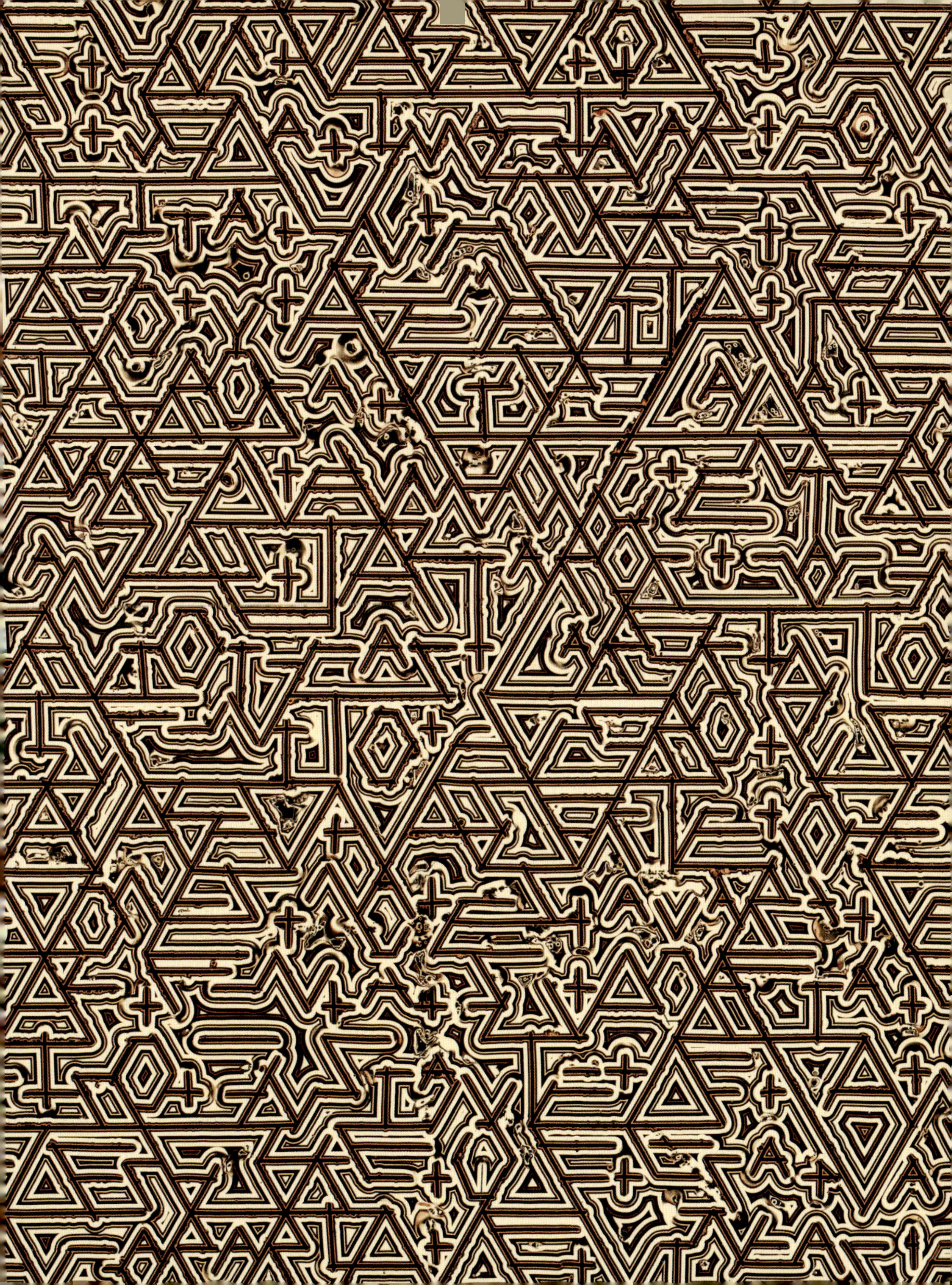

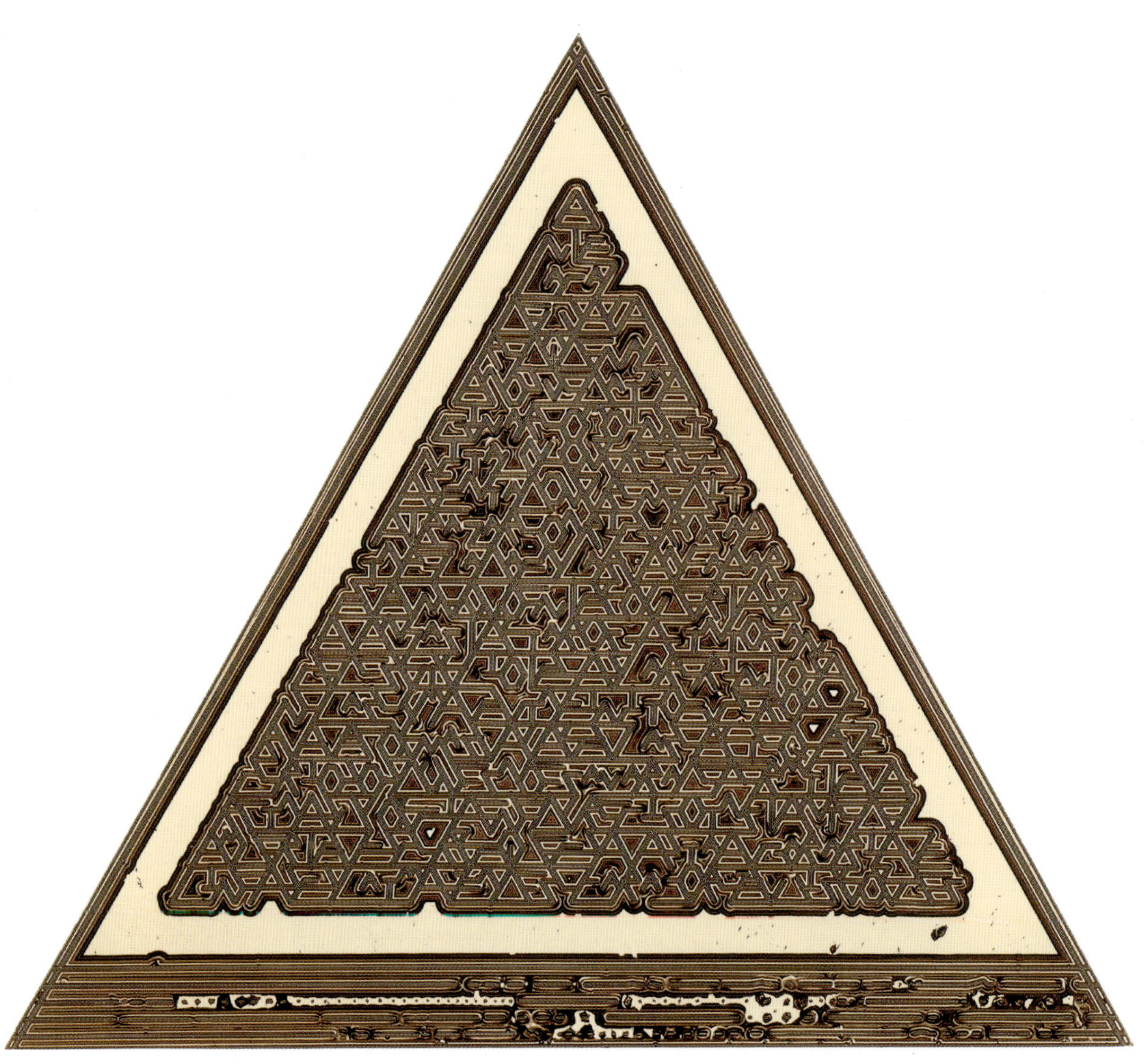

Pierre Cordier (b.1933)

Chemigram 15/9/91 'from La Suma of Jorge Luis Borges'
1991

Chemigram on gelatin silver paper
62 x 70 cm

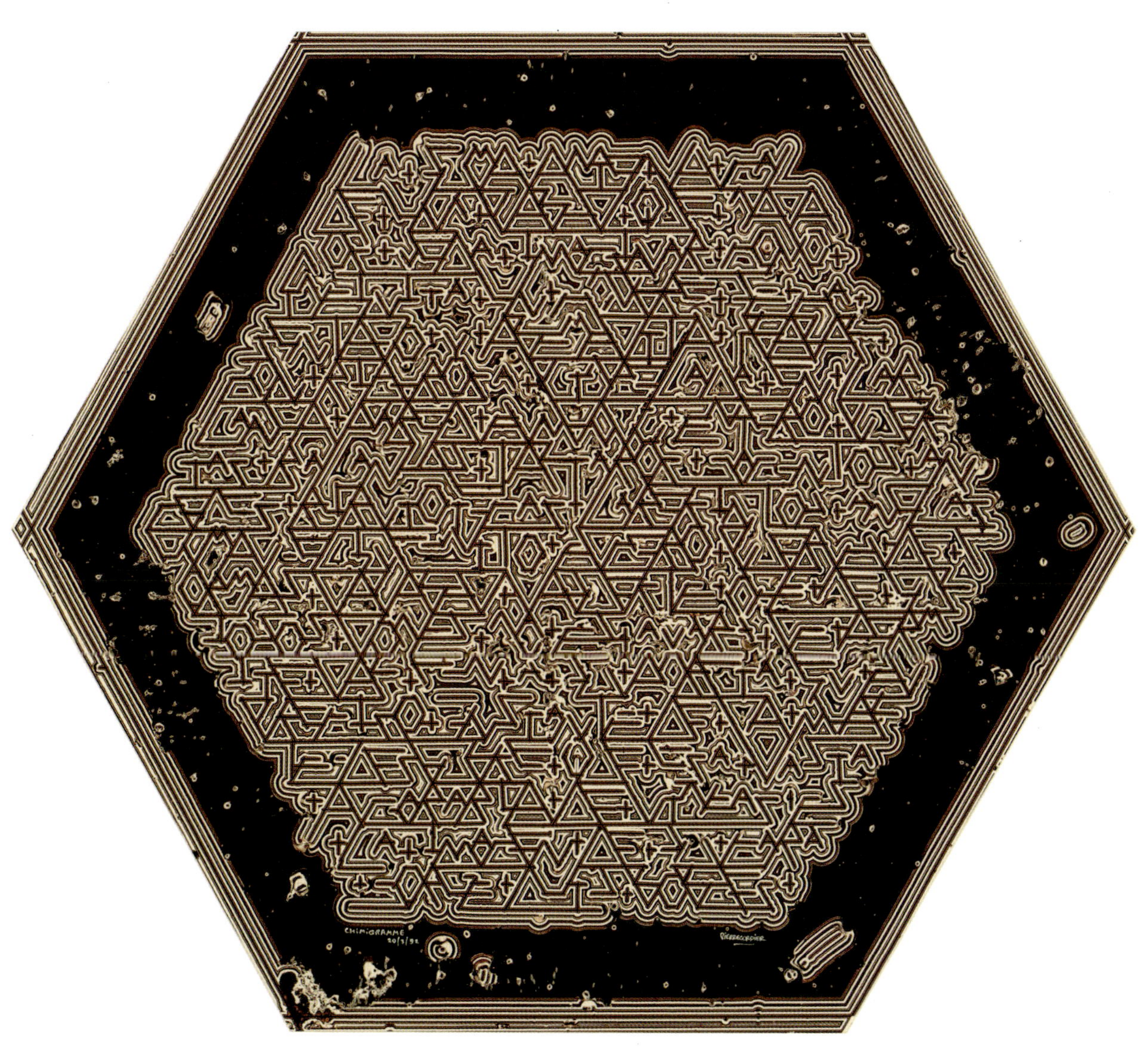

Pierre Cordier (b.1933)

Chemigram 20/3/92 'from La Suma of Jorge Luis Borges'
1992

Chemigram on gelatin silver paper
53 x 61 cm

(detail p.117)

Cordier's fondness for labyrinthine patterns, this time in the form of words, is shown in these works that reference the Argentinian writer, poet and philosopher Jorge Luis Borges. They are composed of letter forms that spell out Borges's poem *La Suma*. The letters, however, are almost impossible to decipher, their shapes joining together as paths forking in different directions.

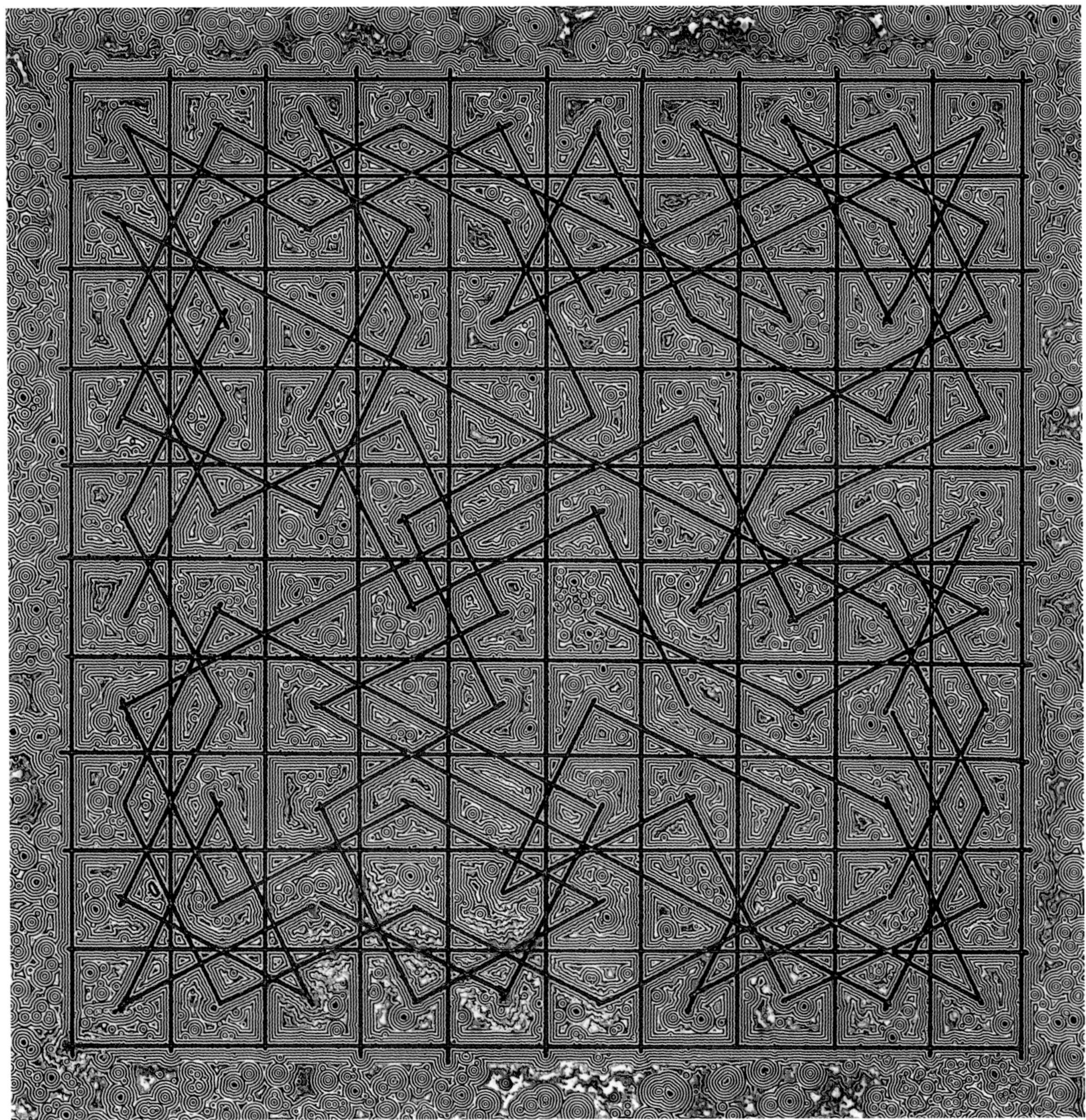

Pierre Cordier (b.1933)

Chemigram 31/7/01
'Hommage à Georges Perec'
2001

Chemigram on gelatin silver paper
15.1 x 14.9 cm

Georges Perec's major work, *Life: A User's Manual* (1978), tells the story of a Paris apartment building and its inhabitants. The apartments form a 10 x 10 grid, which serves as the structure of the book's narrative. Each is dealt with according to the moves made in the 'knight's tour', a chess-based mathematical problem in which the knight must visit each square exactly once.

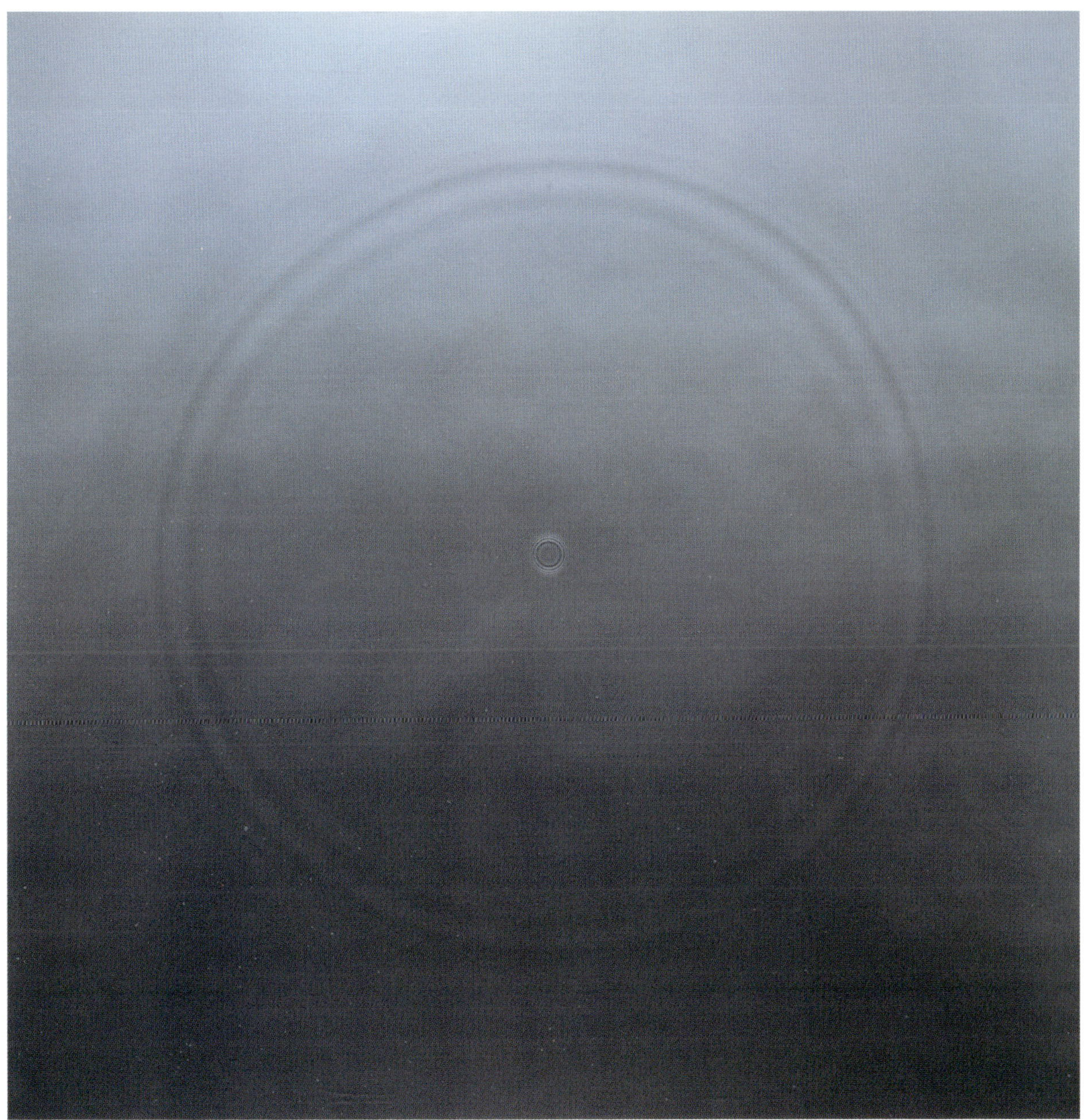

Adam Fuss (b.1961)

Ark
1990

Gelatin silver print
140 x 140 cm

This work was created by placing a sheet of photographic paper in a tray of water, letting a single drop fall into the still surface and firing a flash to record the event. The image has a fine range of grey tones delineating the undulating wave. The spreading circles signify the infinite possibilities of development.

Adam Fuss (b.1961)

Invocation
1992

Dye destruction print
101.6 x 76 cm

To make this piece, a mother briefly placed her child on photographic paper that had been submerged in a tray of shallow water. The resulting image – created by firing flashlight directly at the paper – captures not only the child's outline but also the ripples in the water caused by its movements. Fuss's image is a kind of baptism, but its title also means an earnest appeal or prayer to a supernatural being for psychological or spiritual inspiration.

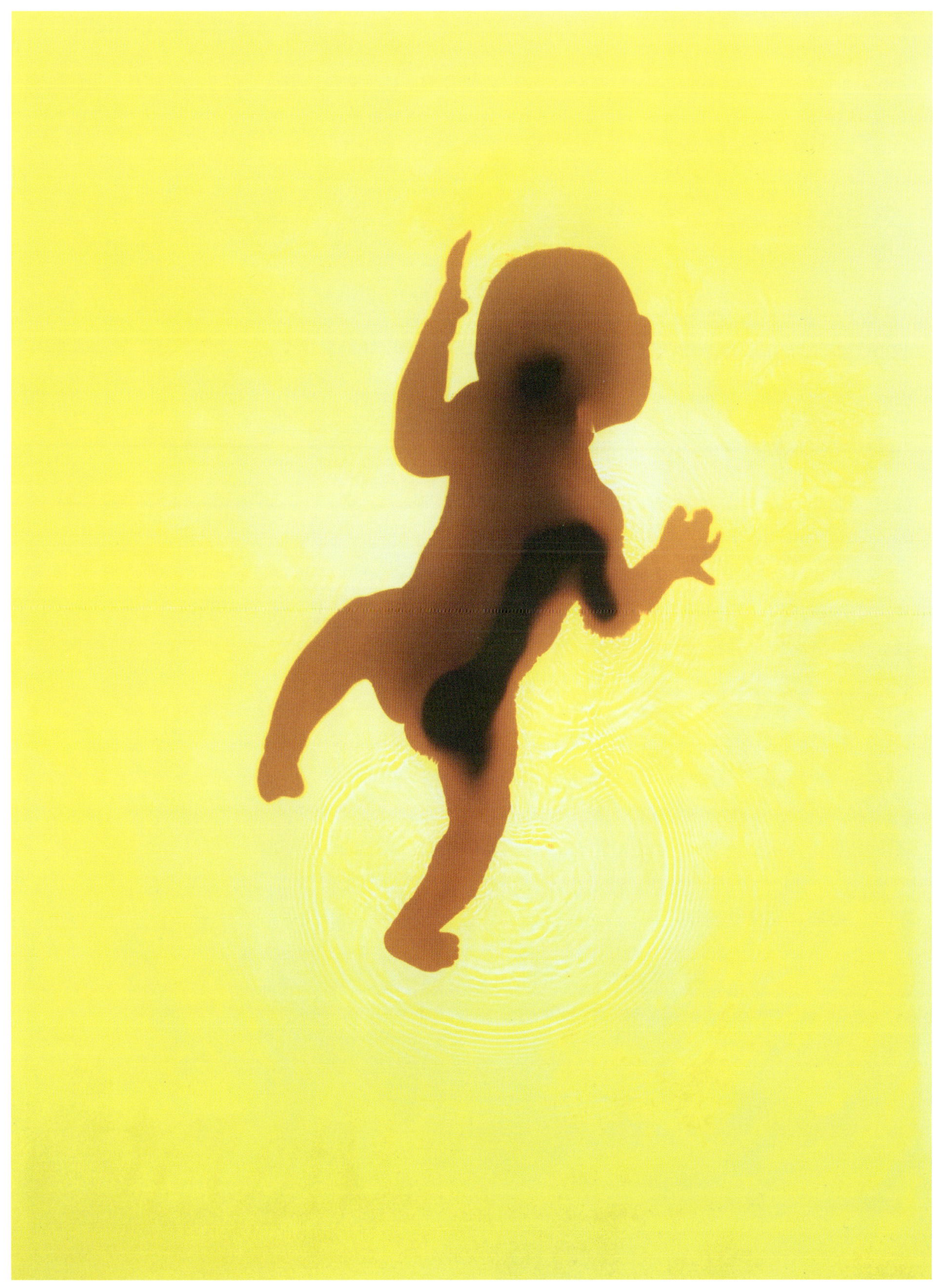

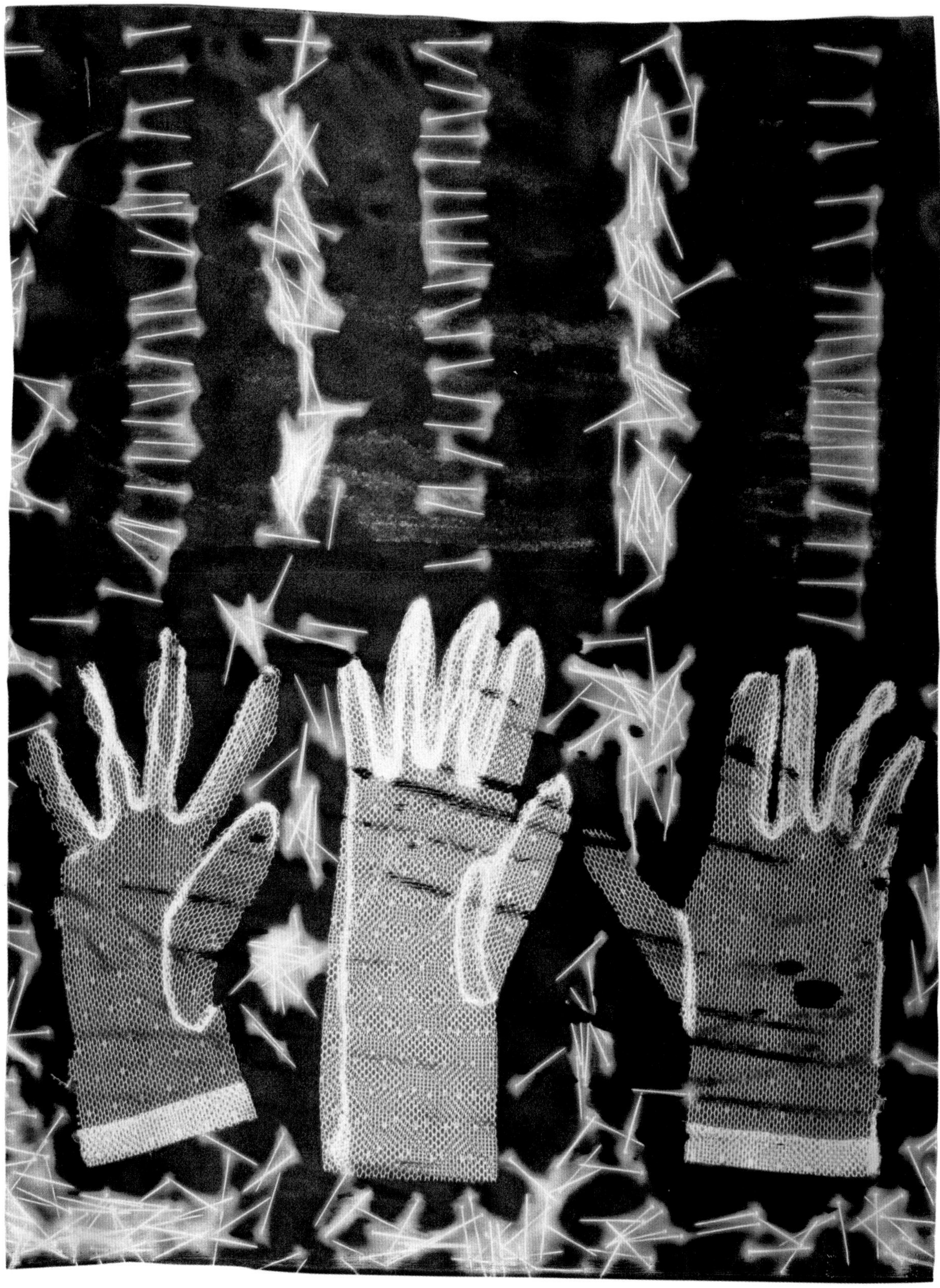

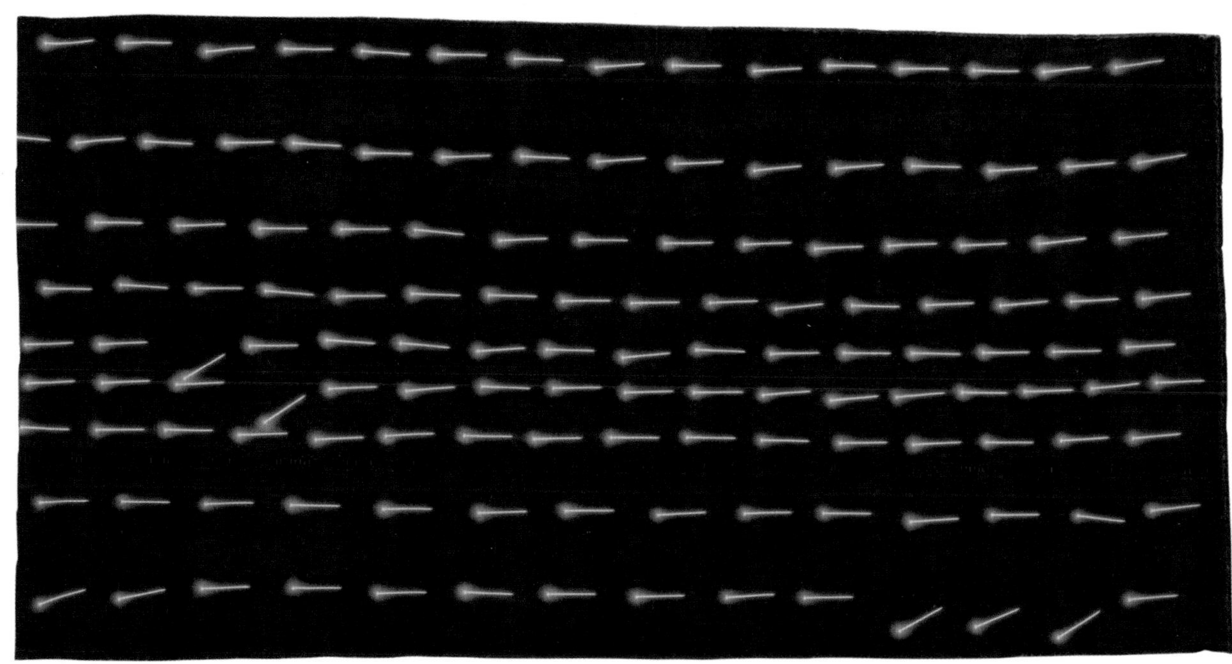

Rebecca Earley (b.1970)

Pins and Gloves
1995
Heat photogram printed polyoctose satin microfibre
44.5 x 58.8 cm

Pin Stripe
1995
Heat photogram printed polyoctose satin microfibre
36.8 x 73.5 cm

These are unique fabric samples made using a heat photogram process pioneered by Earley, a textile designer. The patterns were made by coating objects with heat-sensitive dyes and then heat-pressing them onto synthetic microfibre fabric. The metal pins act as conductors and create a glowing effect, as if charged with electricity.

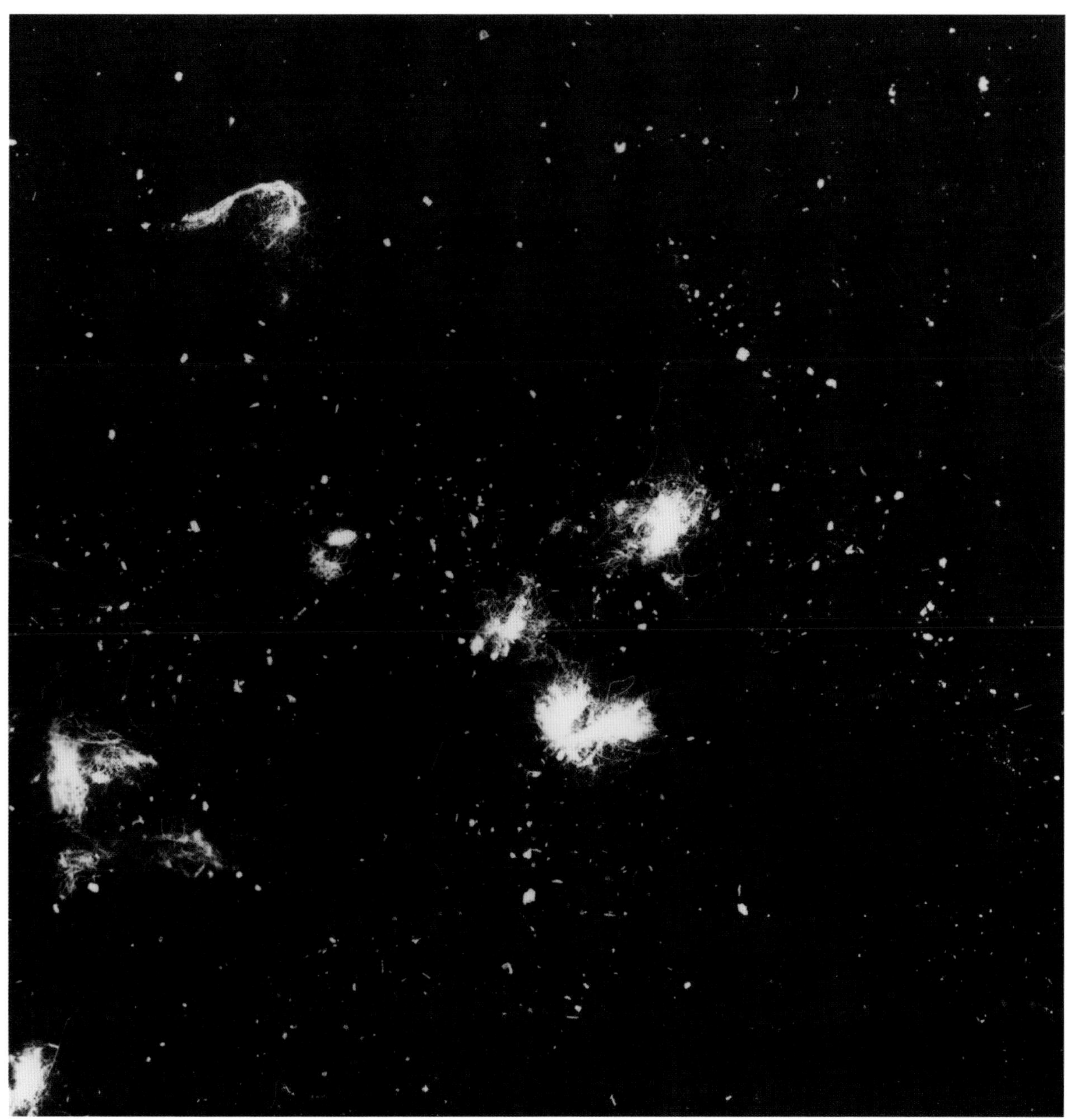

Cornelia Parker (b.1956)

Bated Breath: Fluff and Dust from the Whispering Gallery, St Paul's Cathedral, London
1997

Gelatin silver print
29 x 29 cm

Parker describes her making of this image: 'I was on my hands and knees in the hushed gallery, trying to cope with my fear of heights, when I focused on the felted layer of dust that had collected on the edges of the parapet. This dust formed an accumulated acoustic, built up over time by the thousands of whispering visitors. Later, trapped between the glass, the fluff and dust was used as a negative to produce a photogram.'

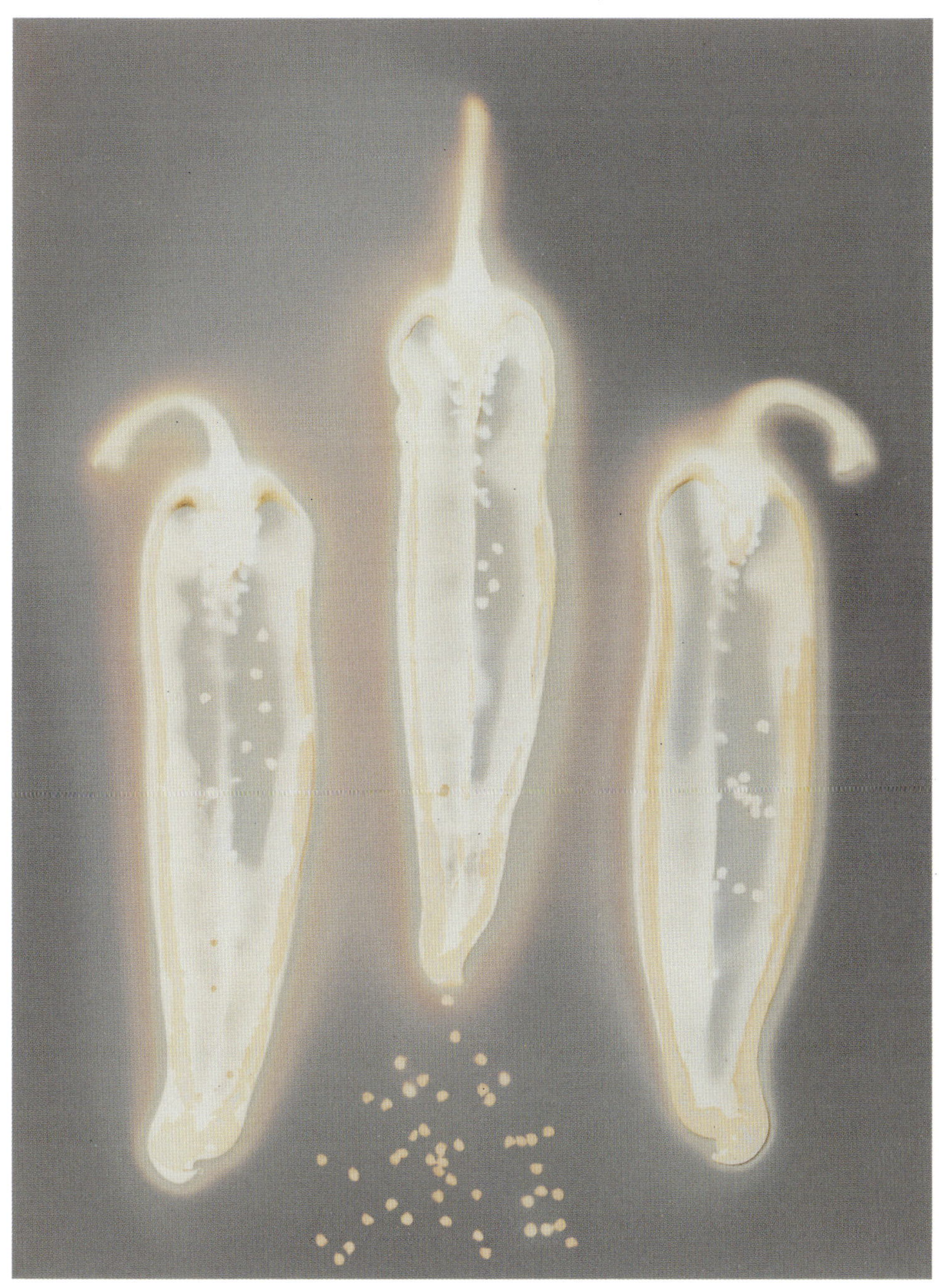

Angela Easterling (b.1944)

Ramiro Peppers
2000

Gelatin silver print
40.5 x 30.5 cm

Easterling's photograms are dependent upon variables in exposure time, light source, humidity and the combination of the organic materials employed when reacting in direct contact with sensitized paper. The plant materials generate their own particular colours when combined with photographic chemicals on standard black and white paper. Here the peppers created a yellow and purple glow.

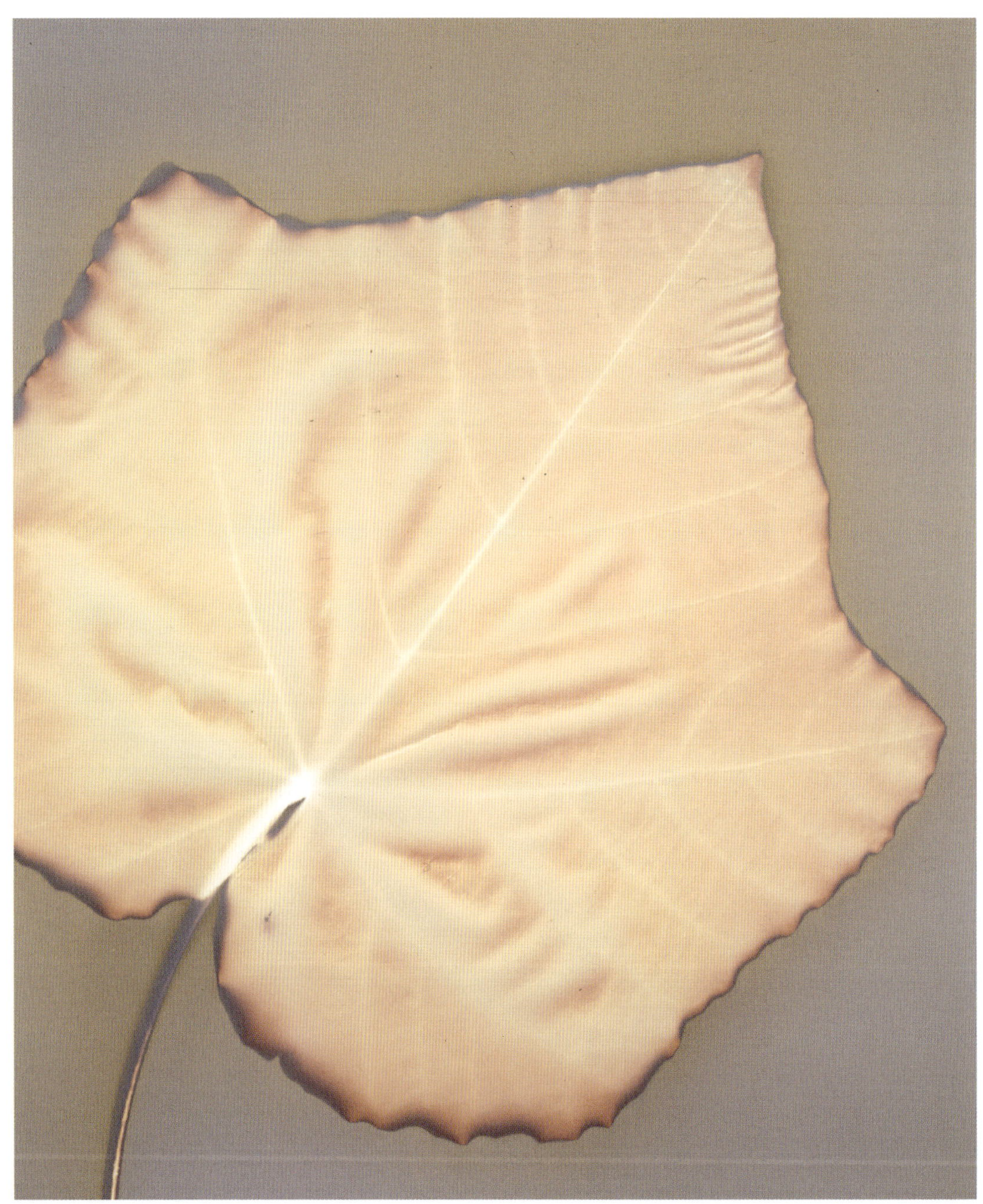

Angela Easterling (b.1944)

Ochroma lagopus (Balsa)
2001

Gelatin silver print
47.5 x 40 cm

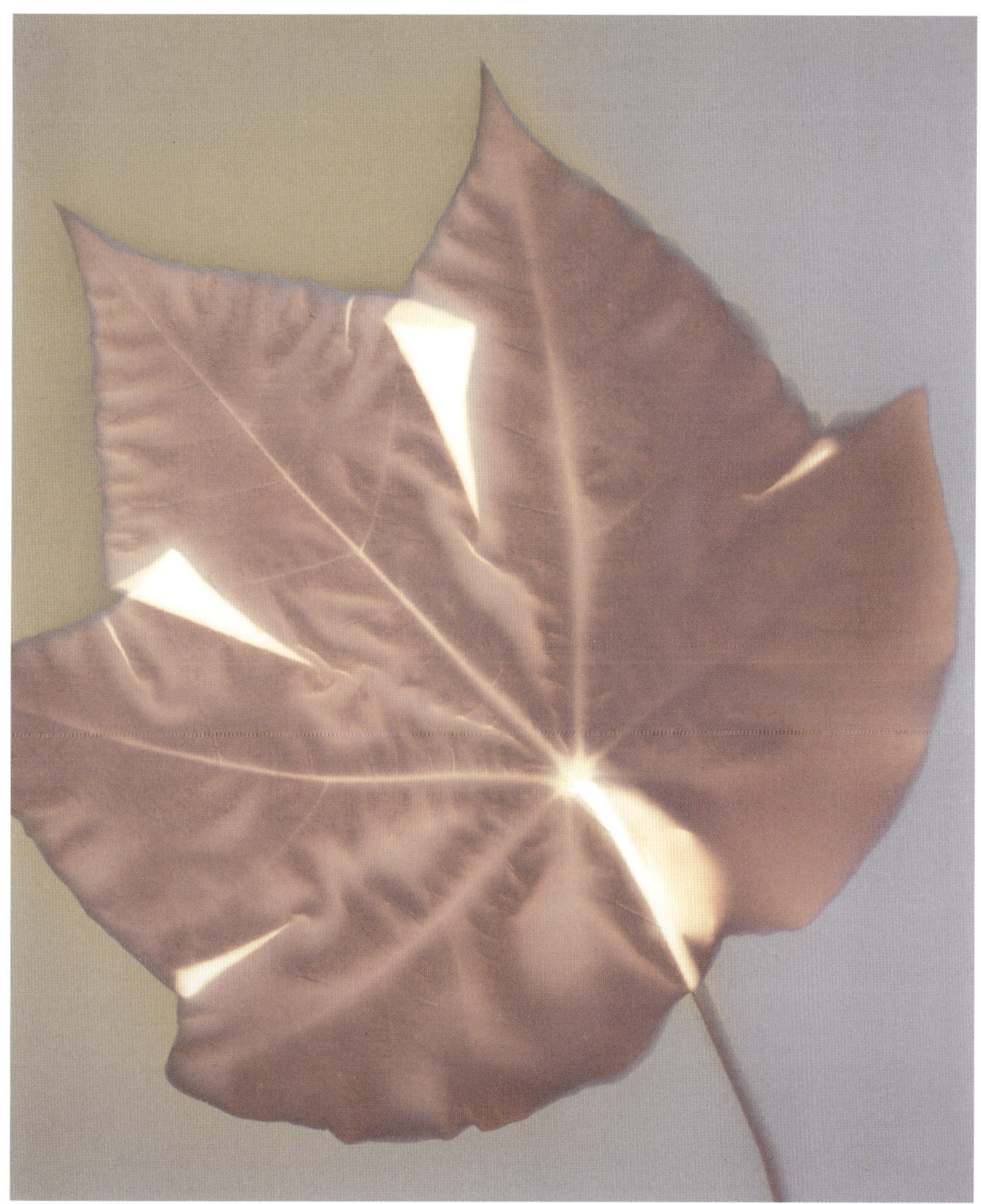

Angela Easterling (b.1944)

Sterculia quinqueloba (Large-leaved Star Chestnut)
2001

Gelatin silver print
47.5 x 40 cm

Easterling demonstrates here the difference in density between leaves high up on a tree, through which light must pass, like the chestnut leaf, and those nearer the ground, like the thinner and thus more translucent balsa leaf, which need to absorb as much of the available light as possible.

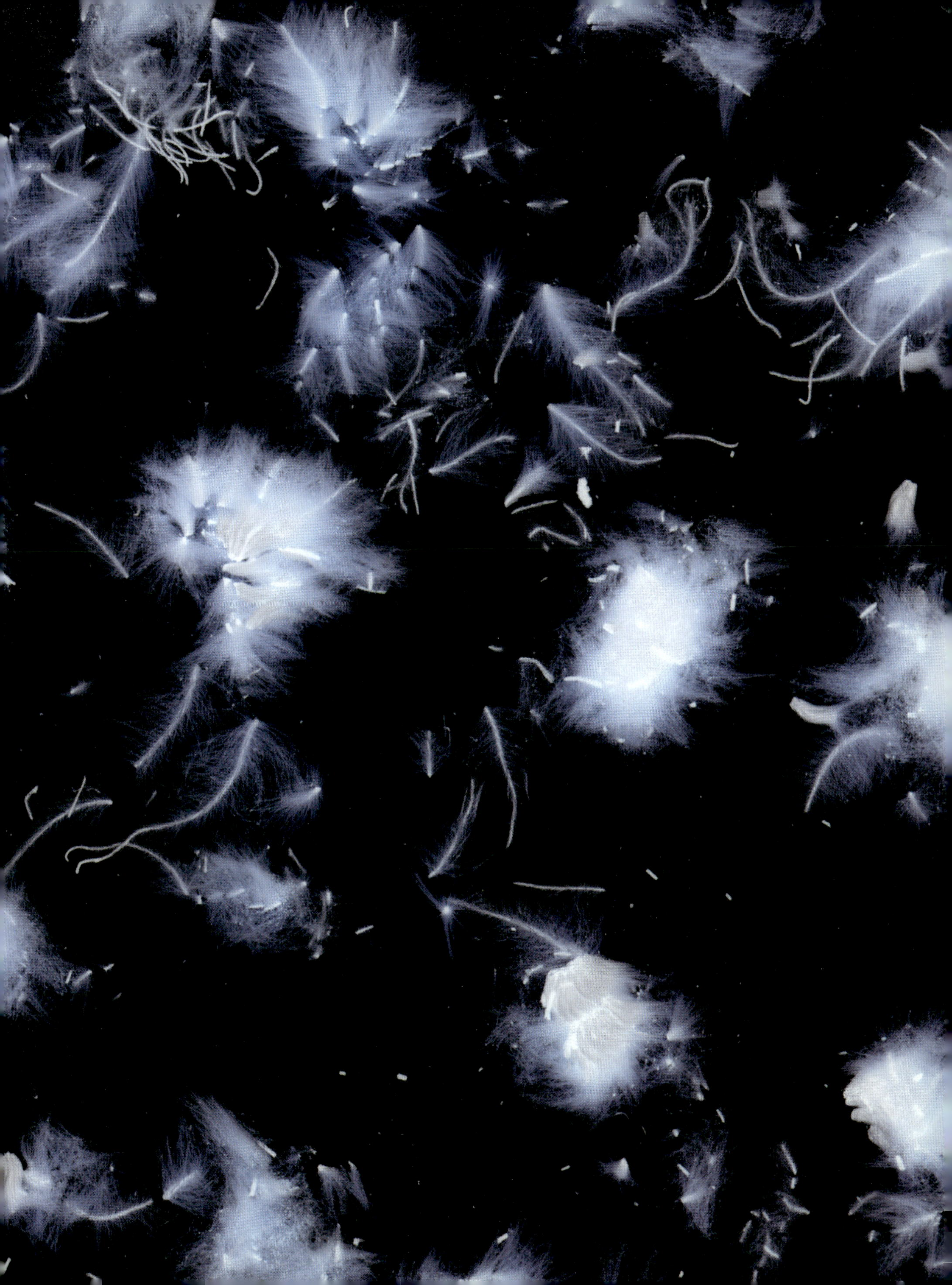

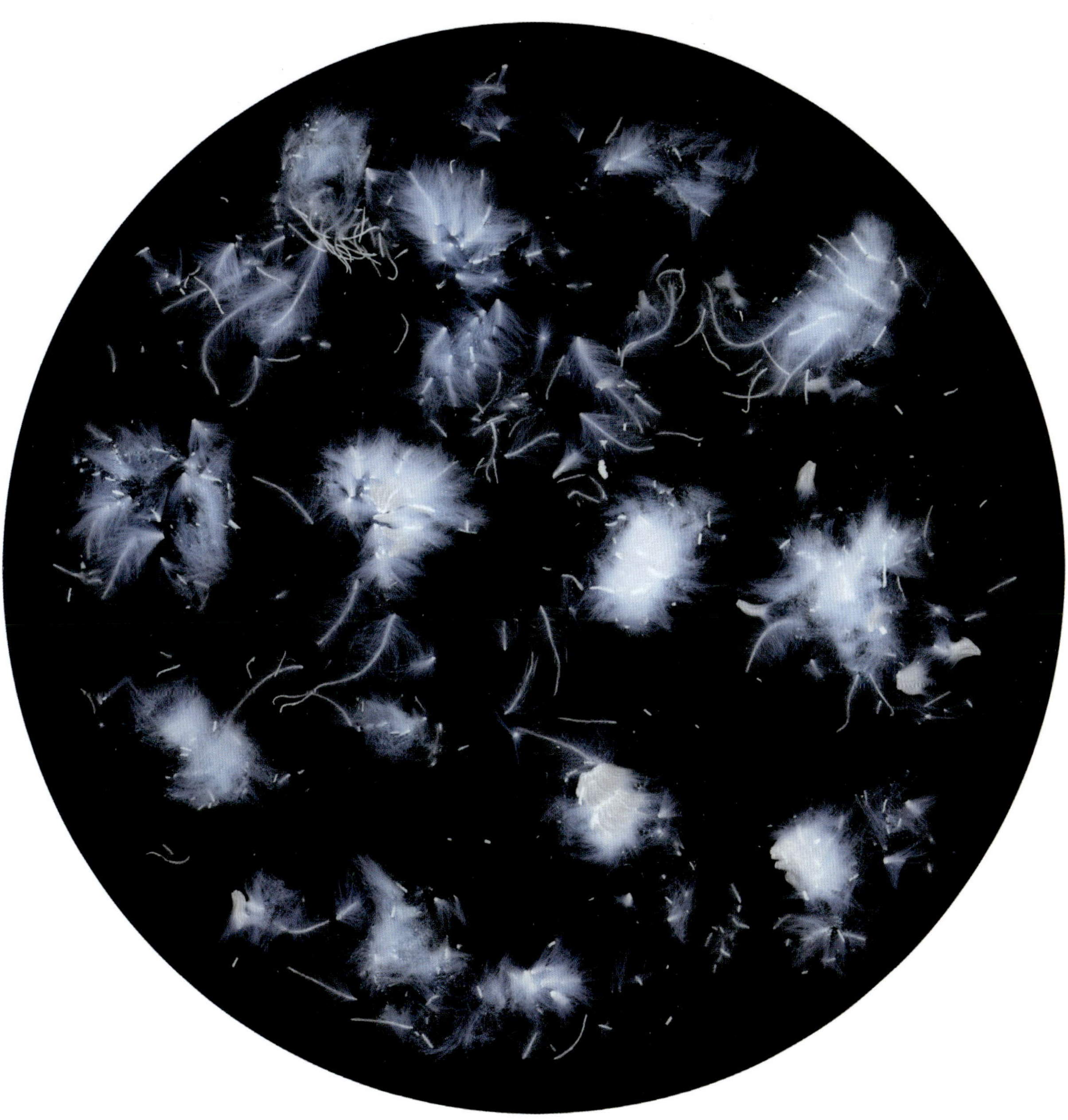

Barbara and Zafer Baran (b.1956 and 1955)

Ephemera #98
2002

Pigment print
105 x 87.5 cm (framed)

(detail p.135)

As its title suggests, the *Ephemera* series is concerned with issues of transience and permanence. The works consciously refer back to the nineteenth-century botanical photograms of William Henry Fox Talbot and Anna Atkins, retaining the spirit of their enquiry but updating the photogram techniques with digital technology.

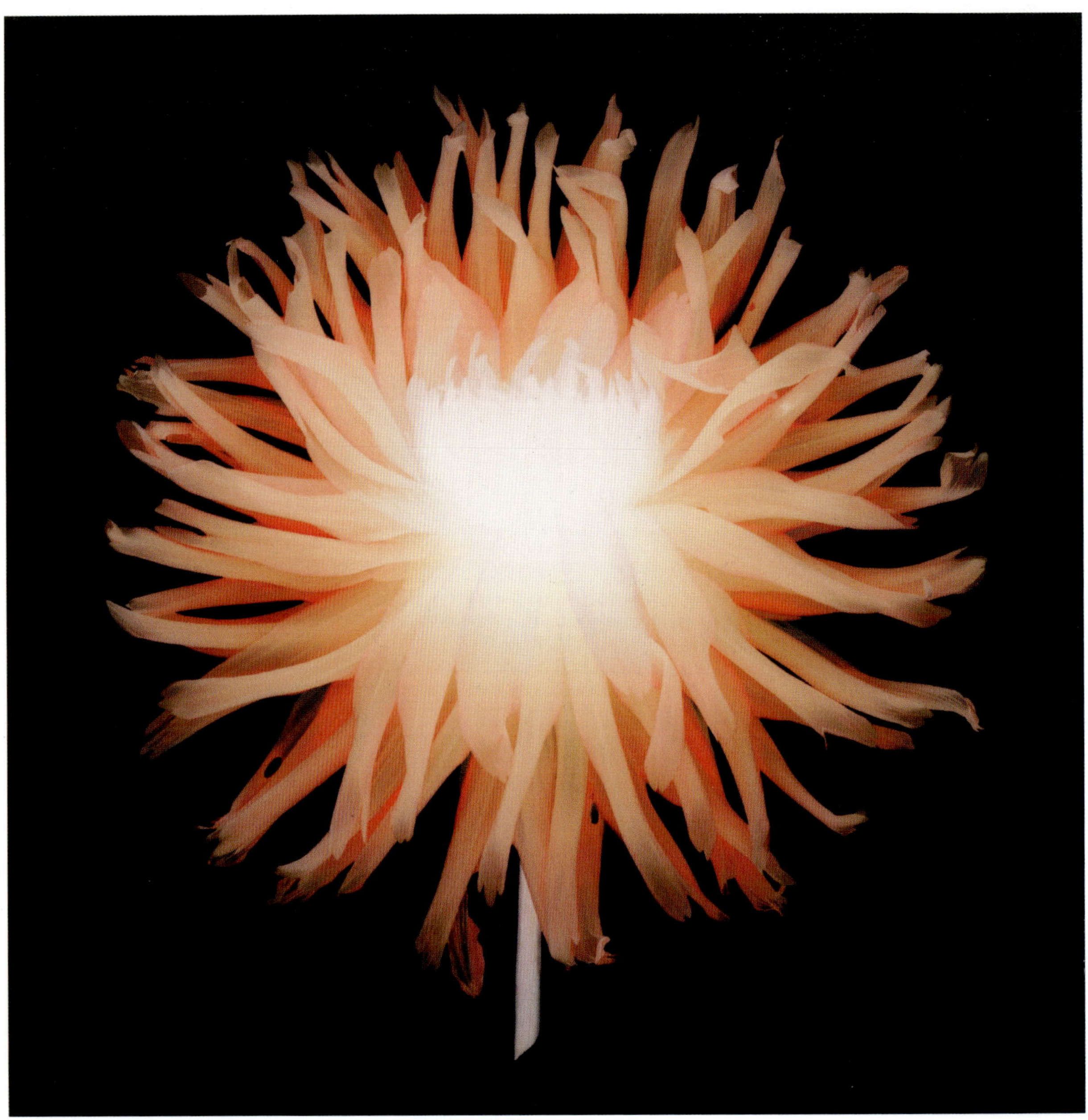

Barbara and Zafer Baran (b.1956 and 1955)

Dahlia #120
from the series *The Flower Cabinet*
2003

Pigment print
31.9 x 31.9 cm

This luminous image was made by placing a flower directly onto a scanner; light passing through the translucent petals revealed its hidden parts. It is part of a series commissioned by Royal Mail and was used as the basis for a set of postage stamps celebrating the Royal Horticultural Society bicentenary in 2004.

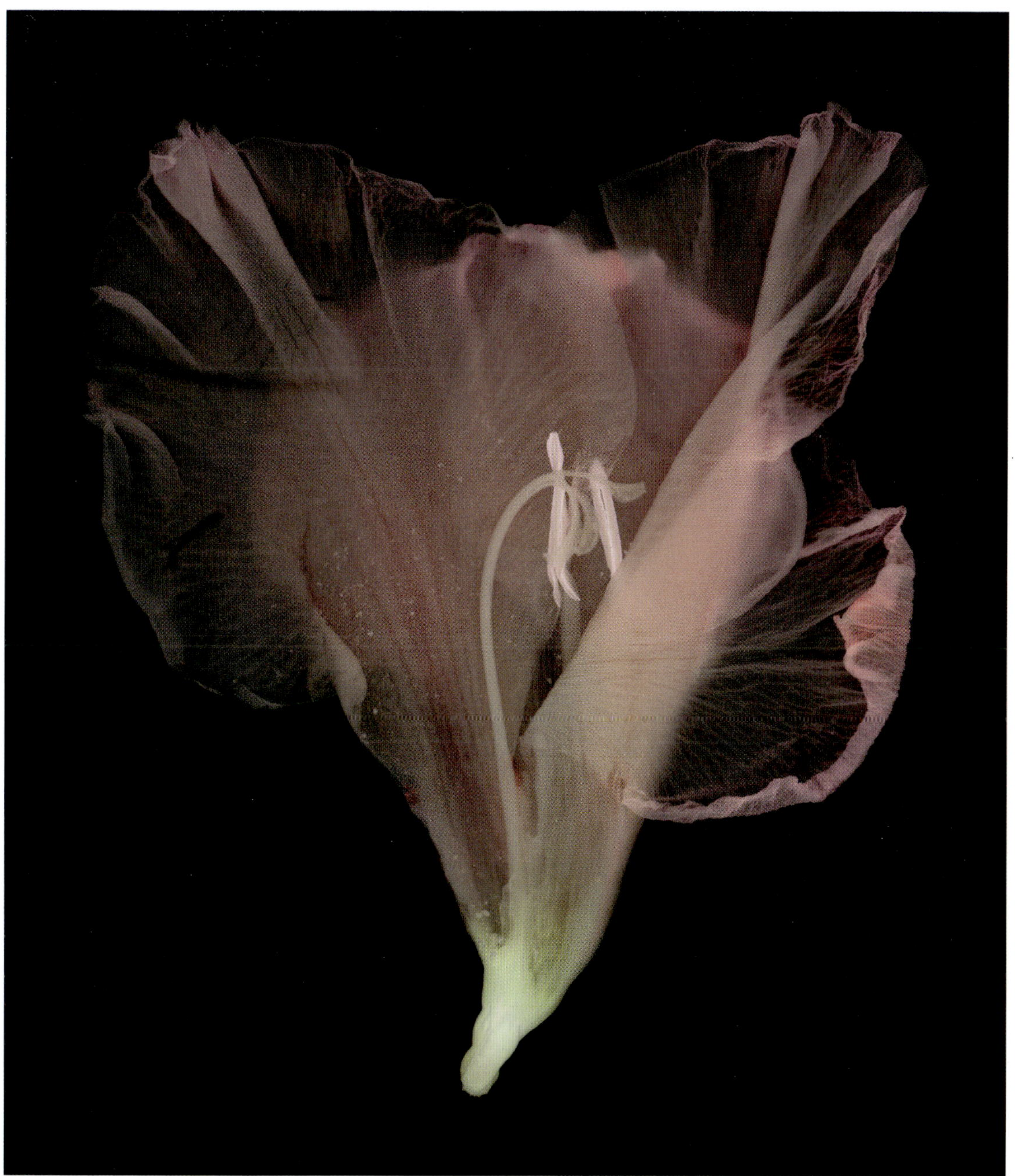

Barbara and Zafer Baran (b.1956 and 1955)

Ephemera #179
2002

Pigment print
99 x 87.5 cm (framed)

Despite the possibility for digital manipulation with scannergrams, Barbara and Zafer Baran rarely alter the images aside from basic cropping. The colours and compositions are formed directly on the scanner plate.

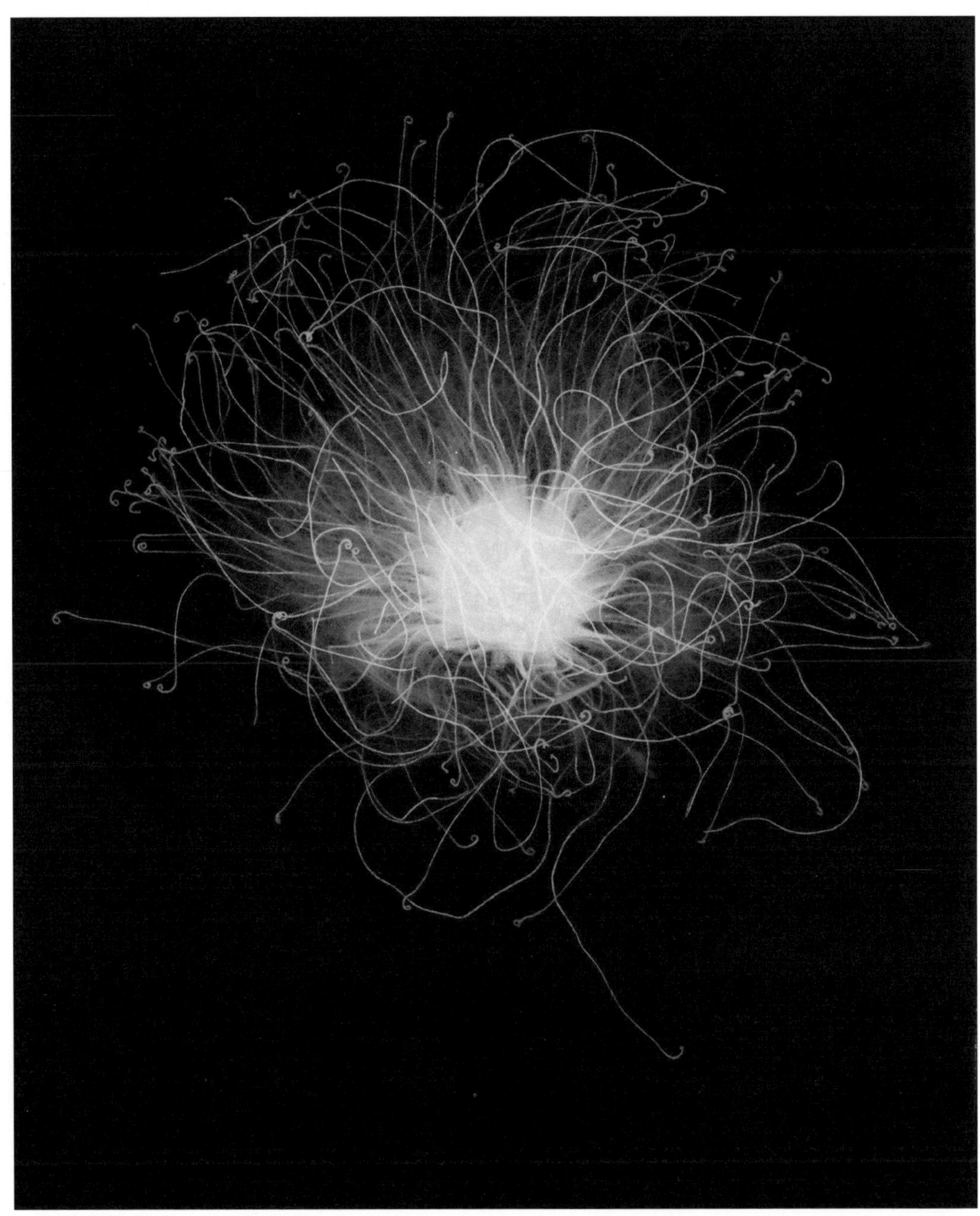

Barbara and Zafer Baran (b.1956 and 1955)

Ephemera #113
2002

Pigment print
105 x 87.5 cm (framed)

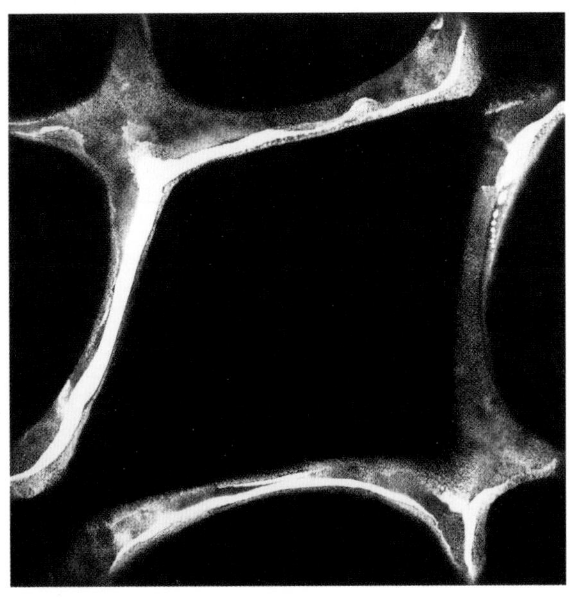
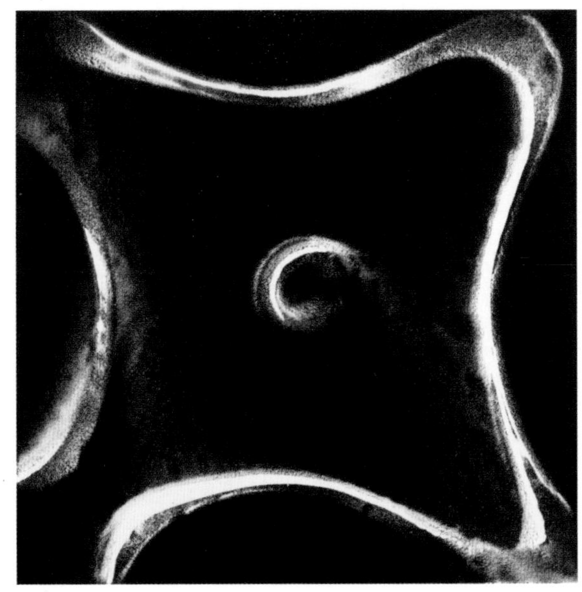
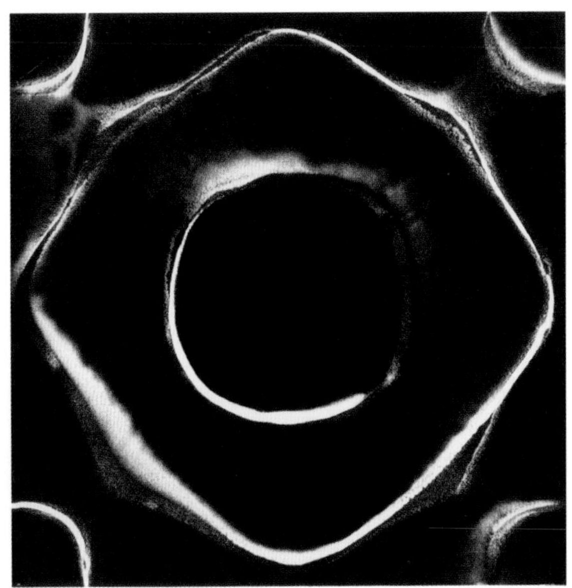
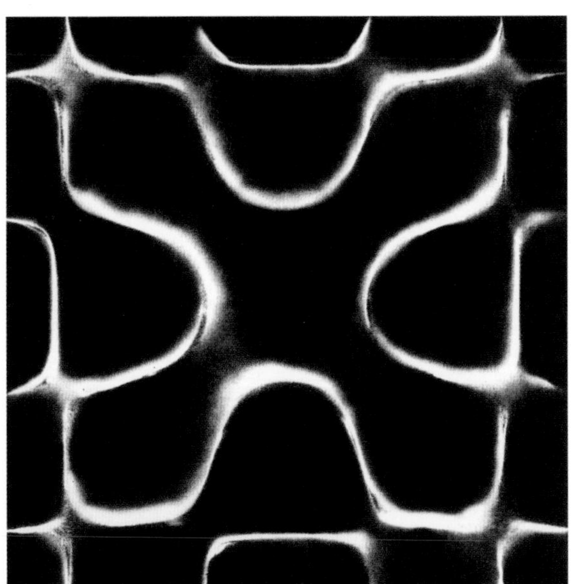

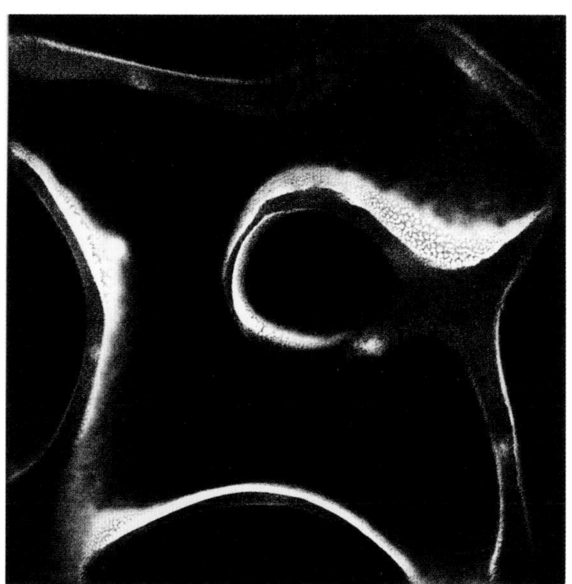
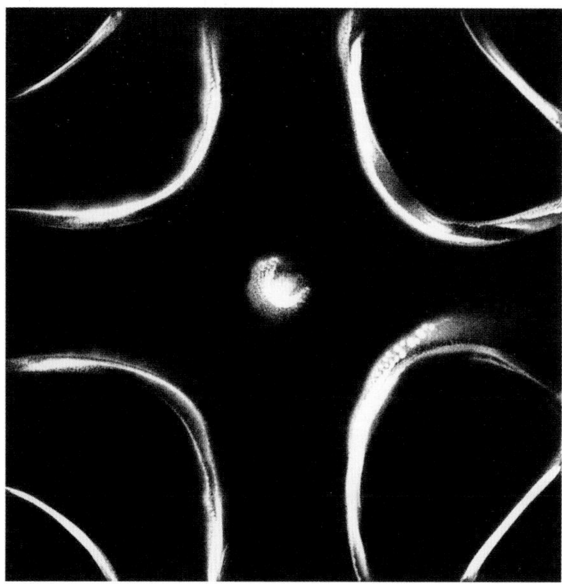
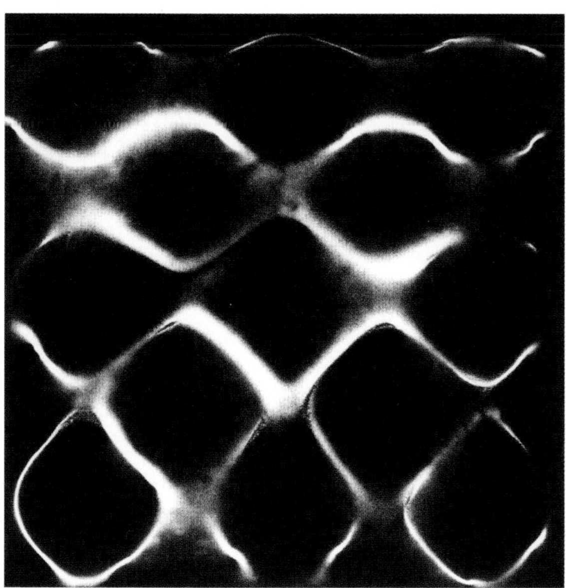
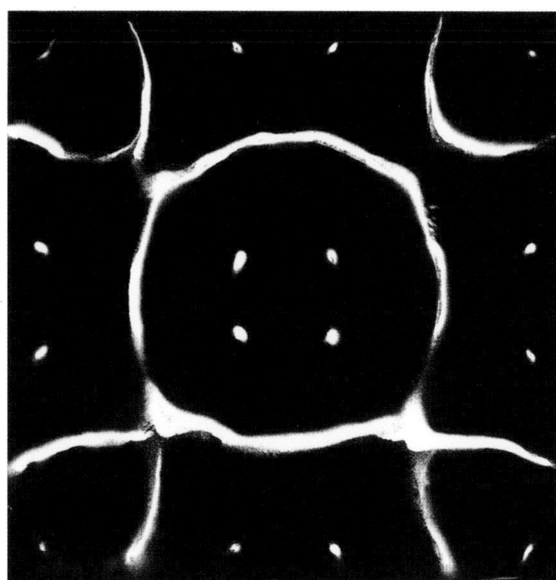

Susan Derges (b.1955)

Chladni
1983

Gelatin silver prints
45 x 45 cm each

Ernst Chladni was an eighteenth-century physicist who researched the visualization of sound waves. He discovered that fine sand on a square metal plate formed geometrical patterns when a violin bow was vibrated across the edge of the plate. Derges made these images in a similar fashion, but with carborundum powder on photographic paper to produce photograms.

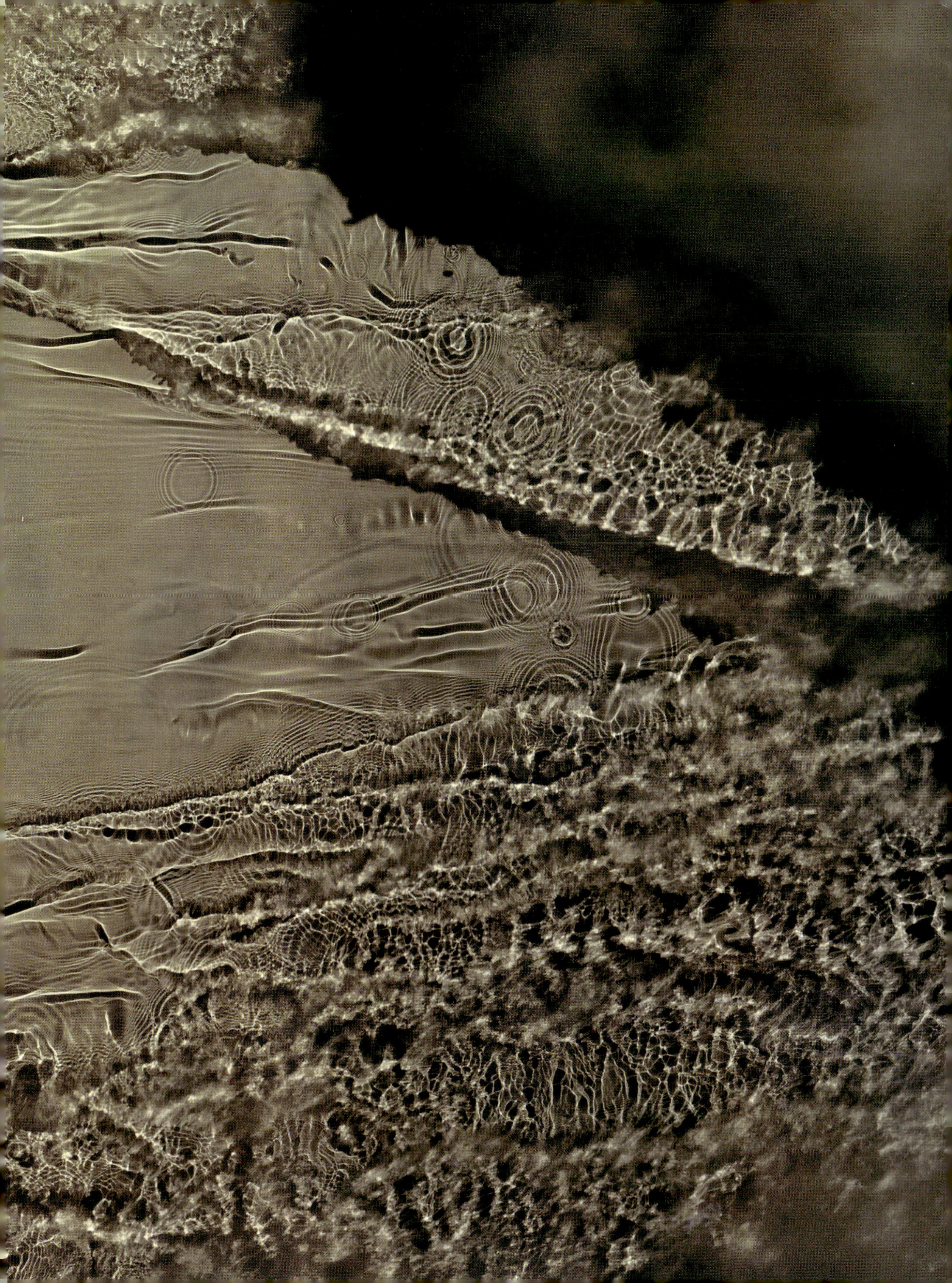

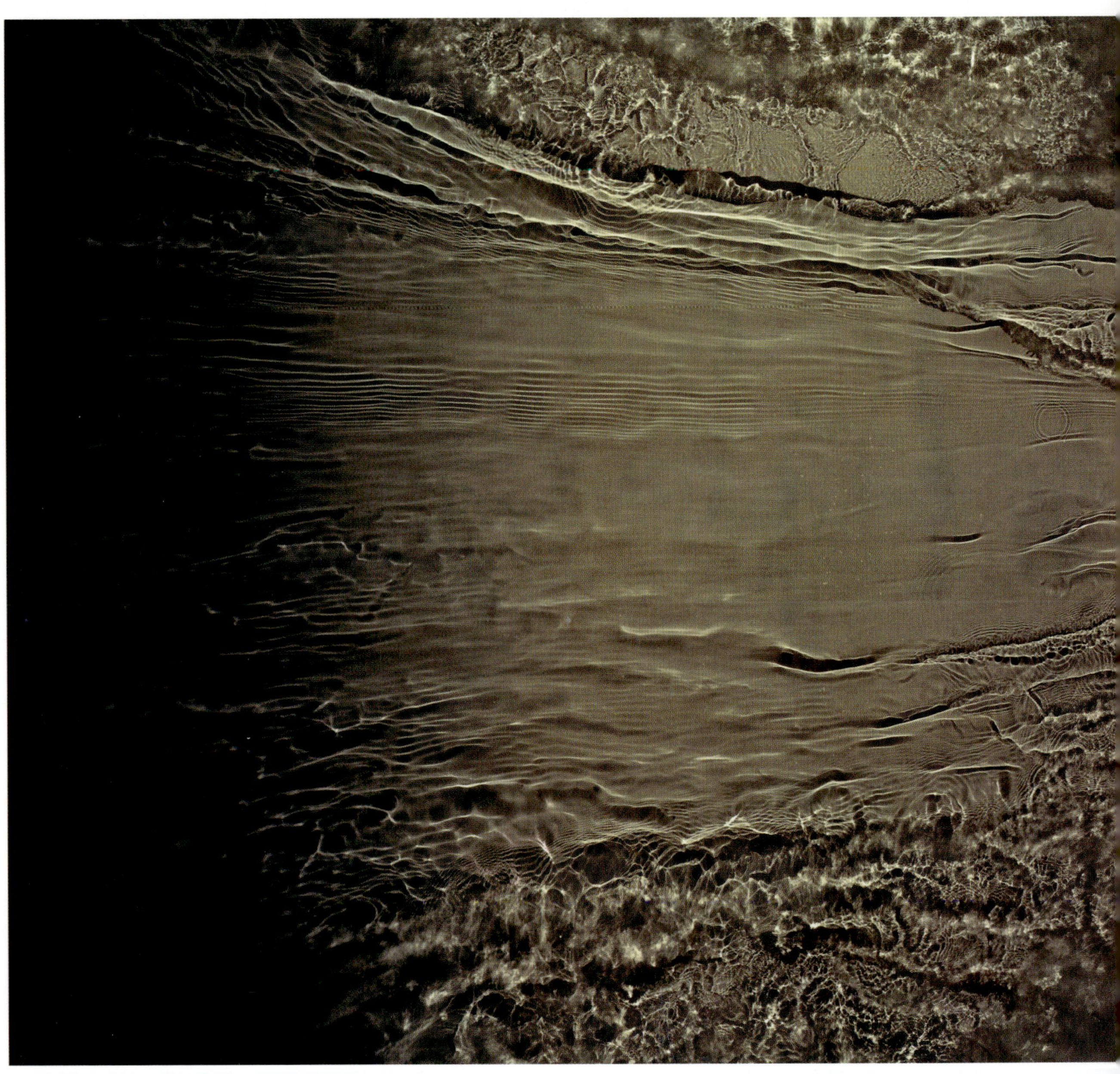

Susan Derges (b.1955)

Eden 5
2004

Dye destruction print
101.5 x 243.8 cm

(detail p.145)

Working outdoors at night, Derges submerged photographic paper below the surface of a river. The paper was then exposed to a microsecond of flashlight. The process embraces chance, for although her knowledge of the river's movement gave her an indication of images she would produce, the final result could be seen only after processing.

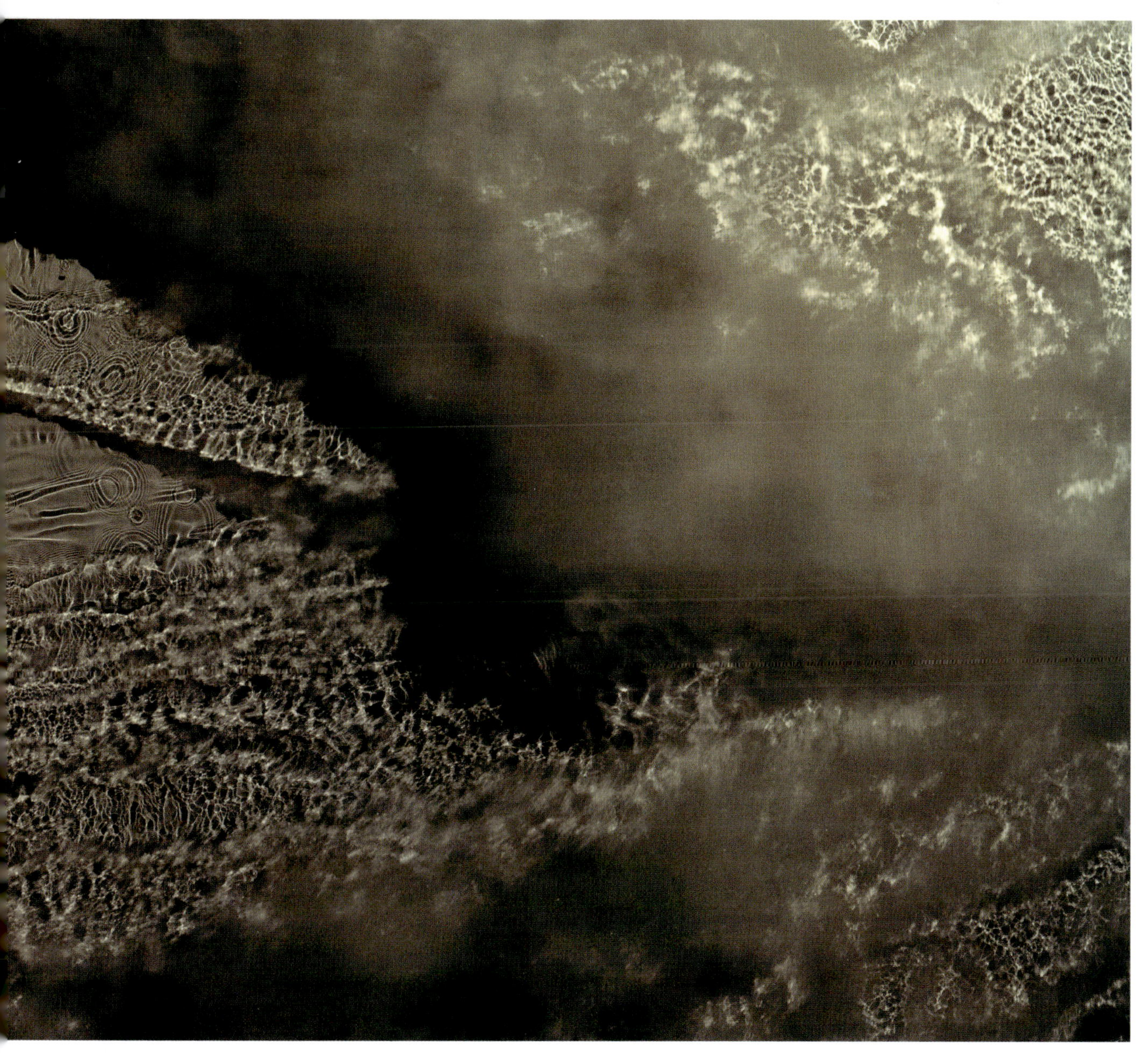

Eden 5 is part of a series made for a residency at the Eden Project gardens in Cornwall. They show the many different wave forms that Derges has carefully examined over the years. Like other artists and philosophers, she is exploring the idea that natural patterns are the signs of deeply hidden affinities – visible signs that point to the invisible.

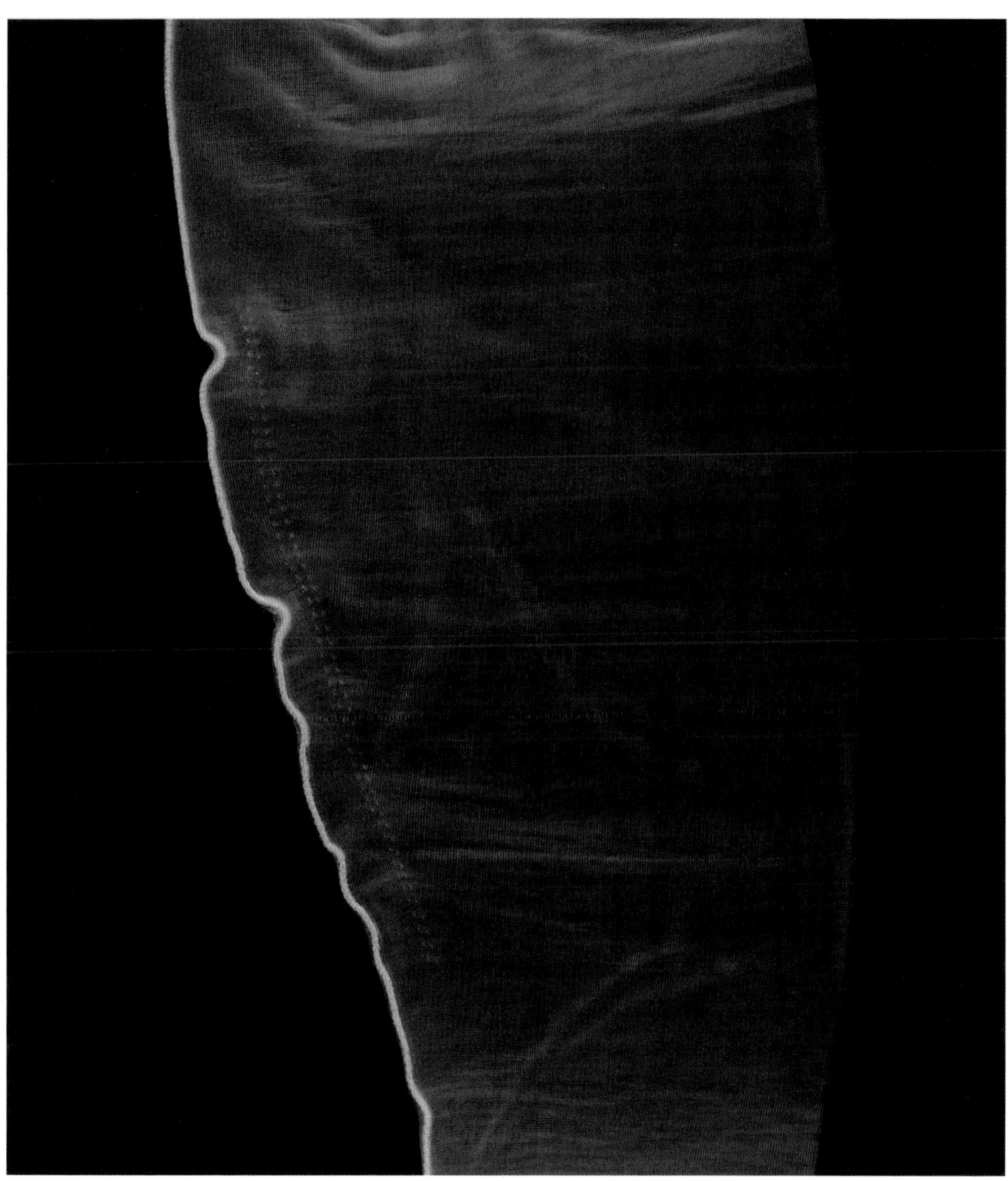

Elaine Duigenan (b.1964)

Dior
2005

Digital pigment print
41.9 x 29.8 cm

Duigenan is interested in what she calls 'intimate archaeology', using the scannergram technique to reassess familiar things. Here, she focuses on the synthetic material of nylon stockings, first marketed in New York in 1940. By cropping the object, she creates a semi-abstract image, accentuating the material's form, texture and transparency.

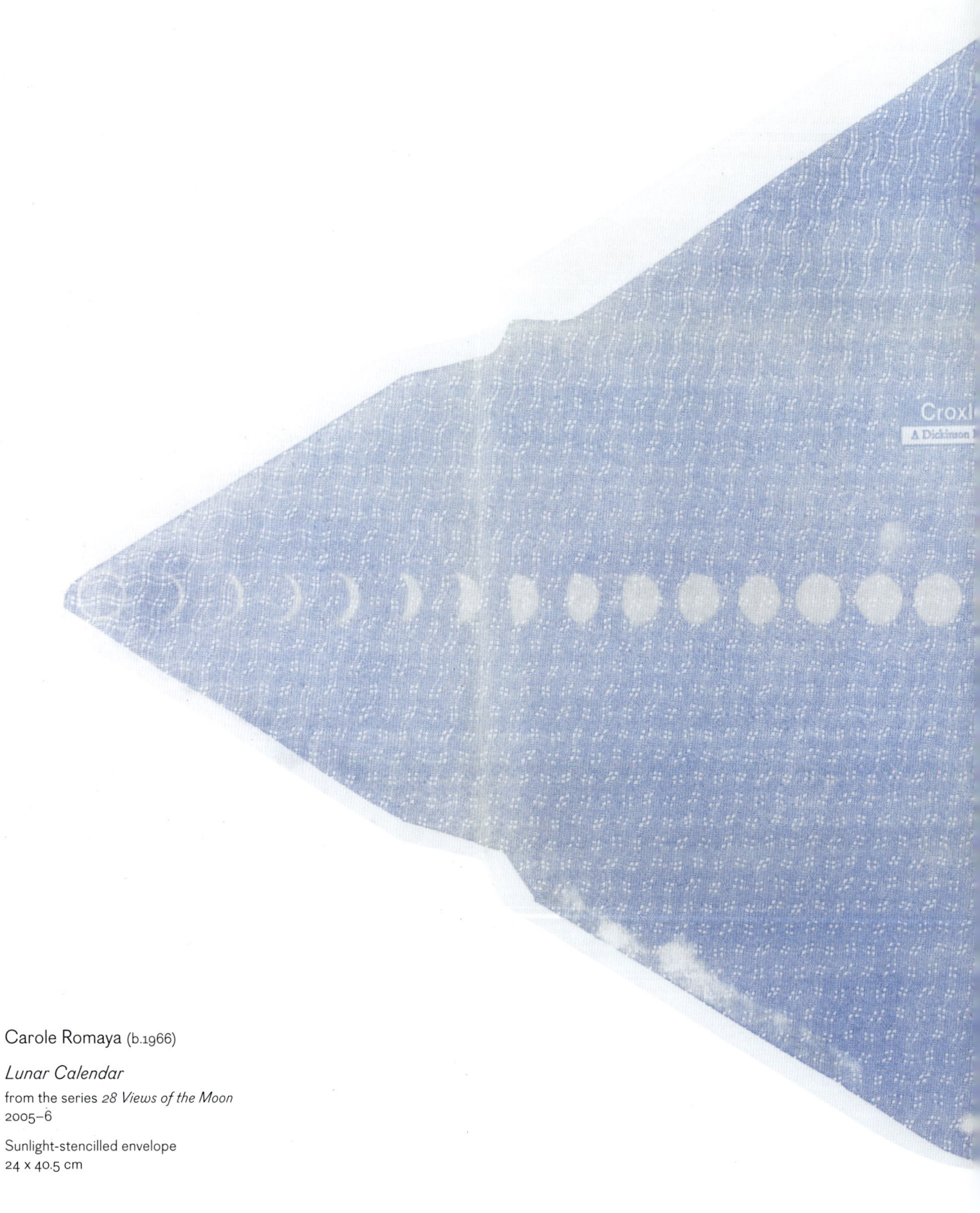

Carole Romaya (b.1966)

Lunar Calendar

from the series *28 Views of the Moon*
2005–6

Sunlight-stencilled envelope
24 x 40.5 cm

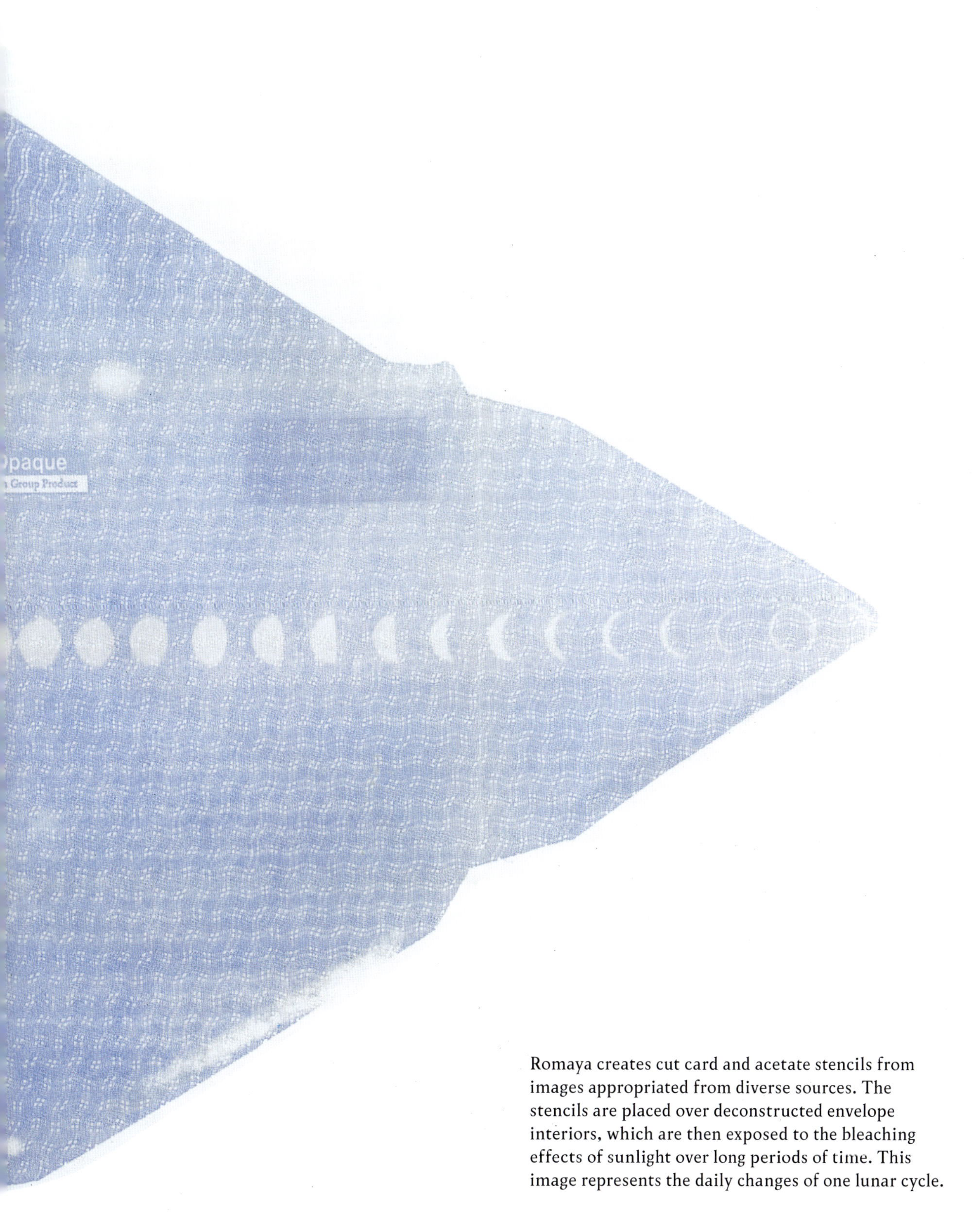

Romaya creates cut card and acetate stencils from images appropriated from diverse sources. The stencils are placed over deconstructed envelope interiors, which are then exposed to the bleaching effects of sunlight over long periods of time. This image represents the daily changes of one lunar cycle.

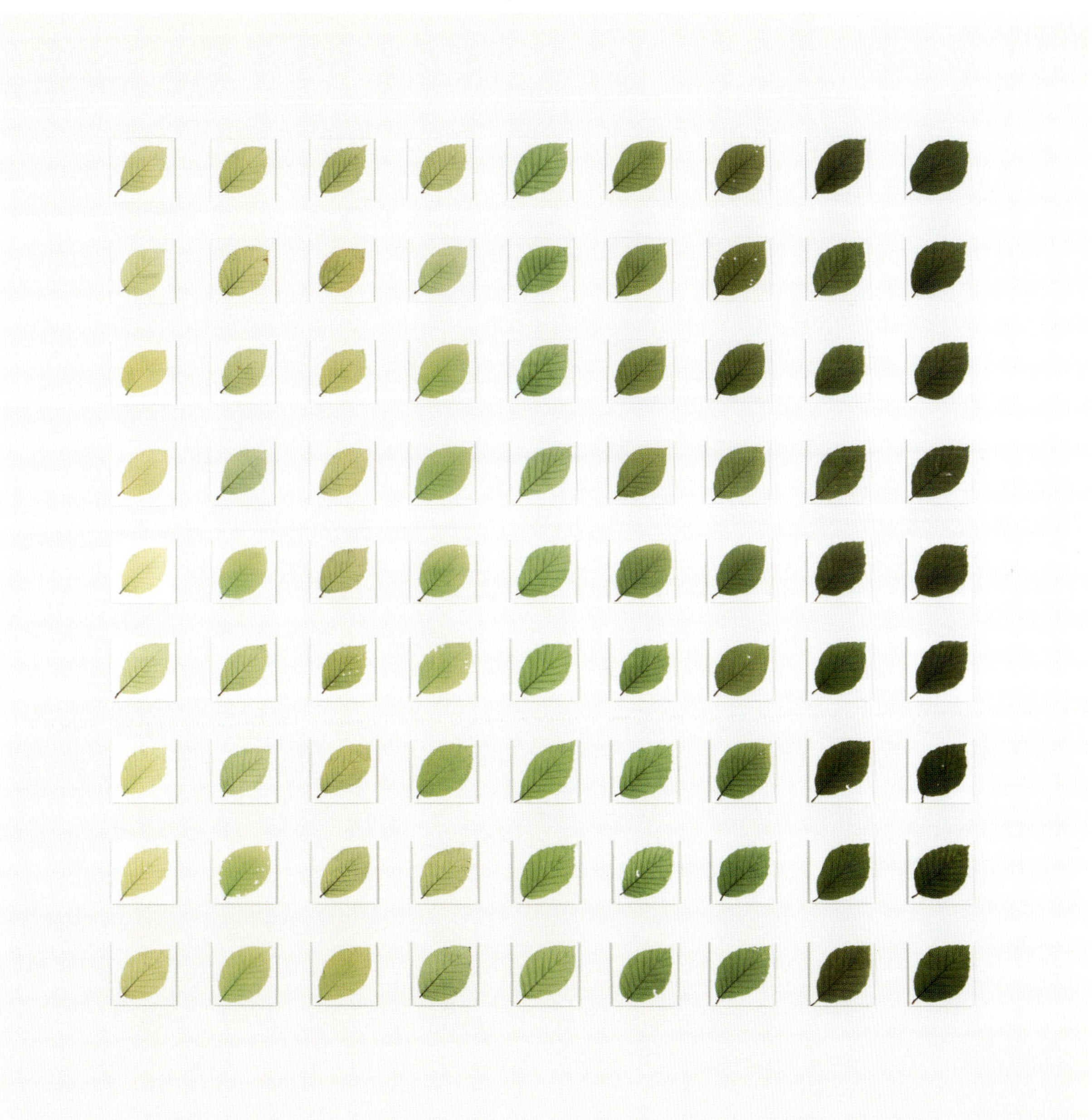

Garry Fabian Miller (b.1957)

Breathing in the Beech Wood, Homeland, Dartmoor, Twenty-Four Days of Sunlight, May 2004
2004

Dye destruction prints
162 x 162 cm

To make this image, Miller gathered leaves over twenty-four days in spring. He placed them into a photographic enlarger, using the leaves instead of a negative or transparency to project their image onto photographic paper. Each vertical row represents one day of collecting and printing. The arrangement shows the gradual effect of chlorophyll entering the leaf to make it green. It offers a comparison between this process and photography, both of which rely on the transforming power of light.

I live on the Green Hill
and when visiting
the City, the V+A
offers respite and
light.
– a thinking light
– light of colour
and beauty
Illumination,
a sense of home

Garry Fabian Miller

Dartmoor
Spring 2007

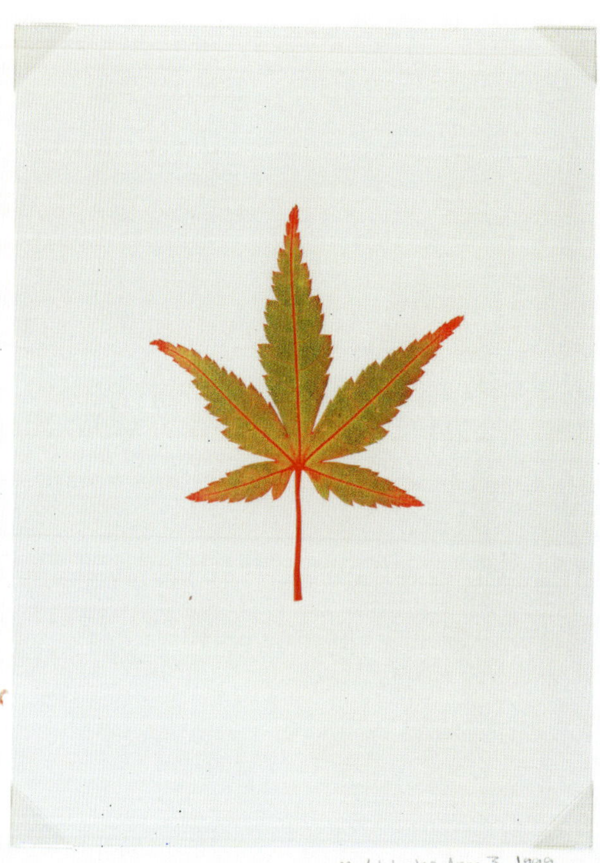

Garry Fabian Miller (b.1957)

Dartmoor, Spring 2007
2007

Dye destruction print and handwritten text
29.7 x 42 cm

Contribution to the Victoria and Albert Museum's 150th Anniversary Album

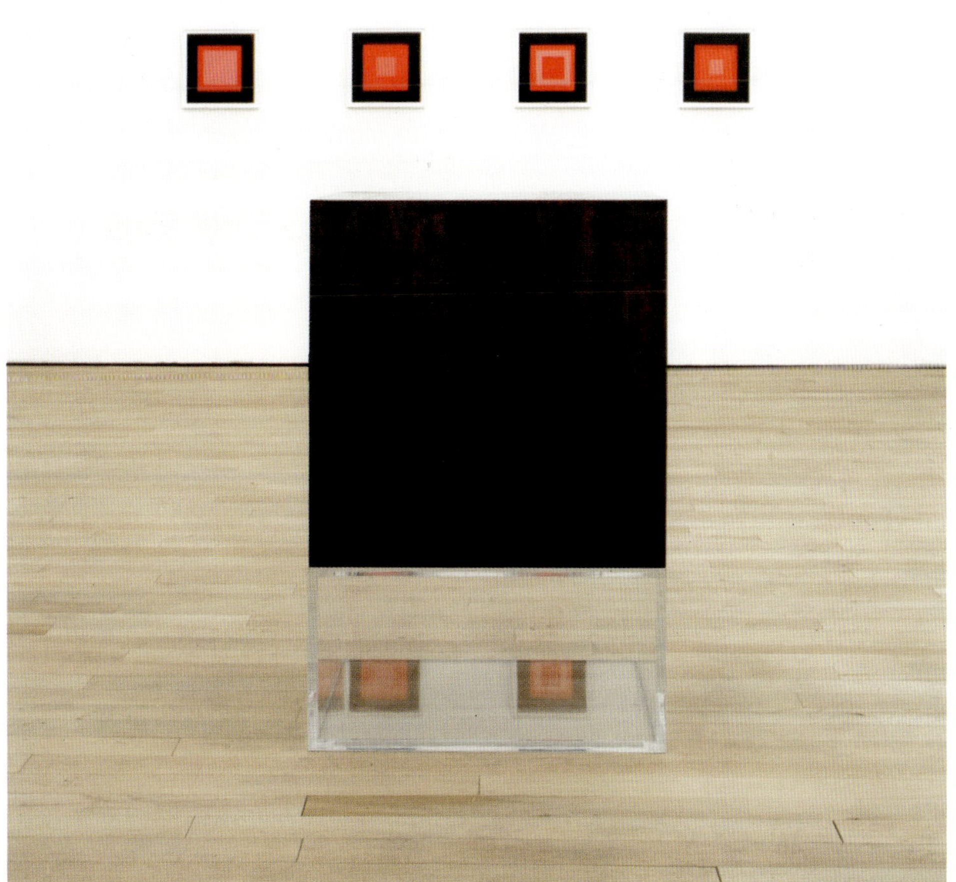

Garry Fabian Miller (b.1957)

Year One
2005–6

Dye destruction prints in wooden cabinet
108 x 72 x 71 cm (cabinet)

Since 1992, Miller has made abstracted images in the darkroom using light shining through glass vessels and over shapes fashioned from card. For *Year One*, he made one work every day over the course of a year. These were distilled into a set of twelve, one for each month. Titles were given according to the Celtic 'Coligny' calendar. Presented in the drawers of a display cabinet, the result is a sustained investigation into form and colour alongside the cycle of the year.

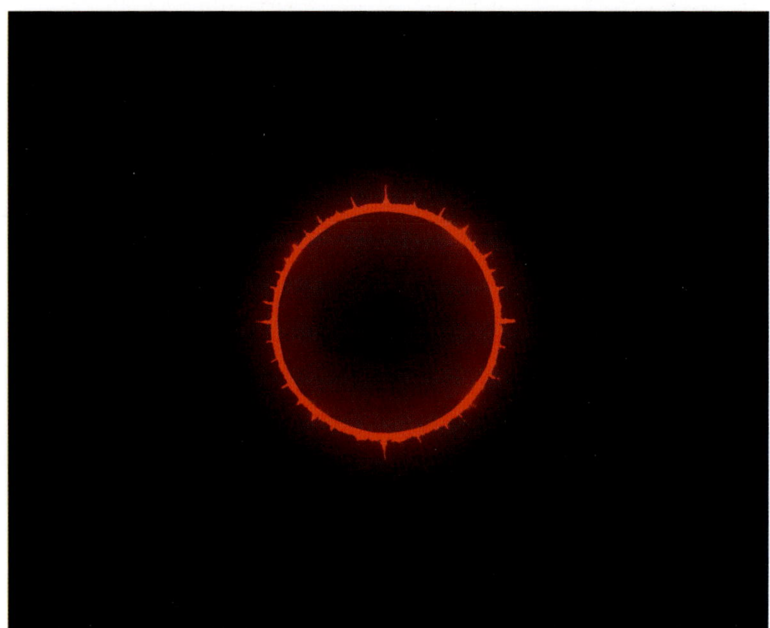

Year One: Samonios
30.5 x 40.5 cm

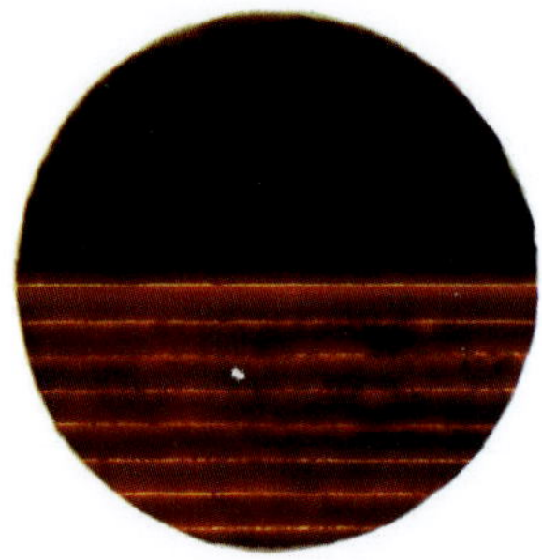

Year One: Dumannios
30.5 x 40.5 cm

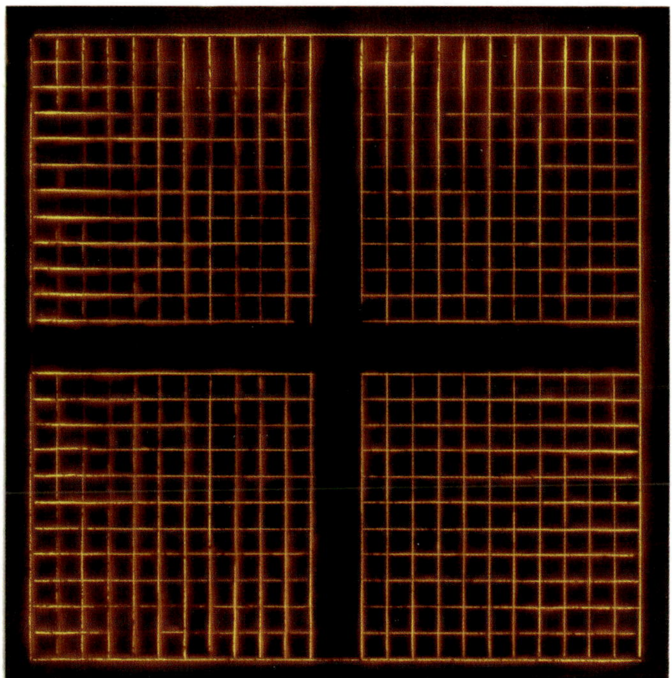

Year One: Riuros
40.5 x 40.5 cm

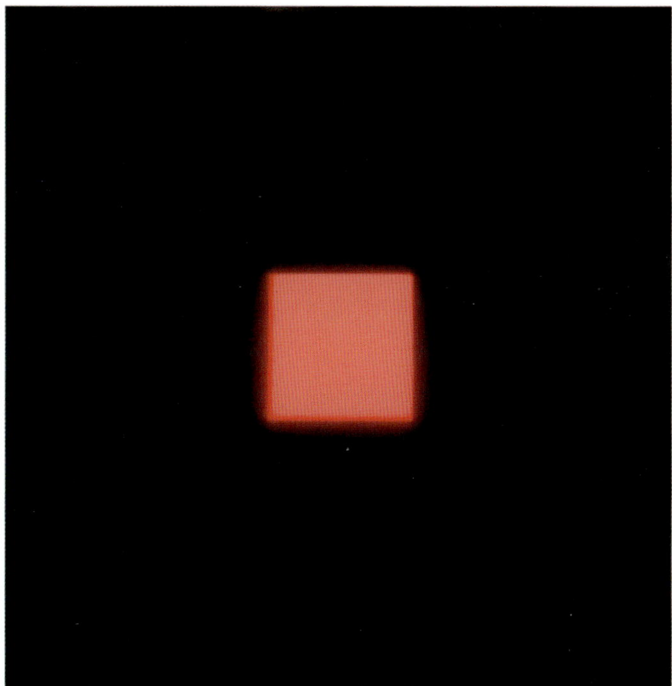

Year One: Anagantios
40.5 x 40.5 cm

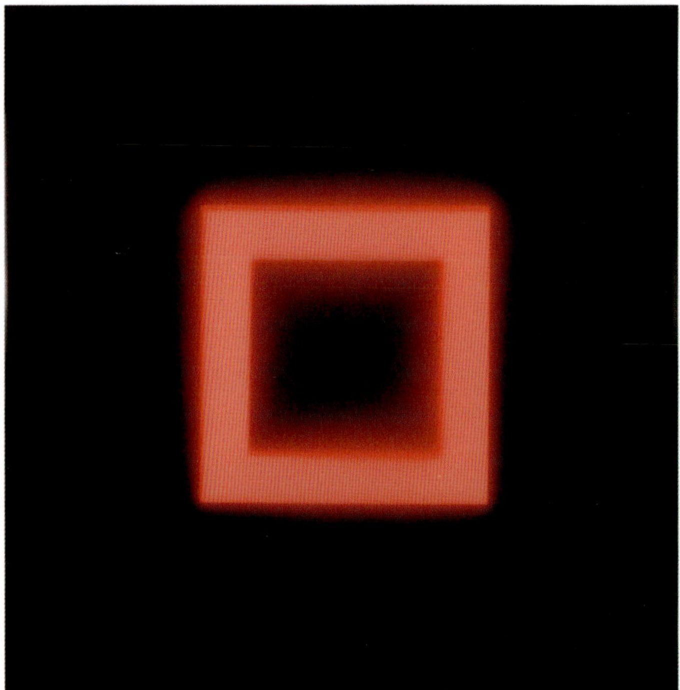

Year One: Ogronios
40.5 x 40.5 cm

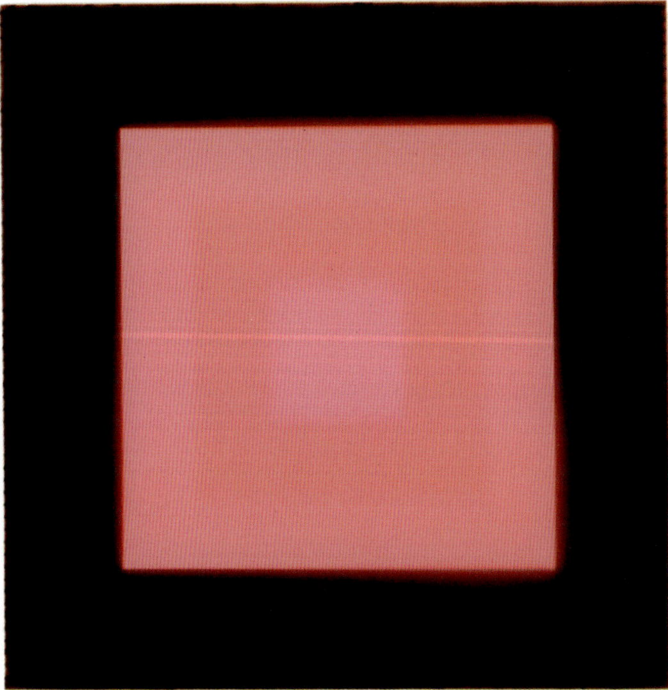

Year One: Cutios
40.5 x 40.5 cm

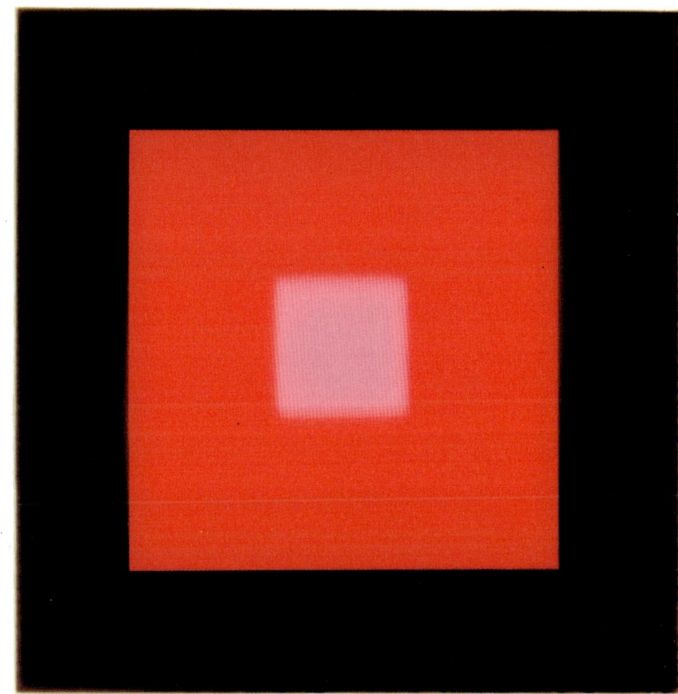

Year One: Giamonios
40.5 x 40.5 cm

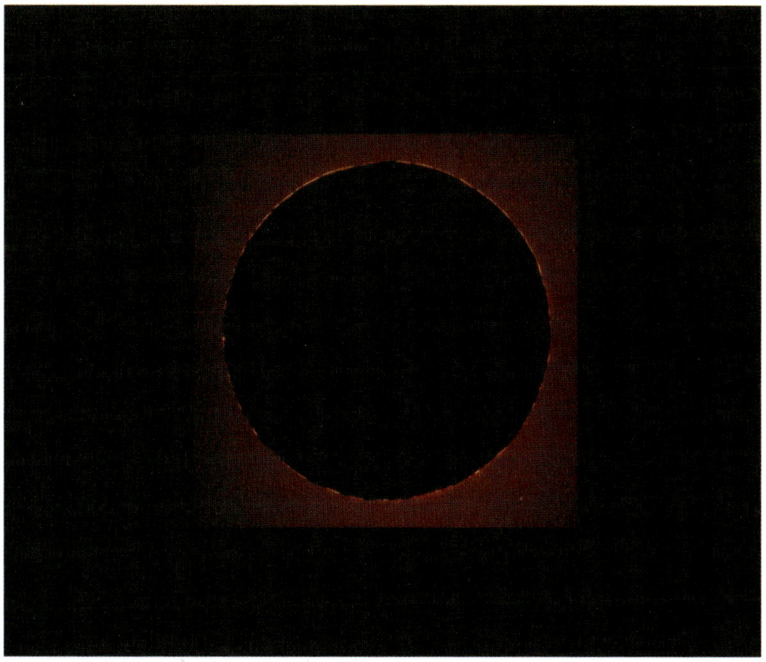

Year One: Simivisionios
40.5 x 50.5 cm

Year One: Equos
40.5 x 50.5 cm

Year One: Elembiuos
50.5 x 40.5 cm

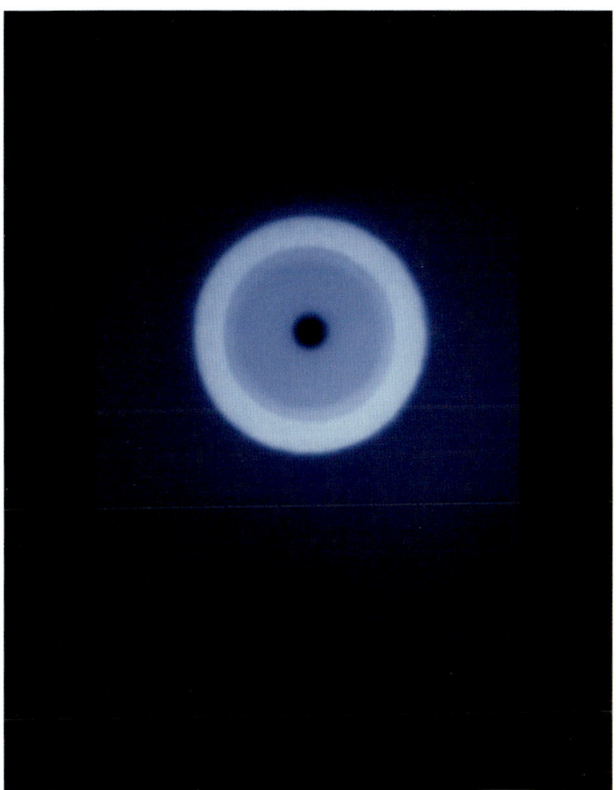

Year One: Edrinios
50.5 x 40.5 cm

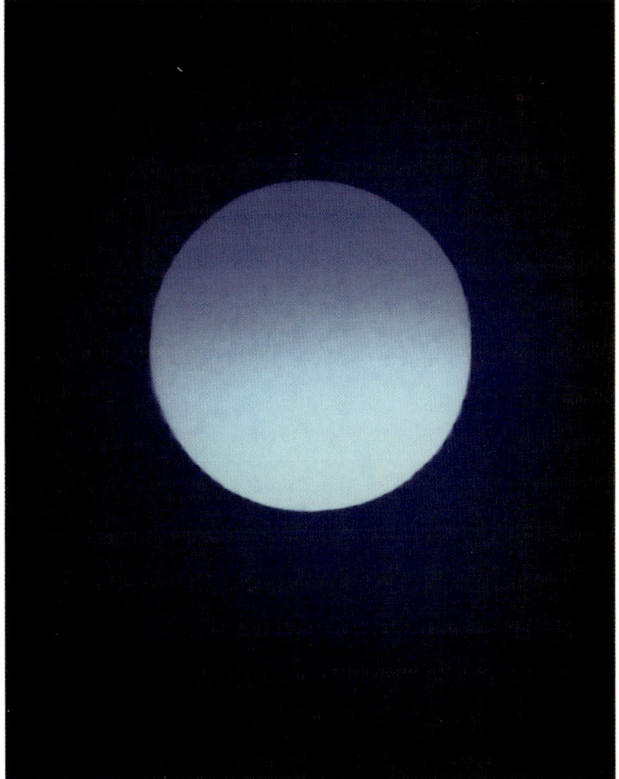

Year One: Cantios
50.5 x 40.5 cm

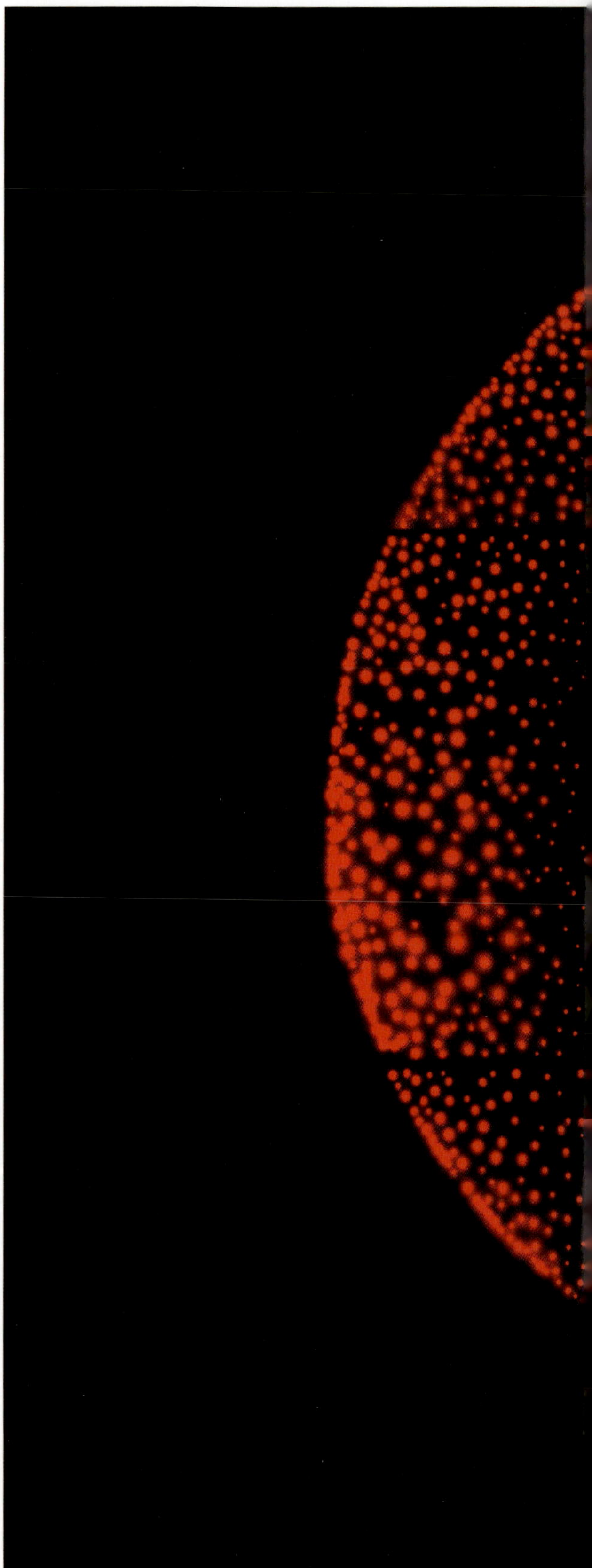

Garry Fabian Miller (b.1957)

Exposure (five hours of light)
1 July 2005
2005

Dye destruction prints
160 x 190 cm

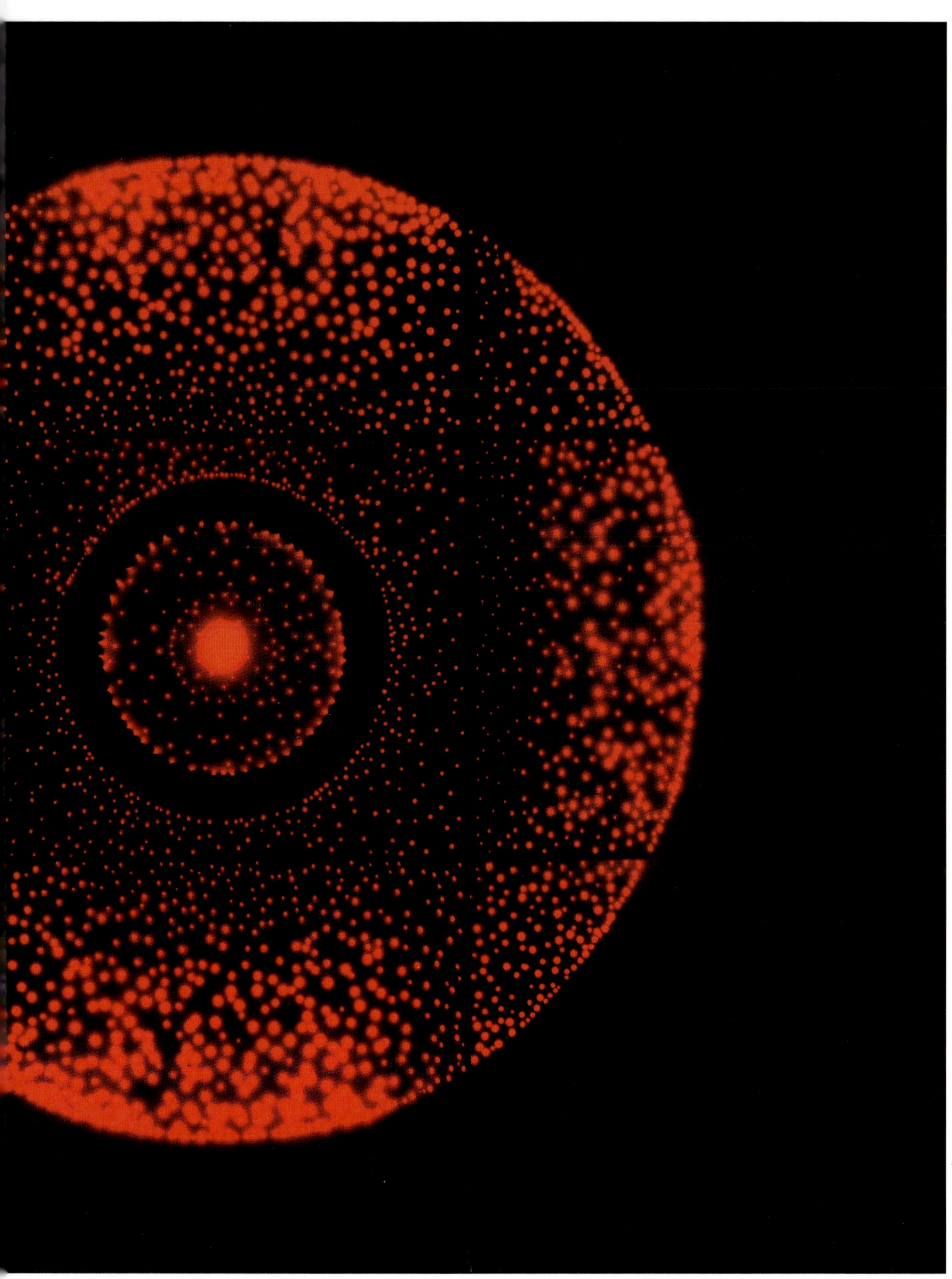

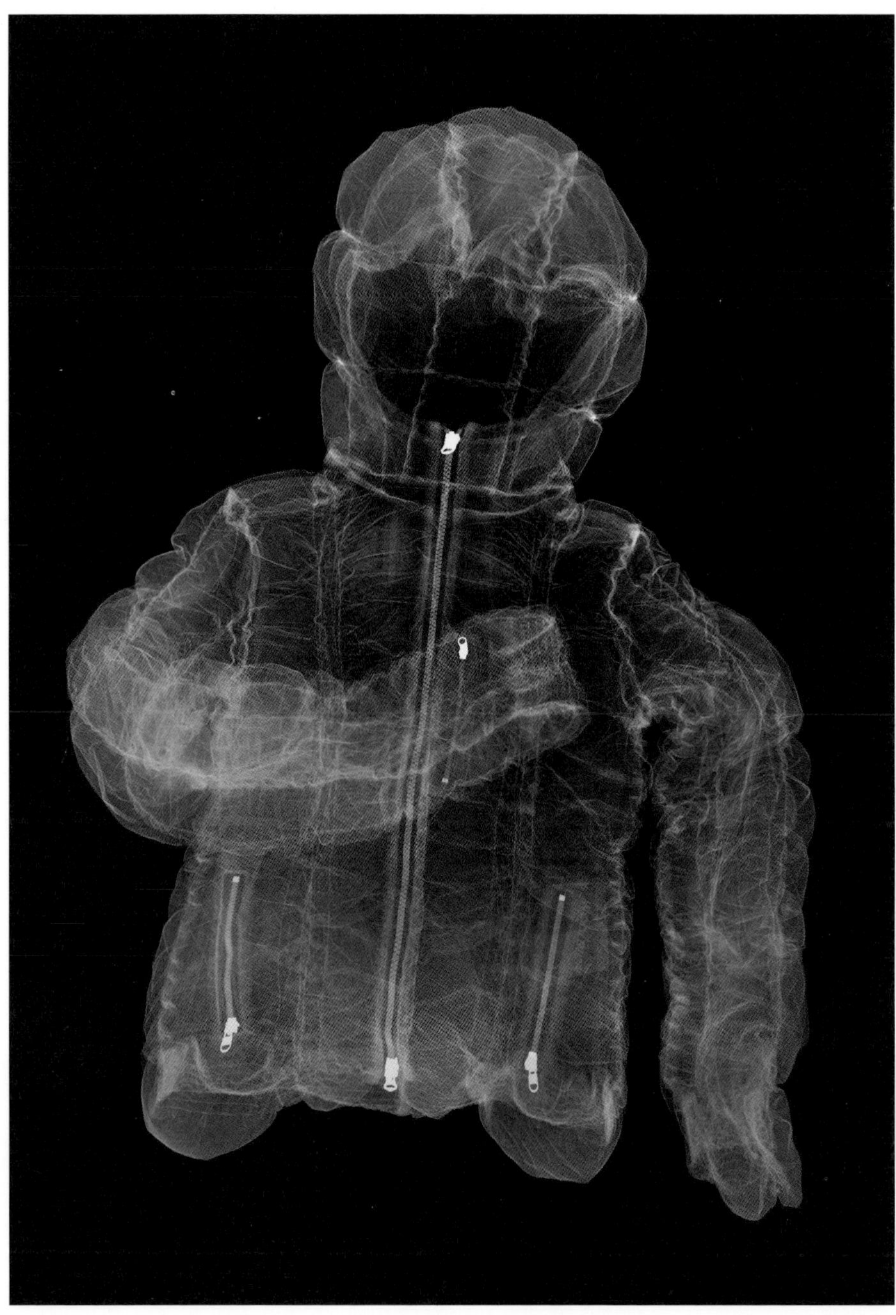

Nick Veasey (b.1962)

Puffa Jacket
2008

Digital C-type print
41.9 x 29.7 cm

Veasey's X-ray artworks counter a world obsessed with surface appearance by stripping back the layers to show what is hidden beneath. This image provides a fresh look at fashion illustration, and was part of a magazine feature documenting the winners of the Sportswear International Fashion Awards. The X-ray reveals the tracks and folds of material and the skeletal network of stitches that shape a jacket.

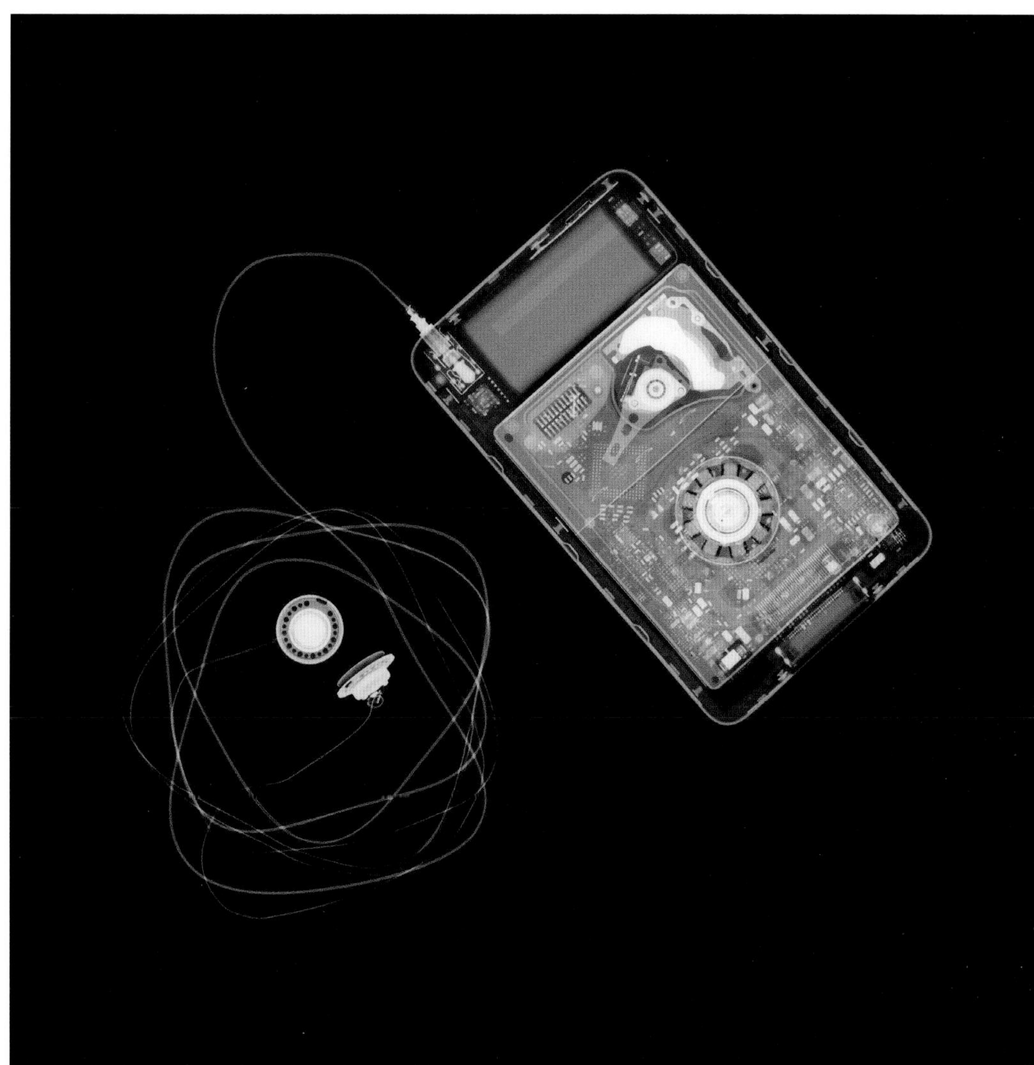

Nick Veasey (b.1962)

i-Pod
2008

Digital C-type print
86 x 85.8 cm

Veasey's X-ray images often reveal the skill and ingenuity that go into design and manufacture. His works depict a wide range of classic products, from small electronic devices to large vehicles. He also delights in appropriating for artistic ends a technology that has become commonplace in security and surveillance.

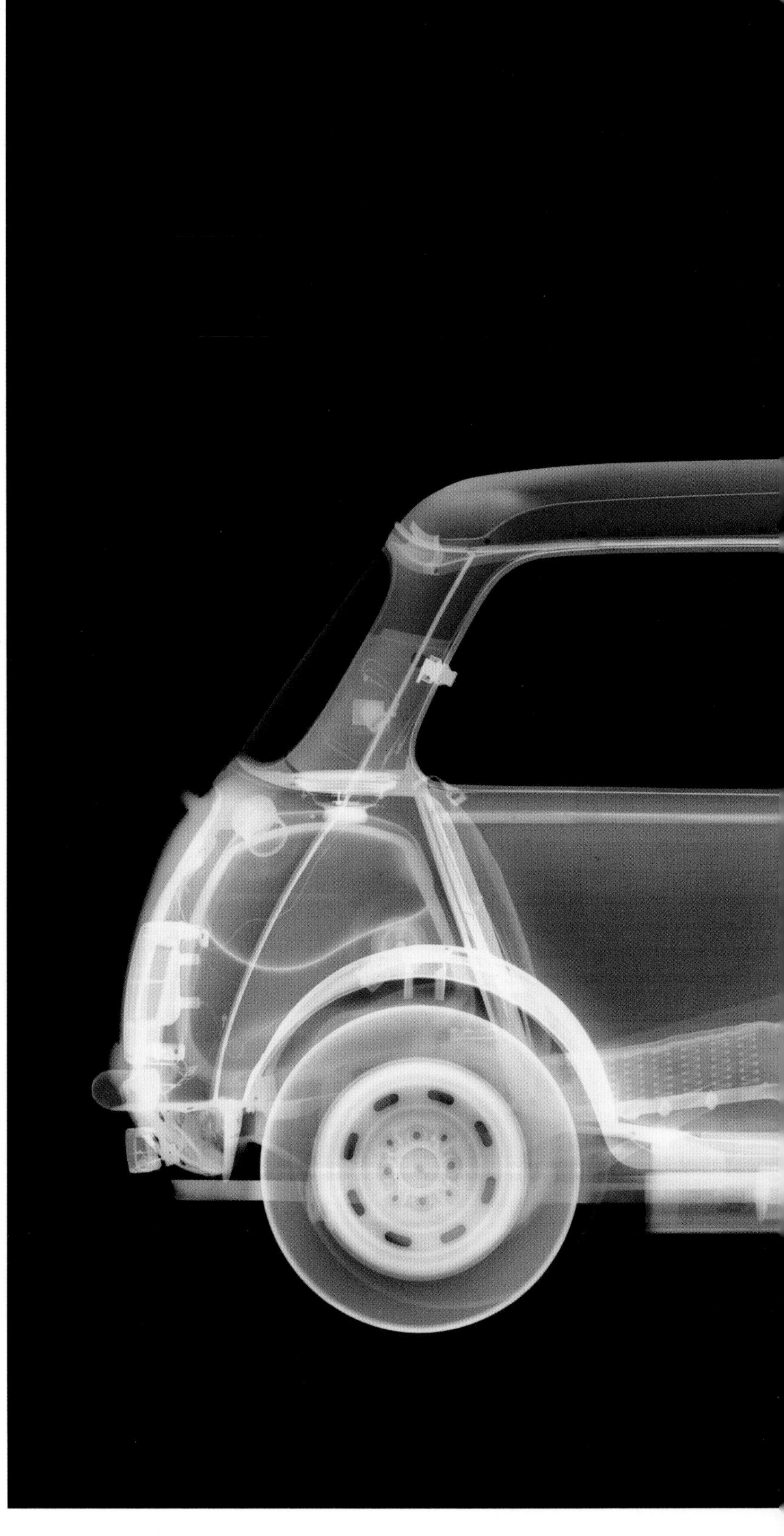

Nick Veasey (b.1962)

Mini
2008

Digital C-type print
85.5 x 120.8 cm

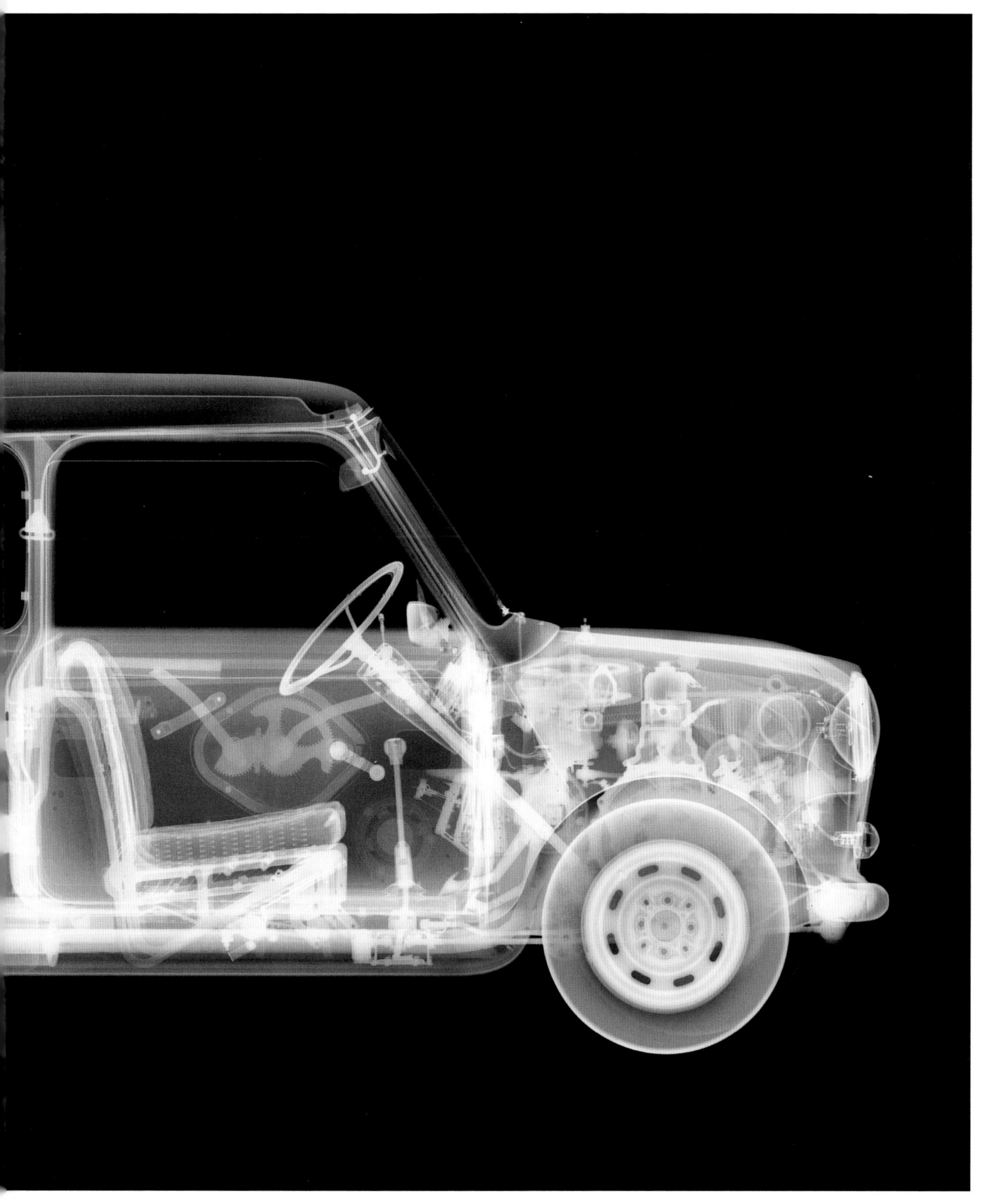

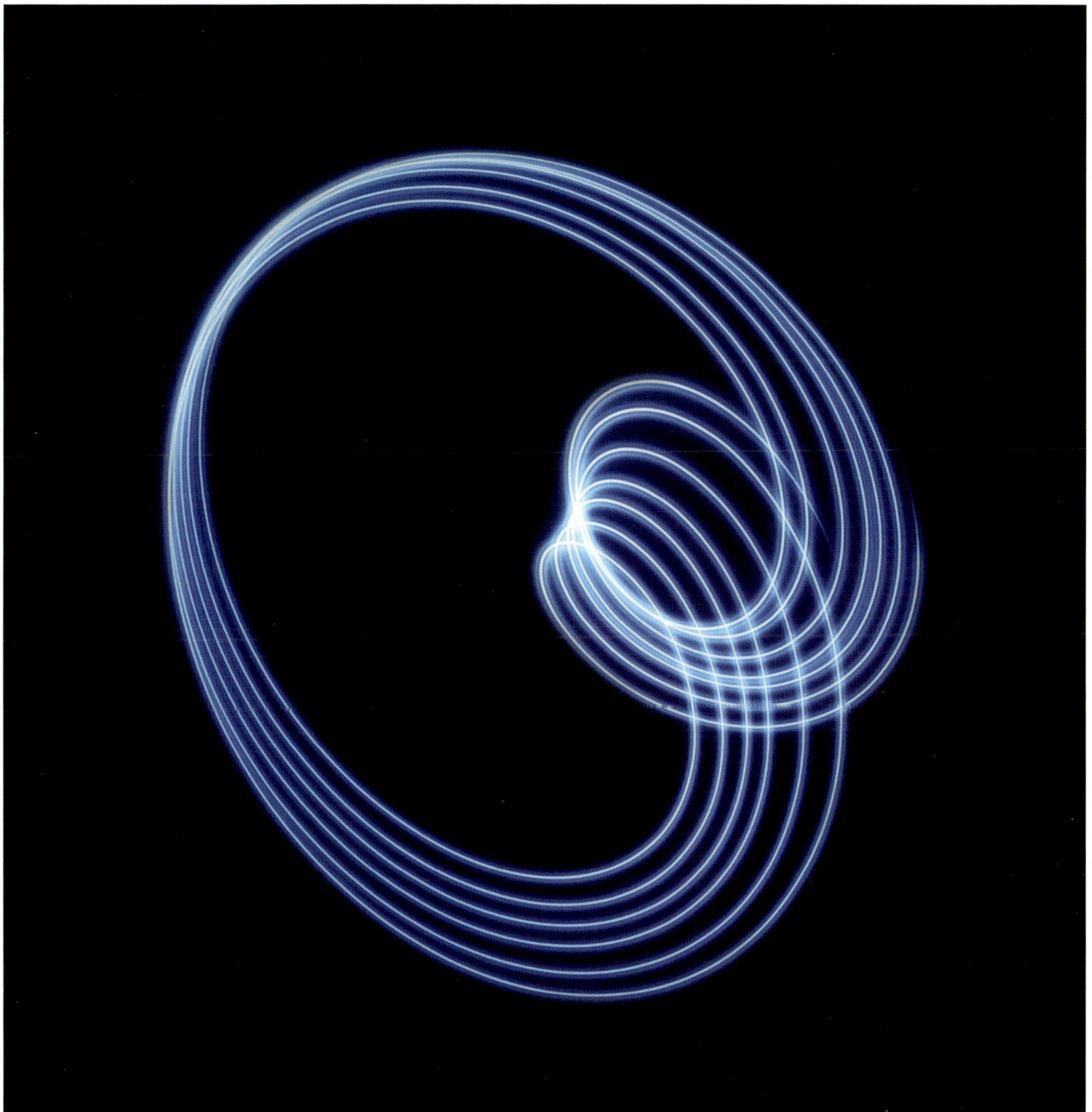

Rob and Nick Carter (b.1968 and 1969)

RN622 Harmonograph VI
2006

Dye destruction print
91 x 91 cm

This unique drawing with light is part of a series using patterns created by the harmonograph, a Victorian scientific device used to trace intervals that occur in music and other wave forms. Rob and Nick Carter made their own contemporary version: a light swinging from the ceiling like a pendulum traces its pattern on a sheet of photographic paper fixed to a rotating board below. This pattern is known as a 'rotary octave'.

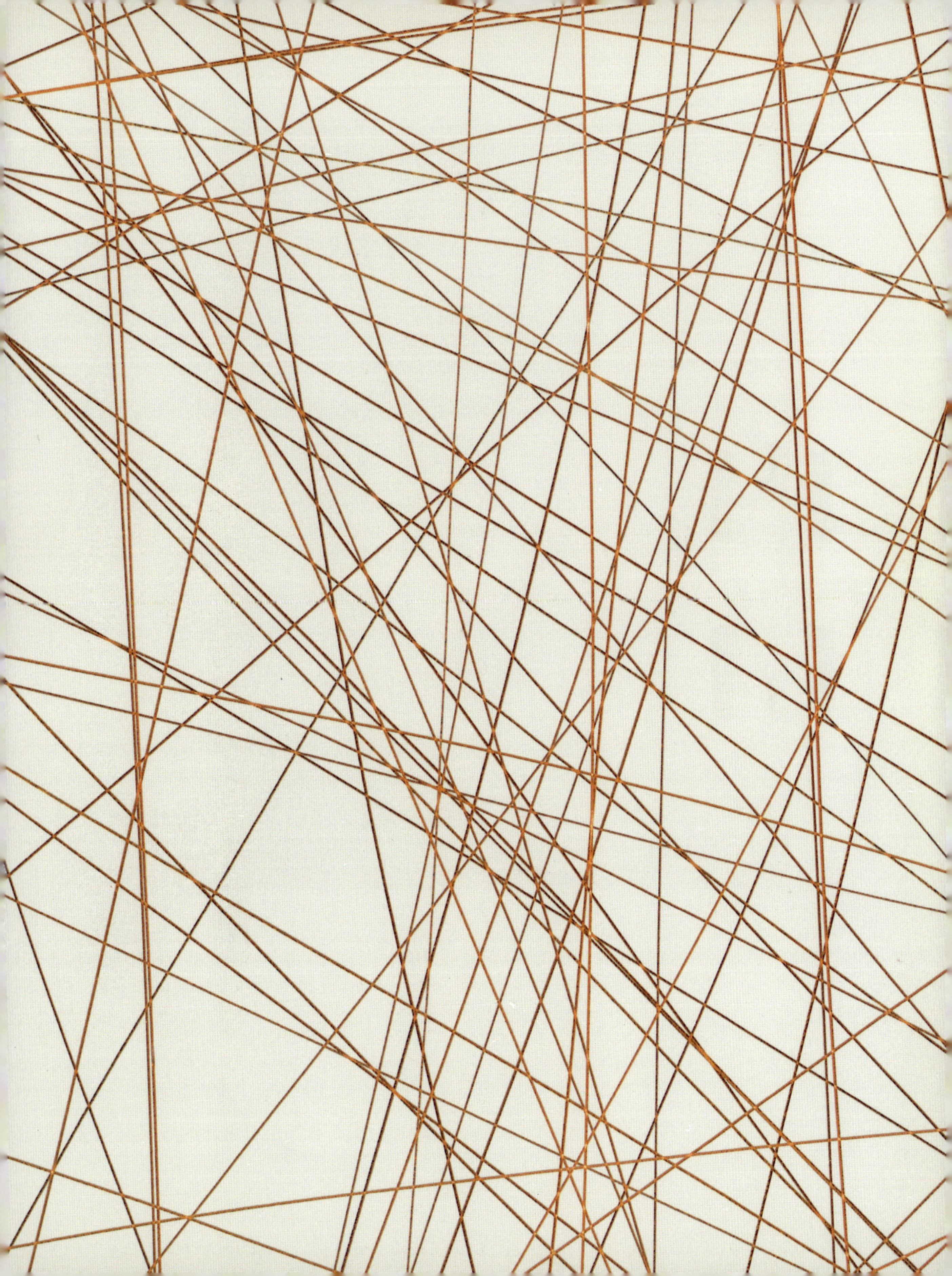

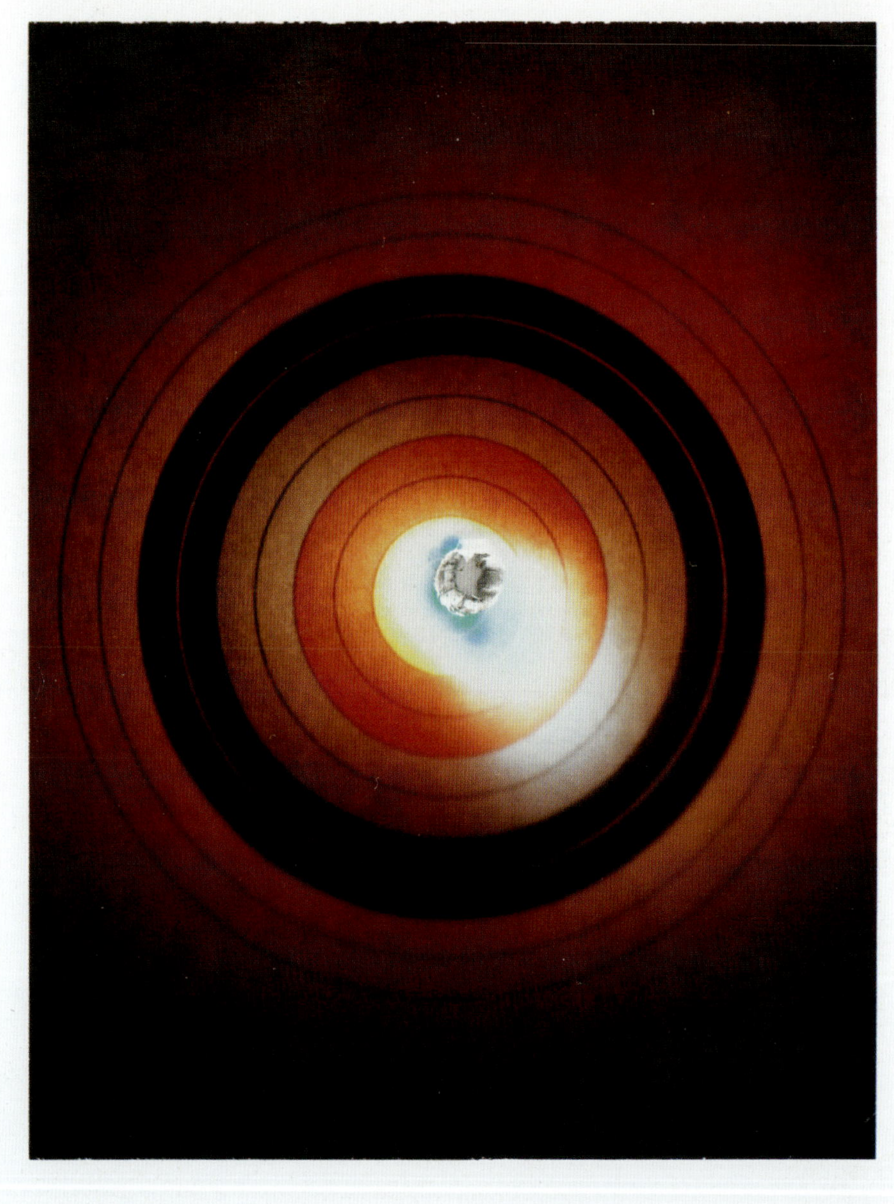

Marco Breuer (b.1966)

Untitled (Target)
2015

Polaroid contact print shot with .22 rifle
11 x 8.5 cm

Breuer coaxes a range of colours and textures from his photographic paper by augmenting traditional methods of exposure, developing and printing with folding, scratching, burning, piercing, abrading and other interventions. The surfaces bear the marks of touch, demonstrating the same fragility and variety as a living organism. Most traditional photographs record a single instant; by contrast, Breuer's accumulate scars over time.

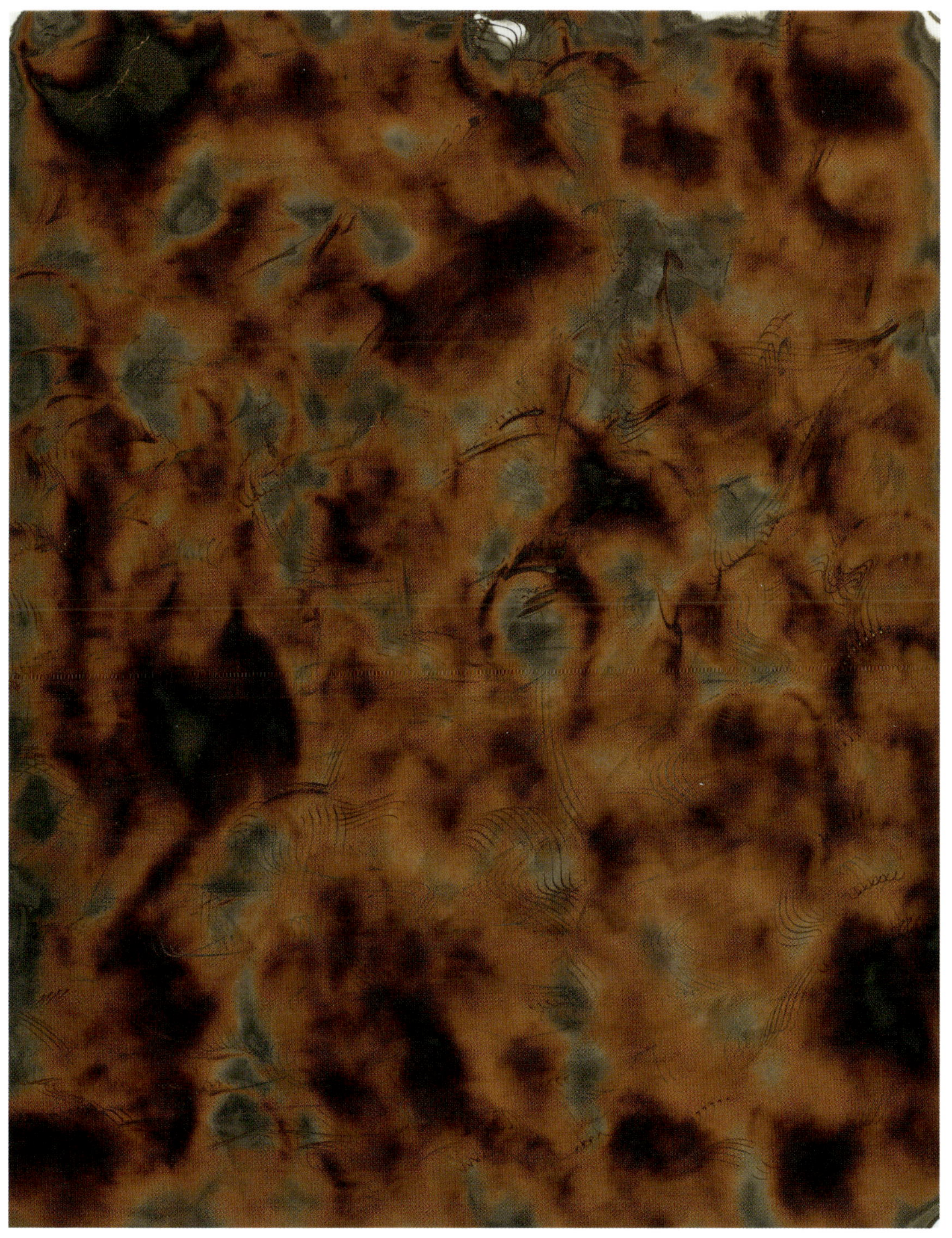

Marco Breuer (b.1966)

Untitled (Tip)
1999

Gelatin silver paper, burned
25 x 19.5 cm

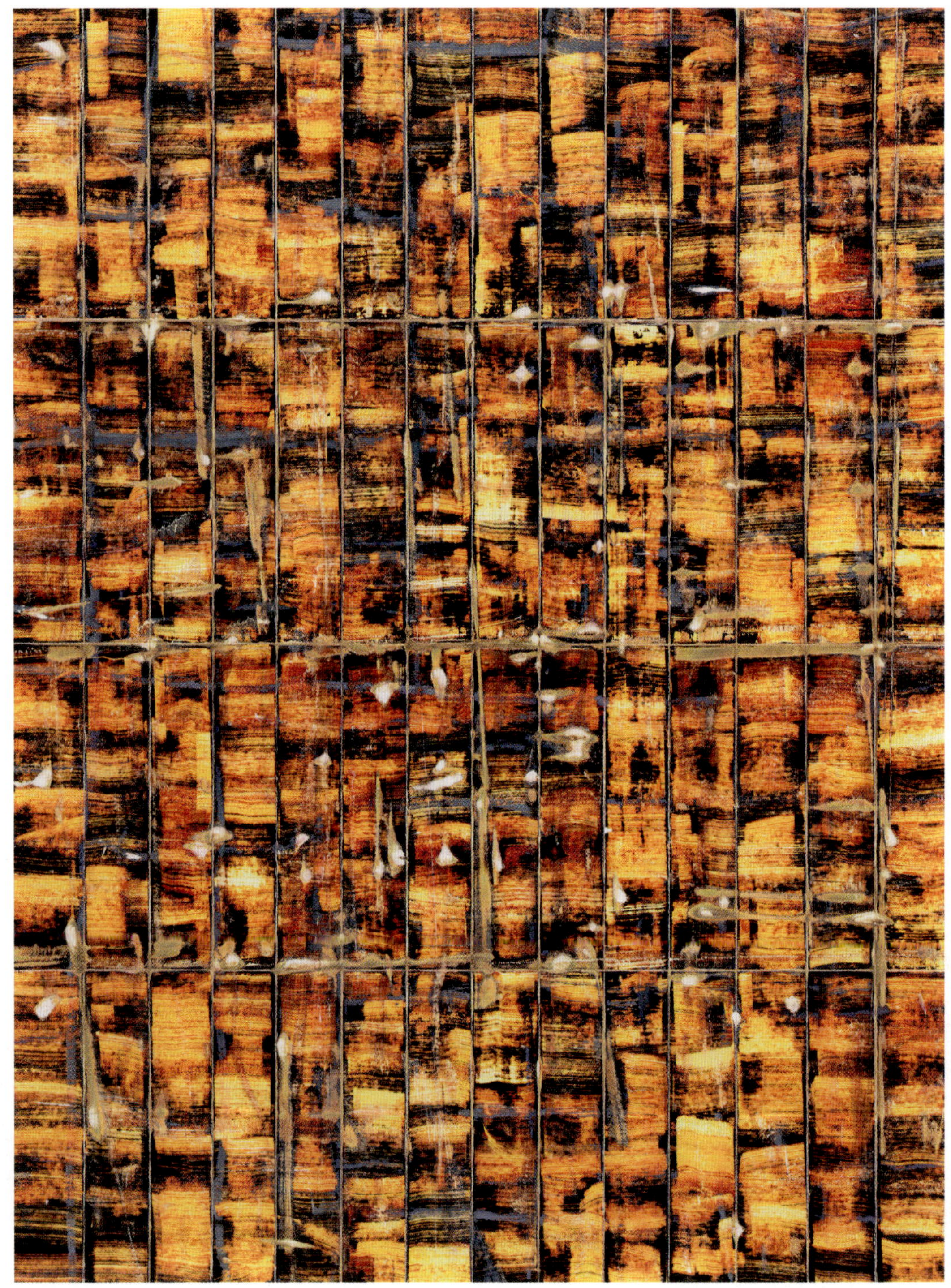

Marco Breuer (b.1966)

Untitled (C-1656)
2014

Chromogenic paper, folded, burned and scratched
57 x 42.5 cm

Marco Breuer (b.1966)

Pan (C-424)
2004

Chromogenic paper, scratched
60 x 50 cm

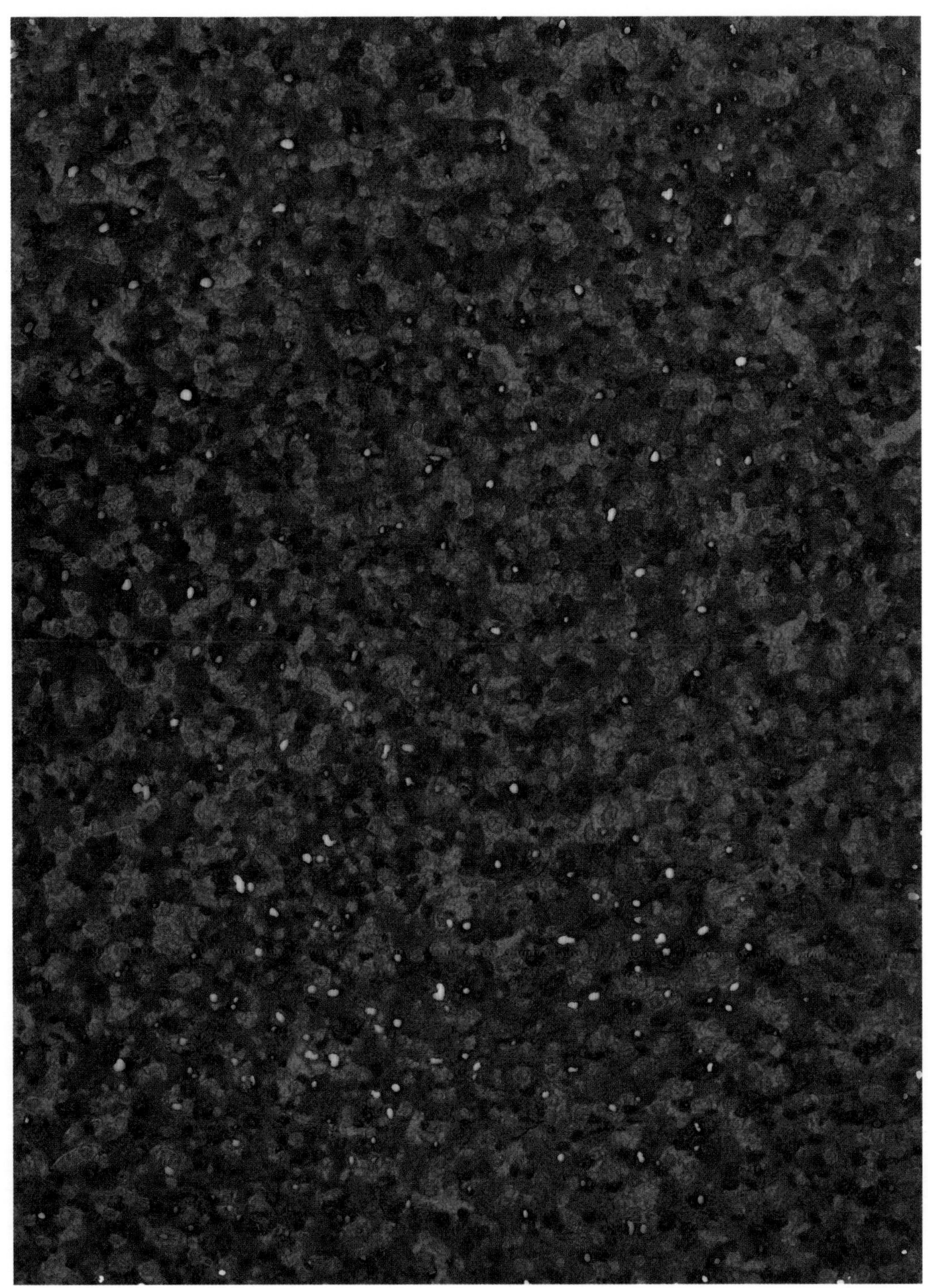

Marco Breuer (b.1966)

Untitled (E-77)
2005

Gum bichromate on Fabriano paper
48 x 35.5 cm

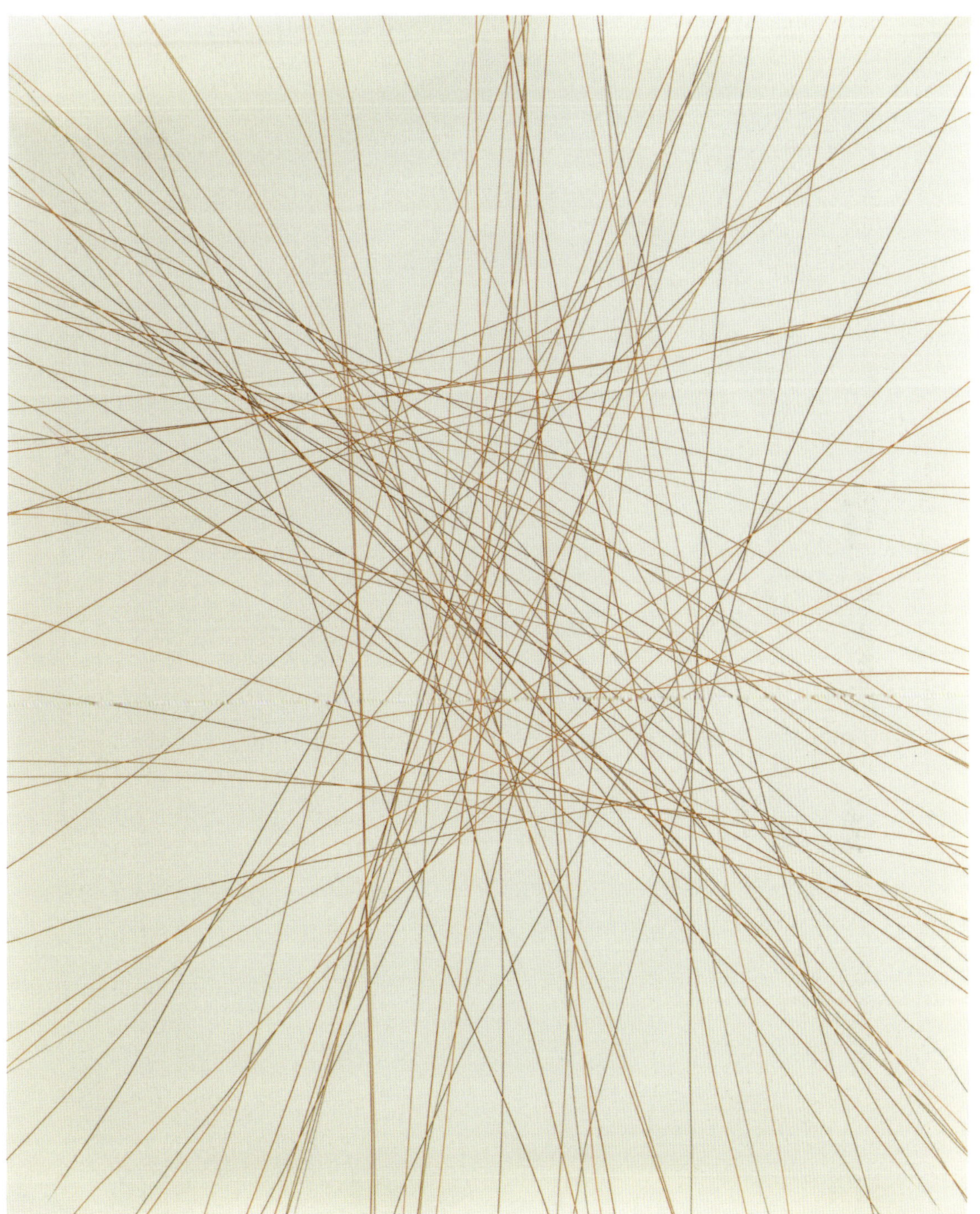

Marco Breuer (b.1966)

Approx. (C-939)
2009

Chromogenic paper, scratched
56.4 x 46.5 cm

(detail p.171)

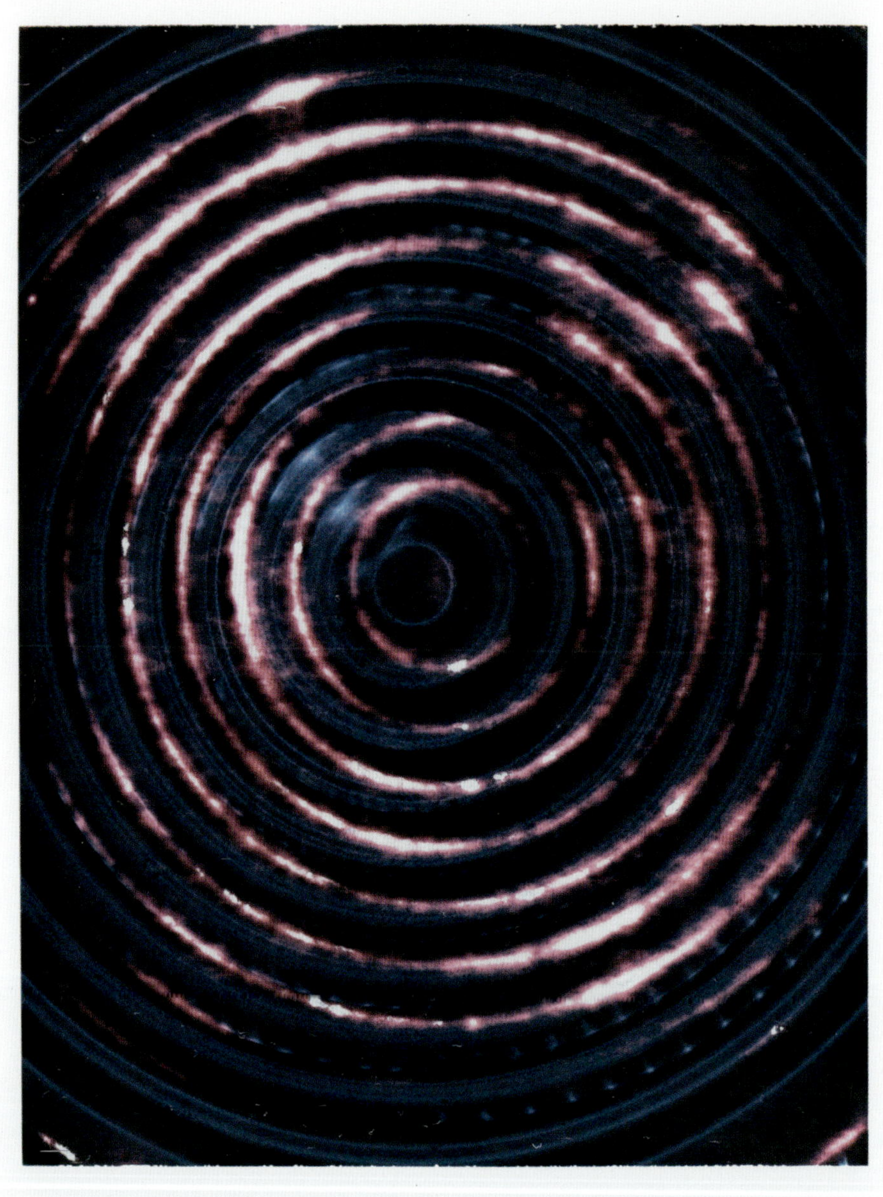

Marco Breuer (b.1966)

Untitled (Plate)
2015

Polaroid photograph, abraded
11 x 8.5 cm

Hiroshi Sugimoto (b.1948)

Lightning Fields, 225
2009

Gelatin silver print
58.4 x 49.5 cm

(detail p.2)

Sugimoto's *Lightning Fields* series was influenced in part by a desire to recreate William Henry Fox Talbot's research into static electricity. This photograph captures the electrical discharge produced between a Van de Graaff generator and a metal table top on which a sheet of negative film was placed. The print is an enlargement from the negative. The scale of the fleeting natural phenomenon is ambiguous and as unique as a bolt of lightning.

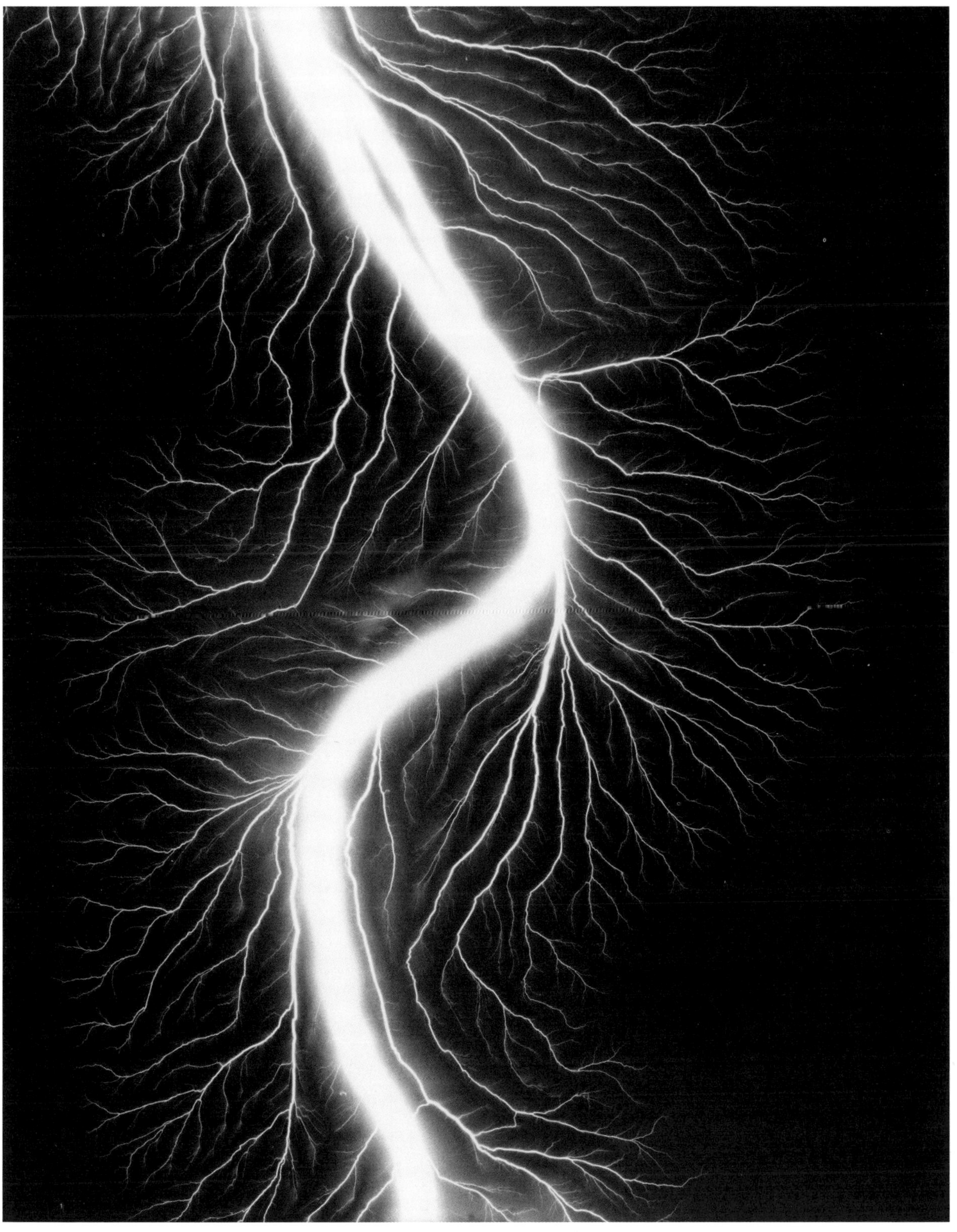

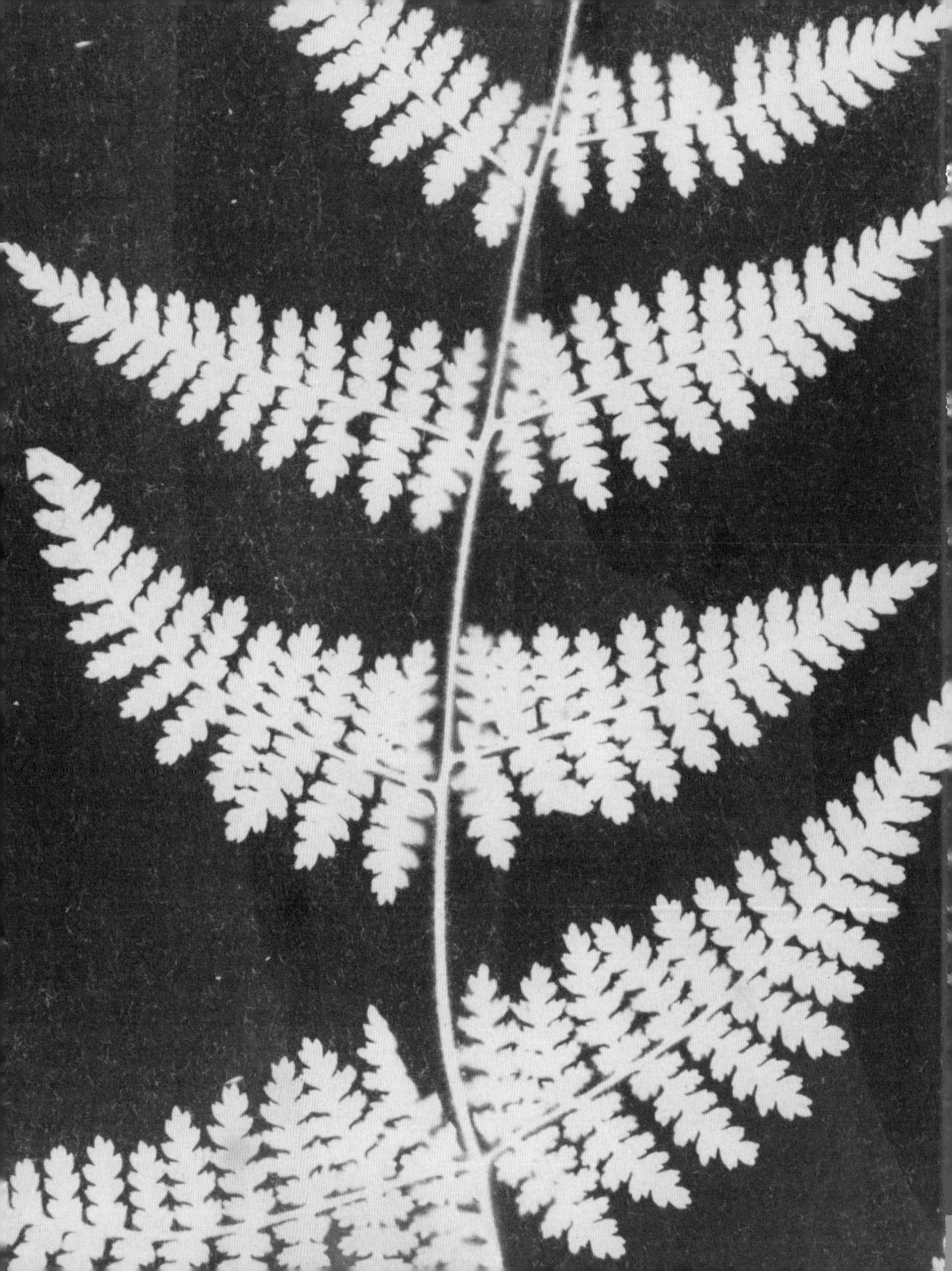

Glossary of Processes and Techniques

Albumen print

The albumen print was invented in 1850 and was the most common type of print for the next forty years. It produced a clearer image than its predecessor, the salted paper print. An albumen print was made by coating paper with a layer of egg white and salt to create a smooth surface. The paper was then coated with a layer of silver nitrate. The salt and silver nitrate combined to form light-sensitive silver salts. This double-coated paper could then be placed in contact with a negative and exposed to the sun to produce a print. Prints typically have a soft sheen and are coloured a variety of shades of brown.

C-type print

A C-type print, usually made from a colour negative, is a colour print in which the print material has at least three emulsion layers of light-sensitive silver salts. Each layer is sensitized to a different primary colour – either red, blue or green – and so records different information about the colour make-up of the image. During printing, chemicals are added that form dyes of the appropriate colour in the emulsion layers. It is the most common type of analogue colour photograph.

Calotype

William Henry Fox Talbot discovered the calotype negative process in late 1840 and patented it in 1841. It is the direct ancestor of modern photography because it took advantage of a latent image to capture a short exposure in the camera, and then brought this to full density in the darkroom using a chemical developer. Because the image was contained in the fabric of the paper rather than on a surface coating or emulsion, the paper fibres tended to show through in the prints, making them, in the words of contemporary critics, 'Rembrandtish'.

Carbon print

Carbon printing was introduced from 1864. A sheet of paper was coated with a layer of light-sensitive gelatin which contained a permanent pigment (often carbon). It was then exposed to daylight under a negative. Carbon prints can be produced in a variety of colours, ranging from rich sepia tones to cooler shades of grey and blue. Because of their resistance to fading they were much used in the 1870s and 1880s for book illustration and commercial editions of photographs.

Chemigram

A chemigram is made directly on photosensitive paper. Working in full light, the chemistry of photographic developer gives the blacks, and fixer the whites. Varnish, wax or oil coated on the paper can create images impossible to realize by any other means. The maker has the choice between creating controlled forms and forms that are the effects of chance, or a combination of the two.

Chromogenic paper

A colour printing paper designed for use with a colour transparency or negative, this print material has at least three emulsion layers of silver salts, sensitized to one of the three primary colours: blue, green and red. During exposure to a negative or transparency, an image is formed in each layer, which, after development, forms dyes on the white base of the paper stock that appear as a single image in full colour.

Cliché-verre

Cliché-verre is a photograph made from a hand-drawn negative. The design is drawn or painted onto a sheet of glass, or, alternatively, scratched onto a piece of glass that has been made opaque by being painted over or blackened with smoke. The sheet of glass is then placed on a sheet of sensitized paper and exposed to light. The blackened area of the glass acts as a stencil, creating an image on the paper below only where light was able to pass through the glass.

Cyanotype

The cyanotype process for making prints was invented by Sir John Herschel in 1842 and came from his discovery of the light-sensitivity of iron salts. A sheet of paper was brushed with iron salt solutions and dried in the dark. The object to be reproduced – a plant specimen, a drawing or a negative – was then placed on the sheet in direct sunlight. After about fifteen minutes a white impression of the subject formed on a blue background. The paper was then washed in water where oxidation produced the brilliant blue – or cyan – that gave the process its name.

Dye destruction print

Dye destruction prints are made using direct positive colour paper. This paper was originally introduced in 1963 for printing colour transparencies or negatives. It is coated with at least three layers of emulsion, each of which is sensitized to one of the three primary colours. Each layer also contains a dye related to that colour. During development of the image, any unexposed dyes are bleached out (hence 'dye destruction'). The remaining dyes form a full-colour image. The technique is also known by its technical description, 'silver dye bleach processes', and its trade name, Ilfochrome (formerly Cibachrome).

Gelatin silver print

Introduced in 1871, gelatin silver prints are made using paper that has been coated with gelatin containing silver salts. Where light strikes the silver salts, they become dark. The image is then developed out (rather than printed out), using chemical developer. The paper itself can have a matt or gloss surface, and the image can be toned.

Gum bichromate

This type of printing, popular in the early twentieth century, allowed a high degree of control and artistic manipulation. The paper is brushed with a coating of gum arabic, water, pigment and potassium (or ammonium) bichromate, and usually exposed in contact with a negative. Brushing or washing the surface could dissolve areas of the coating hardened more or less by exposure, thus changing contrast and adding effects reminiscent of drawing or painting.

Heliograph

Joseph Nicéphore Niépce invented this process in which he first coated a pewter plate with light-sensitive Bitumen of Judea (asphaltum). Taking an existing engraving on paper, he waxed it to make it translucent and placed it on the plate in the sun. Its rays hardened the bitumen under the light areas of the image. The plate was washed with a solvent, which removed the unexposed areas, and etched in acid. It was then ready for inking and printing. Recent technical analysis of the Niépce plates in the Victoria and Albert Museum has revealed the use of another light-solidified material, which resembles the resin obtained when heating lavender oil, and a range of levels of etching and hand-tooling over the plates. Niépce also experimented with the plates inside a camera, producing the earliest known surviving photograph made in a camera, *View from the Window at Le Gras* (1826 or 1827), held in The Gernsheim Collection, Harry Ransom Center, The University of Texas at Austin.

Hologram

This image in three dimensions is made on a photographic plate, though not strictly a photograph. There are several kinds of holograms, many of which involve complex processes. Transmission holograms are made by directing one of two parts of a laser beam towards an emulsion on a glass plate. The other part of the beam is directed towards the subject and reflected towards the emulsion.

The coincidence of the two beams produces a mixture of patterns that are recorded with their similarities and differences together on the plate. When the plate is illuminated again by a laser, an image that appears to have three dimensions is produced and is altered in the perception of its dimensionality as the person viewing the plate moves.

Luminogram

A variation of the photogram (see below). In a luminogram, light falling directly on the paper forms the image. Objects placed between the light and the paper (but not touching the paper) will filter or block the light, depending on whether they are transparent or opaque.

Paper negative

See calotype, *and* photogenic drawing.

Photocopy

Commercial photocopying was introduced by the Xerox company in 1959. Most current photocopiers rely on xerography technology, a dry process using electrostatic charges on a light-sensitive photoreceptor to first attract and then transfer toner powder onto paper in the form of an image. Heat, pressure or a combination of both is then used to fuse the toner onto the paper.

Photogenic drawing

'Photogenic drawing' was William Henry Fox Talbot's name for the results of his first cameraless photographic process, invented in 1834, perfected in 1835 and announced to the public in 1839. In its simplest form a smooth high-quality sheet of writing paper was immersed in a solution of table salt and then dried. Talbot brushed the paper with a solution of silver nitrate. This combined with the salt to produce silver chloride, which is light-sensitive. Small objects such as leaves and lace could then be placed on the paper and exposed to sunlight. This produced a light image of the object against a dark background; in other words, a negative image. No developer was involved – solar energy did all the work. The technique was also used in small cameras (his wife once called these 'mousetraps') and could produce negatives with exposures approaching an hour.

Photogram

The term 'photogram' appeared in *The Times* newspaper as early as 1857, and was used with increasing frequency from the 1890s, though it did not refer to cameraless contact processes at this time. The modern use of the term seems to have appeared around 1925, and refers to the process of placing an object in contact with a photosensitive surface and, in the dark, exposing both to light. Where the object blocks the light, either partially or fully, its shadow is recorded on the paper. The photogram artist is not able to predict the results in the viewfinder of a camera, and often works in the dark. The final image is only apparent after physical and chemical manipulation or development.

Photographic and photoglyphic engraving

These are methods of photographically producing copper or steel printing plates that can then be used in a conventional press. The first was patented by William Henry Fox Talbot in 1852, and the second by him in 1858. At first, a copper or steel plate was coated with a gelatin solution made light-sensitive with potassium bichromate. The object to be depicted, such as a leaf or piece of fabric, was placed on top. Exposure to daylight hardened the areas not covered by the object. The unhardened areas were then washed off and the plate etched in acid. With etching complete, the gelatin was removed and the plate could then be printed. The addition of screens or other graining allowed Talbot to devise his second process, which had a much wider tonal range. A glass photographic positive was put over the sensitized plate and used to make the image. Nature made the faithful original photographic drawing, but, in the final prints, carbon-based ink relied on nothing light-sensitive and preserved the original image for posterity. This was the direct forerunner of the photogravure process.

Photogravure

Photogravure is a process for reproducing photographs in large editions in ink. It uses gelatin to transfer the image, usually from a black and white negative, to a copper printing plate. The gelatin carries the image because it hardens in proportion to its exposure to light. Areas of the gelatin not exposed stay soft and can be dissolved away in water. What remains is a gelatin version of the image, which is pressed onto a copper plate. The plate is then placed in an acid bath. Where the gelatin is thick, the acid eats the metal away slowly; where the gelatin is thin or absent, the acid eats faster. Consequently, the plate is etched to different depths according to the tones of the original image. When inked for printing, the varying depths hold different amounts of ink.

Pigment print

This form of digital print is made via an inkjet printer. As a form of art reproduction, inkjet prints became more widely available in the 1980s, when digital printer technology improved and printers became less expensive. The first inkjet prints were created with Iris printers, developed by Iris Graphics, Inc., and are therefore sometimes known as Iris prints. High-quality versions are sometimes termed giclée prints. Some types of digital inkjet printing use pigments rather than ink or dyes. Pigment particles embed into the receiving paper and are therefore more permanent.

Polaroid

This instant film, introduced in 1947, gave an almost immediate positive print, achieved by developing chemicals being already present in the film. The film is designed to be used in an instant camera that initiates the developing process.

Radiograph

Radiography is the imaging technique using X-rays that pass through an object and are captured directly behind it on photographic film, or, more recently, on digital sensors. The first X-ray images were made in Germany by Wilhelm Röntgen in late 1895.

Salted paper print (salt print)

Salted paper prints are nothing more than William Henry Fox Talbot's original photogenic drawing paper, and refer to when his original printing-out paper was used to make prints rather than negatives. The developed calotype negative, while more sensitive to light and thus of advantage in the camera, was far less suitable for printing. Its complexity and fickleness were unnecessary complications, and its tones were judged to be less pleasant. Salt prints, once fixed, naturally have a range of reddish to purplish-brown tones. Since the image is within the paper fibres with no surface coating, it suffers some loss of detail but gains in aesthetic appeal. Starting in the 1850s, with the increased industrialization of photography, salt prints quickly yielded to factory-made albumen paper, but in the 1890s they enjoyed a revival in the hands of 'pictorialist' art photographers.

Scannergram (scanography)

The process of directly capturing digitized images of objects uses a flatbed 'photo' scanner. Commercial flatbed colour scanners were intended to copy paper documents, but they became increasingly available and affordable in the 1990s and led to experimentation by artists. The scanner's limited depth of field means that three-dimensional objects placed on it only appear in focus about 12 mm from the surface, yet the image resolution is comparatively high compared with standard digital camera capture.

X-ray

See radiograph.

Further Reading

BOOKS

Christina Z. Anderson, *Experimental Photography Workbook* (Bozeman, MT 2012)

Marco Antonini et al., *Experimental Photography: A Handbook of Techniques* (London 2015)

Simon Baker and Emmanuelle de L'Ecotais, *Shape of Light: 100 Years of Photography and Abstract Art* (London 2018)

Gordon Baldwin, *Looking at Photographs: A Guide to Technical Terms* (Los Angeles and London, 1991)

Martin Barnes, *Shadow Catchers: Camera-less Photography*, second edition (London 2012)

Geoffrey Batchen, *Emanations: The Art of the Cameraless Photograph* (New York 2016)

Virginia Heckert, *Light, Paper, Process: Reinventing Photography* (Los Angeles 2015)

Gottfried Jäger, Rolf H. Krauss, and Beate Reese, *Concrete Photography / Konkrete Fotografie* (Bielefeld and Berlin, 2005)

Christopher James, *The Book of Alternative Photographic Processes*, third edition (Boston, MA 2015)

Corey Keller (ed.), *Brought to Light: Photography and the Invisible, 1840–1900* (New Haven, CT 2009)

Sarah Kennel, Diane Waggoner, and Alice Carver-Kubik, *In the Darkroom: An Illustrated Guide to Photographic Processes Before the Digital Age* (Washington DC and London, 2010)

Luis Nadeau, *Encyclopedia of Printing, Photographic and Photomechanical Processes* (New Brunswick, NJ 1989)

Lyle Rexer, *The Edge of Vision: The Rise of Abstraction in Photography* (New York 2009)

WEBSITES

www.alternativephotography.com/processes/
www.photoconservation.com

Picture Credits

The following list of artists provides, for reference, Victoria and Albert Museum object numbers for included works. Those with collection reference letters RPS belong to the Royal Photographic Society Collection, Victoria and Albert Museum, acquired with the generous assistance of the Heritage Lottery Fund and Art Fund.

heritage lottery fund
LOTTERY FUNDED
Art Fund_

Anna Atkins (1799–1871)
p.39 PH.379-1981
p.40 PH.380-1981
p.41 PH.382-1981
p.42 PH.381-1981

E. & J. Baldwin Photographic Portrait Studio (fl.1880s)
pp.47–9 E.9:6, 10, 2, 3, 9 and 4-2009

Barbara and Zafer Baran (b.1956 and 1955)
pp.135 (detail) and 137 E.340-2005
p.138 E.343-2005
p.139 E.341-2005
p.140 E.336-2005
All given by the artists.
Courtesy the artists

Bart's Hospital X-ray Unit
pp.64–5 RPS.1237-2018

Josef Breitenbach (1896–1984)
p.76 E.18-1999
© Josef and Yaye Breitenbach Charitable Foundation. Courtesy Gitterman Gallery

Marco Breuer (b.1966)
pp.171 (detail) and 177 E.740-2017
p.172 E.747-2017
p.173 E.742-2017
p.174 E.741-2017
p.175 E.739-2017
p.176 E.743-2017
p.178 E.748-2017
All purchased with the support of the V&A Photographs Acquisition Group.
© Marco Breuer. Courtesy Yossi Milo Gallery, New York

Christopher Bucklow (b.1957)
p.110 E.70-1997
Given by the artist in memory of Ray Smith.
p.111 E.238-1999
© Christopher Bucklow

Alan Archibald Campbell-Swinton (1863–1930)
p.50 RPS.1239-2018

Rob and Nick Carter (b.1968 and 1969)
p.169 E.904-2010
Given by the artists.
© Rob and Nick Carter

Helen Chadwick (1953–1996)
pp.12 (detail) and 109 E.648-2016
p.108 PH.146-1986
© The Artist's Estate. Courtesy Richard Saltoun Gallery, London

Pierre Cordier (b.1933)
pp.113 (detail) and 115 E.858-2010
Purchased through the generosity of HH Sheikh Saud bin Mohamad bin Ali Al-Thani, with further support from Basil Hyman.
p.114 E.328-2018
Purchased with the support of the V&A Photographs Acquisition Group.
p.116 E.329-2018
Given by the artist.
pp.117 (detail) and 119 E.859-2010
Given by the artist.
p.118 E.330-2018
Given by the artist.
p.120 E.856-2010
Given by the artist.
© Pierre Cordier

Jean-Baptiste-Camille Corot (1796–1875)
p.45 E.2923-1921

Susan Derges (b.1955)
pp.142–3 E.2810 to 2817-1990
pp.145 (detail) and 146–7 E.445-2010
All given by the artist.
© Susan Derges

Elaine Duigenan (b.1964)
p.149 E.28-2007
Given by the artist.
© Elaine Duigenan

Rebecca Earley (b.1970)
p.126 T.122-1997
p.127 T.123-1997
© Rebecca Earley

Angela Easterling (b.1944)
p.131 E.1425-2001
p.132 E.1429-2001
Given by the Eden Project.
p.133 E.1430-2001
Given by the Eden Project.
© Angela Easterling

Harold Edgerton (1903–1990)
pp.1 (detail) and 84 E.579-1997
© Harold Edgerton/MIT. Courtesy of Palm Press, Inc.

Frances Ellis (fl. 1960s)
pp.98–9 RPS.1238-2018

Johann Carl Enslen (1759–1848)
p.35 RPS.1661-2017

John Arthur Fairfax Fozzard (1905–1993)
p.73 RPS.1215-2018

Adam Fuss (b.1961)
p.123 E.1589-1991
p.125 E.693-1993
© Adam Fuss. Courtesy Cheim & Read, New York

Susan Gamble (b.1957)
p.106 PH.149:2-1986
p.107 PH.149:1-1986
© Susan Gamble

Arnold M. Gilbert (1921–2001)
p.104 E.1236-1991
p.105 E.1237-1991
© The Artist's Estate.

James Green and James H. Gardiner (fl.1890s)
p.52 RPS.1630:10-2018
p.53 RPS.1630:7-2018

Robert Heinecken (1931–2006)
pp.93–7 E.840:3, 21, 27, 10, 22-2003
Purchased through the Cecil Beaton Fund.
© Robert Friedli Heinecken Estate. Courtesy of Rhona Hoffman Gallery

Nicolaas Henneman (1813–1898)
p.26 RPS.101-2017

Calvert Richard Jones (1802–1877)
p.36 PH.66-1983

Garry Fabian Miller (b.1957)
p.153 E.529-2005
Courtesy of HackelBury Fine Art, London.
p.154 E.477:58-2008
Given by the artist.
pp.155–61 E.1186:1 to 13-2012
Courtesy of Ingleby Gallery.
pp.162–3 E.326-2018
Given by the artist.
© Garry Fabian Miller

Curtis Moffat (1887–1949)
p.59 E.880-2003
p.60 E.2555-2007
p.61 E.2557-2007
p.62 E.2554-2007
All given by Penelope Smail.

László Moholy-Nagy (1895–1946)
p.55 E.801-1997
p.56 CIRC.224-1974

Floris Neusüss (b.1937)
p.85 E.74-2011
© Floris Neusüss

Floris Neusüss and Renate Heyne (b.1937 and 1947)
p.87 E.293-2012
Given by the artists.
p.88 E.325-2018
Given by the artists.
p.89 E.324-2018
Given by the artists.
p.91 E.462-2011
© Floris Neusüss and Renate Heyne

Joseph Nicéphore Niépce (1765–1833)
p.14 RPS.3-2017
p.15 RPS.1-2017
p.16 RPS.2-2017

Cornelia Parker (b.1956)
p.129 E.490-1998
Courtesy the artist and Frith Street Gallery, London

Ernest Payne (1862–early 20th century)
p.51 RPS.1208-2018

Man Ray (1890–1976)
pp.67–70 E.1650, 1648, 1646, 1654-2001
All purchased with the generous support of the Friends of the V&A and Art Fund.
© Man Ray Trust/ADAGP, Paris and DACS, London 2018

Carole Romaya (b.1966)
pp.150–51 E.1380-2010
Given by the artist.
© Carole Romaya

Henry Holmes Smith (1909–1986)
p.79 1132-1975
p.80 1131-1975
p.81 1135-1975
© Smith Family Trust. Courtesy Gitterman Gallery

Frederick Sommer (1905–1999)
p.83 E.995-1993
© Frederick & Frances Sommer Foundation

Jean-Pierre Sudre (1921–1977)
pp.101 (detail) and 103 E.327-2018
Given by Dylan Haskins.
© Jean-Pierre Sudre. Courtesy Gitterman Gallery

Hiroshi Sugimoto (b.1948)
pp.2 (detail) and 181 E.223-2018
Purchased with the support of the V&A Photographs Acquisition Group.
© Hiroshi Sugimoto. Courtesy of Marian Goodman Gallery

William Henry Fox Talbot (1800–1877)
pp.6 (detail) and 32 RPS.246-2017
p.19 RPS.55-2017
p.20 RPS.59-2017
p.22 RPS.13-2017
pp.23 and 182 (detail) RPS.97-2017
p.24 RPS.39-2017
p.27 RPS.114-2017
p.28 RPS.158-2017
p.29 RPS.110-2017
p.31 RPS.242 to 245-2017
p.33 RPS.211-2017

William Henry Fox Talbot (1800–1877)
or **Nicolaas Henneman** (1813–1898)
p.25 RPS.93-2017

Franciszka and Stefan Themerson (1907–1988 and 1910–1988)
pp.74–5 PH.23-1987
© Themerson Estate

Nick Veasey (b.1962)
p.164 E.403-2009
p.165 E.446-2010
pp.166–7 E.447-2010
All given by the artist.
© Nick Veasey

Index

Page numbers in **bold** refer to main entries
Page numbers in *italics* refer to illustrations

The Victoria and Albert Museum is the world's leading museum of art and design. Photography has been at the core of its collection since the museum's foundation in 1852. Today, with over 800,000 images dating from 1839 to the present, its photography collection is one of the largest and most spectacular in the world.

The **V&A Photography Library** is a series of books that explores the museum's vast holdings. Each volume focuses on a particular theme, practice or artist, offering the reader fresh insights into the art and culture of photography.

Martin Barnes is Senior Curator of Photographs at the Victoria and Albert Museum, London, which he joined in 1995. He has curated numerous UK and international touring exhibitions and published widely on historic and contemporary photography.

I am very grateful for the support I received from my colleagues at the Victoria and Albert Museum while I was researching and writing this book, notably: Ellie Atkins, Susanna Brown, Rachael Chambers, Dan Cox, Richard Davis, Simon Fleury, Coralie Hepburn, Lauren Ashley-Irvine, Kathryn Johnson, Erika Lederman, Hannah Newell, Ella Ravilious, Catherine Troiano, Marta Weiss, Tom Windross and the staff of the V&A Photography Studio. Special thanks are due to Kate Stevens, who arrived at just the right moment and made the record-speed production of this book possible. I am deeply grateful to Brian Liddy, and especially indebted to Larry J. Schaaf, for invaluable comments and corrections on William Henry Fox Talbot and early photographic processes. I also thank the team at Thames & Hudson, including commissioning editor Andrew Sanigar, and designer Lewis Chaplin at Loose Joints. Finally, this book would not have been possible without the creative work and generosity of all the photographers, artists and their estates, who kindly gave permission to reproduce their images. I dedicate it with love to Lydia and little Eden.

M.B.